D1355947

Seasons in the Sun

Also by Impress Sport

Rugby League. In Its Own Words
The Dream Season
Stevo's Super League Diary

Seasons in the Sun

A Rugby Revolution

Edited by Tony Hannan
& featuring contributions by

Dave Hadfield	Ray French
Mike Rylance	Ian Laybourn
Christopher Irvine	Gareth Walker
Paul Rowley	Malcolm Andrews
John Ledger	Graham Clay
David Lawrenson	Angela Powers
Mike Latham	Dave Woods
Harry Edgar	Trevor Hunt
Andy Wilson	Tony Hannan

impress
SPORT LIMITED

Copyright Tony Hannan and contributors 2005

Photography by Dave Williams at www.rlphotos.com & Graham Clay

First published in Great Britain in 2005 by
IMPRESS SPORT LIMITED
Fountain Chambers
Fountain Street
Halifax
HX1 1LW

ISBN 0-9547884-4-3

A catalogue record for this book is available from the British Library.

Designed and produced by Impress Sport
Printed in Malta

"Some reporters came for a funeral
and had to write about a party"
- RFL CHIEF EXECUTIVE MAURICE LINDSAY
Charlety Stadium, Paris, March 1996

ACKNOWLEDGMENTS

The editor and publishers of *Seasons in the Sun* are grateful to each of the book's contributors. In order of appearance: Dave Hadfield (*The Independent*), Christopher Irvine (*The Times*), Malcolm Andrews (*Rugby Leaguer & League Express*), Mike Rylance (author - *The Forbidden Game*), John Ledger (*Yorkshire Post*), David Lawrenson (*The Observer*), Mike Latham (BBC Radio Lancashire), Harry Edgar (*Rugby League Journal*), Andy Wilson (*The Guardian*), Ian Laybourn (Press Association), Gareth Walker (*The People*), Ray French (BBC television and *League Weekly*), Angela Powers (Sky Sports), Dave Woods (BBC Radio Five Live) and Trevor Hunt (BBC GMR). We would also like to thank all the rugby league writers and broadcasters who aren't in the book - we love you all, but the budget has been stretched further than Terry Newton's suspension as it is!

In addition to the above, we would like to single Paul Rowley out for thanks; a glowing example of the inspirational athletes who continue to grace every level of the game, whatever the off-field politics.

Dave Williams and Sig Kasatkin of www.rlphotos.com deserve a pat on the back for supplying the bulk of the pictures. The rest are from the personal collections of Graham Clay and Martin Robson. League Publications Ltd's *Gillette Rugby League Yearbook* has been a priceless source of statistical reference. Our thanks go to the fine gentlemen who are its editors, Tim Butcher and Daniel Spencer.

Finally, a snoop must be cocked at those critics who, since 1895, have confidently predicted the demise of this great game, oblivious to its resilience, culture and proud place in the affections of generations. Whatever the trials and (often self-inflicted) troubles that come its way, whatever the hurdles, rugby league has always bounced back and it always will.

CONTENTS

Introduction

Tony Hannan

"Fev is Fev. Cas is Cas. Stick your merger up your ...!".

As a summary of the widespread reaction to the arrival of Super League one short decade ago, those words on a banner at Featherstone's Post Office Road would take some beating. Fair enough, "ass" might not be the term usually adopted for the nether regions in the land of Pontefract cakes and nutty slack, but even in darkest Fev they've heard of poetic scansion. Nor were those grim-faced protesters suggesting that everybody's favourite super villain, Maurice Lindsay, rode into town on a donkey. And even if he did, there was no room at the Traveller's Rest. The message at that Good Friday local derby in 1995, potentially the last between those two famous old clubs, was clear. This is our game. Hands off.

A decade on and with cheerleaders, post-try muzak, squad numbers, squares in the air, (occasionally amusing) mascots, ice creams, salary caps, state-of-the-art stadiums, face-painted toddlers, "scooting" hookers, play-offs, Old Trafford Grand Finals and the occasional ray of sunshine all an accepted part of the top-flight rugby league experience, there will be those who wonder what all the fuss was about. If you, dear reader, are of that breed, perhaps the very sort of open-minded new fan whom the all-singing, all-dancing Super League was designed (in that word's loosest sense) to attract, a leaf through the following pages should prove both entertaining and enlightening. Even for those of an older vintage, who have either hung on gamely for the ride or given the game up as a bad job, there is lots to mull over, diligently recalled by many of rugby league's best-known writers, journalists and broadcasters.

Before we unleash our dogs of jaw, however, it is worth briefly taking stock of just what exactly was revealed at the end of that fateful meeting at Wigan's Central Park on 8th April 1995. For those of an anally-retentive disposition - and a fascination with statistics is another phenomenon that has spread quicker than Bird Flu over the past decade - there is an exact timeline of events at the back of this book. In a nutshell, the concept's aforementioned British broker-in-chief, Maurice Lindsay, put an end to months of rumour and speculation by confirming that, in tandem with a similar competition in the southern hemisphere, a European Super League would kick-off in 1996, for which media magnate Rupert Murdoch's News Ltd would pay £77million over five years. So far, so astonishing.

In itself, that financial jackpot would have brought out the party hats, especially for a sport in which the majority of clubs were at worst on the verge of bankruptcy and at best just plain skint. As usual, though, the devil was in the detail. And what detail it was, ensuring a public relations earthquake that was felt from Liverpool to Hull, throughout the rest of country and right across the world.

It is not often that a rugby league story gets to lead the BBC's *Nine O'Clock News*, but that is precisely what did happen when the Murdoch organisation's plans for a 14-club inter-continental competition were revealed to an incredulous sporting public. Little old flat cap and whippets rugby league, the exclusive preserve of grimy, soot-filled and muddy northerners was, it seemed, about to come over all glamorous. Never slow to miss a good cliché, that was how vast swathes of the national media portrayed it, anyhow. Of course, the cost to the game's century-old traditions was the real story and they got stuck into that with glee too, particularly as the "devil" to whom rugby league was "selling its soul", Murdoch, was already Establishment enemy number one. Not only would the playing season be switched entirely to summer, but 15 of the sport's most-famous clubs would be forced to merge, producing such exotic new outfits as Cheshire (Warrington and Widnes), Cumbria (Barrow, Carlisle, Whitehaven and Workington), Humberside (Hull and Hull Kingston Rovers), South Yorkshire (Sheffield and Doncaster), Manchester (Oldham and Salford) and Calder (Castleford, Featherstone and Wakefield). Those new clubs would be joined by Bradford Northern, Halifax, Leeds, London, Paris, St Helens, Toulouse and Wigan, with Lindsay and others excitedly talking about future teams in Barcelona, Newcastle, Wales and even Rome.

As we now know, in the space of just 22 days those initial ambitions were scaled down to the extent that the inaugural Super League was, in fact, made up of just 12 clubs: Bradford, Castleford, Halifax, Leeds, London Broncos, Oldham, Paris Saint-Germain, St Helens, Sheffield, Warrington, Wigan and Workington. The price, however, rose to £87m. An apparently interminable courtroom drama meant that the Australian version, which used Frankie Goes to Hollywood's appropriate if rather tactless in the circumstances "*Two Tribes (Go To War)*" as its marketing anthem, didn't get going until 1997. Even then, Super League's 10 antipodean teams - Brisbane Broncos, Cronulla Sharks, Canberra Raiders, Canterbury Bulldogs, Penrith Panthers, Hunter Mariners, Auckland Warriors, Perth Reds, Adelaide Rams and North Queensland Cowboys - ran in direct competition with the Australian Rugby League's Optus Cup, which featured the Gold Coast Chargers, Illawarra Steelers, Sydney City Roosters, North Sydney Bears, Newcastle Knights, Parramatta Eels, Manly Sea Eagles, Wests Magpies, Balmain Tigers, St George Dragons, South Sydney Rabbitohs and South Queensland Crushers. The story of how it all came to pass and subsequent events in this most revolutionary of decades will be found in the pages to come.

Needless to say, on both sides of the world, the original idea hasn't quite worked out as planned. Some innovations, despite initial misgivings, have been hugely successful. Others, those frequently excruciating animal nicknames for example, continue to range from tolerable (if they make some sort of sense) to pointless to deeply annoying. And if there's one thing we can say without fear of contraception, as Hylda Baker used to put it, it is that if *Seasons In The Sun* had been commissioned back in the days of Britpop and Cool Britannia, not only would it have needed a different title, in the case of at least one of its contributors its ejaculations would almost certainly have been premature.

Early in 1998, for example, I remember writing something about the soon-to-be introduced play-offs for *League Express*. Deciding the champions on the basis of a Grand Final would never work, I said. First past the post is just too ingrained in the British sporting psyche, I knowledgeably intoned. Blah, blah and a bit more blah. If you asked me now, of course, I would describe the play-offs as the best thing since sliding defence. Not only has the Grand Final system worked, it has exceeded all expectations and swiftly carved a niche in the British sporting calendar, while inspiring similar events which spice up rugby league's National and amateur leagues in their own right.

I wasn't alone in considering the whole thing contrived, and still wouldn't be if the debates raging on this very subject in rugby union are anything to go by. Yet what we critics failed to grasp is that, yes, the play-off system is contrived, but so what? This is professional sport and therefore part of the entertainment industry. Everything is contrived. Certain soccer coaches and fans might think otherwise, but professional sport's purpose has to be entertainment otherwise what's the point? Amateur sport helps keep you fit, gives you something to organise on a Saturday afternoon or Sunday morning, keeps you out of Ikea, and that's fine. But actually paying people to play sport? Here's half a million quid a week, David. Find an empty field in the middle of nowhere and boot a bag of leather around before sending yourself off. Herr Schumacher, here's enough euros to buy Andorra. Now, drive like a madman around the M60 at half past three in the morning, *bitte*. Where's the sense in that?

No-one who has followed its progress over the last eight years could fail to notice the benefits a play-off system offers. Not only does it ensure that the biggest match of the season is always the last, it gives just about every team something to play for over as long a period as possible. That's even more important in rugby league, where the European competition places available to soccer and rugby union don't currently exist. There are logical sporting reasons why the play-offs are a perfectly fair decider of champions too. For one thing, the current regular season is imbalanced, with some teams playing others three times, rather than home and away. And even if that weren't the case, the play-offs acknowledge consistency by rewarding participants with a proportionately less tricky route to Old Trafford in line with points collected and final positions. The table-topping side wins the League Leaders' Shield and has two chances, both at home if required, of reaching the season finale. The eventual winners, therefore, need not only to show a level of consistency sufficient to get them first into the top six and then as high within that group as possible, but also be capable of handling big-match pressure and turning it on when it really matters. It's the ultimate test. Cup and league rolled into one. Think of it as a Grand Prix without cars, in which each club spends 28 rounds jostling for the best position on the starting grid, ahead of the competition proper.

History, too, is on the side of the play-offs. With the exception of Manningham, who won the first-ever Championship in 1895-96 by virtue of topping a 22-team league table, and some to-ing and fro-ing between Yorkshire and Lancashire senior combination leagues in the aftermath of the Northern Union split (with Leigh the final first-past-the-posters of another combined league in 1905-06), rugby league's champions were always decided by some sort of play-off system until the introduction of two divisions in 1973. This, then, is probably the least new-fangled Super League innovation of all.

What is new, of course, is the term "Grand Final" to describe the Championship decider although, quite frankly, anyone intending to complain about Australian-Americanisms would need at least a day and a half to make their case. Mate, the game is riddled with them. Teams don't attack and defend any more, they concentrate on their off-ence and dee-fence. Changing rooms are "sheds". Passes are "off-loads". Men of the match receive a big "wrap", or is it "rap", I'm never quite sure. At least stand-offs are still stand-offs and not five-eighths. Yet. Then there is the trend of appending Roman numerals to the back of every season, i.e. Super League X for the 10th, Super League VI for the sixth and so on, in the style of the NFL Super Bowl. There are those who positively blanch at the practice; I am not among them. With any luck, it's a sign that the game has finally spotted the benefit of building tradition now to increase credibility further down the line. It may look a bit silly when you're on Super League II, but just wait until you get to Super League XXVIII...

As will be seen in the coming chapters, opinions remain many and varied on every aspect of Super League and no-one is pretending that, with the advent of summer, everything in rugby league's garden was suddenly blooming rosy. Far from it. As Harry Edgar eloquently points out, there is a whole other area of the game - more than one, in fact - in which struggles have if anything intensified over this past 10 years. Super League crowds have risen year after year, with more records broken in 2005, but elsewhere media interest is scant and attendances alarmingly low. Super League may have attracted thousands of new admirers to the sport, but it has also managed to alienate many of those who helped nurture the game through the proud and wintry years that went before. One major reason for that unhappy state of affairs is, as Gareth Walker writes, continued confusion over promotion and relegation. With the arrival of French club Les Catalans in 2006, supported by a three-year safety net ahead of what would appear to be more shifting sands and franchises in 2009, this issue will become even murkier. A pivotal task of the next decade must surely be to devote more time, money, imagination and energy to strengthening the sport from its roots up, wherever they may have taken hold, however long they have been planted.

So, this here summer Super League lark then. The best thing to happen to rugby league, or the worst? Well, while it would stretch credibility to pretend that things have been just dandy since Rupert Murdoch chucked £87m on the table and in effect said "take it or leave it", nor has it been a story of absolute woe. Oversimplification is always best avoided when looking back upon any revolutionary period and the Super League era is no exception. If you have visited Australia recently, for example, or just read the chapter in this book by Malcolm Andrews, you will be aware that while the sport is once again on an upward curve down under and more popular than ever, the wounds remain raw. Super League is still a touchy subject. Nevertheless, from a safe distance of several thousand miles it seems reasonable to point out that the pro-Super League camp, so often portrayed as selfish money-grabbing mercenaries, also contained more than a handful of probably misguided dreamers with the sport's interests at heart, whether in rugby kit, business or track suit. Recall too, if you can, cricket's Kerry Packer-inspired World Series of the

1970s, coloured pyjamas and all; a dollars and television-driven development which caused outrage at the time yet which now, some 30-odd years later, is widely credited with introducing a fresh outlook that inarguably changed cricket for the better.

Conversely, it wasn't only Super League players who accepted big fat "loyalty contracts". ARL-affiliated players did so too and isn't there a case to be made for just a hint of career-preservation in the ARL's blatant populism in banging the drum for tradition and the status quo, as they sought to scare off the big bad wolf Murdoch? A position, by the way, helpfully supported by the same rugby union big-wigs for whom rugby league's successful international expansion would doubtless have meant disaster.

In fact, many of the greed-based arguments originally aimed at Super League echo those hurled at a certain Albert Baskerville and his pioneering "All Golds" - a nickname with deliberate financial connotations intended as an insult - as they set sail on rugby league's first ever international tour back in 1907. Along the way, Baskerville and his union "turn-coats" picked up Aussie legend Dally Messenger in Sydney, thereby helping to launch the "professional" code in Australia. It seems blasphemous to so much as suggest it but here goes anyway. Dally Messenger: rugby league hero or money-grabbing mercenary? Discuss. As a certain gentleman whose name pops up in these pages more than any other, Maurice Lindsay, would doubtless concur, when history comes to judge its heroes and villains, it can simply be a matter of perspective.

And speaking of rugby league heroes...

It takes courage to play rugby league, of that there is no doubt. On the field, there is nowhere to hide; weakness will not only be found out, it will be punished mercilessly, in full view of all. There are no messy rucks or mauls in which to stamp on someone's head, no scrums in which to nibble a cauliflowered ear, no line-outs in which to take a quick breather. Bravery, both physical and mental, is a must. Off the field, too, the sport's history is littered with visionary souls who stood up to be counted when it came to wondering where the sport might go next, often risking ridicule for doing so. For all his faults, our old friend Mr Lindsay might well one day be seen in such a light. If so, he will be joining a list that already includes luminaries like Harry Sunderland, Eddie Waring and the late, great Peter Deakin. There have been many less high-profile figures, too, most recently former Rugby Football League boss David Oxley and Deakin's Bradford-oppo, now RFL Director of Development, Gary Tasker. Maybe even the quietly-effective current RFL executive chairman Richard Lewis.

However, few non-playing personalities in today's game display quite the level of fearlessness shown by its - to my knowledge - only male cheerleader. Before every home game at Wakefield's Belle Vue, there he is, rugby league's very own Billy Elliott, tripping the light fantastic without a care in the world, every bit as talented as the dancing girls around him and entertaining a small if appreciative crowd who know character and what used to be called gumption when they see it.

Of course, if Super League's original proposals had gone through and all those angry Featherstone placards and banners been ignored, our Trinity trouper might now have no club left to dance with at all. Alternatively, he and his friends might have proudly strutted their stuff on the turf of Old Trafford, the so-called "Theatre of Dreams", ahead of the Calder Cats' 2005 Grand Final victory, roared on by over 65,000 people. You know, just like the cheerleaders of that other once-derided merged-outfit Wests Tigers did, in Sydney.

It's an intriguing thought that, isn't it? And, while we are at it, perhaps also a lesson that while rugby league's innate sense of fair play, community, integrity and tradition are qualities very much to be cherished, now and again it can be just as important to have the guts to step out of line.

Sometimes, you should dare to do things differently.

1. Painting the Clouds with Sunshine

Dave Hadfield

Summer. I remember summer. It was a time of year I liked very much indeed. Alright, there was no rugby league - not in this country, at any rate - but it had most other things that make life worthwhile: long, lazy days watching cricket; long, lazy evenings warming your beer outside country pubs; long, lazy walks over the moors, looking for slowly ripening blackberries with your offspring. I liked summer.

And, contrary to what the skin specialists will tell you, summer keeps you young. Listen to Brian Wilson. He might look now like a man shuffling his uncertain way through late middle-age, but when he opens his mouth to sing the Beach Boys' anthems for the season of sun and sand, what comes out is the voice of a 21-year-old. It sounds like proof positive to me.

It therefore went without saying that we had to cherish every minute of summer, every precious moment of freedom from responsibility. My predecessor on *The Independent* used to lay down his quill pen on the night of the Premiership final in May and not pick it up - unless there was an overseas tour, of course, but that is another story - until the first league match of the new season at the end of August. I was never quite as hard-line as that, but I did make the most of my summers and I didn't spend much of them sitting behind a desk.

When I heard, therefore, that a tight-knit group of seasonally-motivated chairmen were agitating for a switch to playing the game in summer, I thought it was the wickedest thing I had ever heard. They were an ill-assorted little band, then and now. Chris Caisley of Bradford Northern, Gary Hetherington of Sheffield Eagles and Jim Quinn of Oldham; with Hetherington now at Leeds, he and Caisley have come to form one of rugby league's great Punch 'n' Judy double acts, forever hitting each over the head with the baby and sending for the police. As for Quinn, he disappeared back to Ireland amid all manner of unanswered questions over what had happened to Watersheddings and why.

They didn't have a lot in common in those days either. One thing, in fact - roofs, or, to be precise, the absence or non-functionality of same. Bradford and Sheffield both played in windswept great bowls of grounds, with precious little protection from weather which, in Bradford's case, was always that bit worse than it was even a couple of streets away. Oldham seemed to me to be typical of a school of thought which was in favour of summer because it meant spending less money fixing roofs that were leaking. Their stadium, although it might be much missed now in view of what has happened since, did not so much shed water as soak it up.

Caisley recalls the original motivation behind the radical idea of summer rugby. "We at Bradford were a summer club. Having such an open stadium, it was something we had wanted to push for for a long time. But the condition of a lot of grounds was nowhere near good enough. Most of them were decrepit and we couldn't see any way we going to get our stadia up to the mark for winter sport."

The Three Wise Men also noted, Caisley says, "how much better the game was in Australia" and wondered how much of that was due to playing in better conditions - the Australian winter being roughly equivalent to our summer, the lucky bastards. They also found another instructive example in that country, where Australian soccer had switched to a summer season, with some success. One reason for that was to avoid the crowd-pulling winter codes of Australian rules and rugby league. The relationship, and thus the problem, in this country was the other way around. The FA Premier League and the unprecedented hype surrounding it was squeezing the life out of the opposition during the winter months. It was harder than ever to attract sponsors, to get column inches in the newspapers, to command any attention at all alongside the monster that top-flight football was becoming. You could argue that it hasn't got much easier in the summer, but Caisley and his cohorts could only see advantages in getting away from that unequal competition and said so in the report the Rugby Football League had commissioned from them. "Soccer was killing everything and, with that lack of investment, we couldn't progress or grow our businesses."

This is where recollections start to diverge. There are those who will tell you that the argument was won at this stage, that the game was on its way to a summer season before Rupert Murdoch's intervention. That is not the way Caisley remembers it.

"Our report came to the conclusion that summer was the way forward for the sport, but it was on a shelf gathering dust at the Rugby League. A lot of clubs were dead against it - Leeds were a good example - and there wasn't enough support for it on the RFL Board. Then came the money from Sky and, all of a sudden, everything clicked into place."

The Bradford chairman is under no illusions that summer rugby was a condition of the Sky deal, not just because that was where they had gaps in their schedule, but also because of the need to co-ordinate the British and Australian seasons. "What they had in mind was for us to play Australian clubs in a Global League. That's what the World Club Challenge was all about in 1997, but unfortunately the gap in standards was exposed, especially at the lower end. If that had come a few years later, we'd have had a meaningful competition."

Caisley, Hetherington, Quinn and Co had won the argument by default. The question now was whether summer rugby could be made to work - and the evidence of that first weekend was, even to the eyes of one of its driving forces, mixed to say the least.

"There were 17,000 on that first night in Paris. If that had been done properly, I don't see why it couldn't have been made to work. Then I was at Oldham the following night and they had the world's worst Tina Turner look-alike on an orange box. They must have looked at that at Sky and said: 'Is this what we paid £87million for?'"

Pre-match entertainment, of course, is a Bradford speciality.

Whilst other big clubs, like Leeds and Wigan, were dipping their toes reluctantly or not at all, the Bulls - as they were now - plunged straight in. A stadium that had been a liability in winter was suddenly a major asset to a club that wanted to draw in a new crowd, draw them in early and entertain them before, during and after the action on the field. They had, in Peter Deakin and Gary Tasker, the right people in place to make it happen.

"The way we did it opened a few eyes right across the region," Caisley says. "The atmosphere when you came into the ground made you feel welcome. Alright, we gave out a lot of tickets, but we captured a whole new audience because most of those people came back. There was a small minority who carped and criticised. I remember one old chap who sat in the stand in an old Bradford Northern shirt, shouting 'Northern, Northern.' It took him a few years before he came over to me and said, 'Mr Caisley, you were right.' Gates went up from the start. We got them in and we kept them, but the first thing we had to do was to get them here."

But what of the game itself? How has that changed in 10 years of summer rugby? Caisley has no doubt that it has improved, but he is careful not to attribute all of that improvement purely to playing in the summer. Even in the winter, he says, players would still have had greater access to better coaching and more advanced training methods. "But playing on top of the ground has made a massive difference. A lot of the old players played much of their careers in the mud. It makes you wonder how good they would have been if they had been playing now. Talk to someone like Paul Medley; he would have loved it."

True enough, but there was a stage when the combination of playing in the summer and the need for the action to be televisual upset the balance of the game. It was so easy to find space that Shaun Edwards memorably described it as being like tick-and-pass. Now though, Caisley says, it is the players who would veto any move back to a winter season.

"They would hate it. In terms of our club, we're bound to like it here, because it suits our particular circumstances, but I think players generally like it this way. You could get away with moving back to winter if every stadium was like the JJB and every pitch was top quality and there are some lower division clubs who might think that they couldn't be any worse off in the winter and they might even be a bit better off."

Caisley is right. There is a low rumble in the National Leagues to the effect that, if Super League is to pull up the drawbridge, why not play at a different time of year? Some clubs have developed a sepia-tinged nostalgia for the days of winter rugby which co-incided for some with times of greater prosperity. I seem to remember plenty of them struggling in those days, though, and the roofs certainly leaked.

As far as Super League is concerned, the argument has surely been settled. Despite two live games on television every weekend, despite all the summer distractions - cricket, beer, blackberries etc - summer has worked at the turnstiles for the elite competition, if not necessarily for those beneath. Quite apart from what the players would think about it, would spectators be able to adapt again to watching throughout the winter, as opposed to just nibbling at its edges at the beginning and end of the Super League season?

Maybe we have all got soft together. Unless we are to start leaving our children up on the hillsides, like the Spartans, to toughen them up, the mass audience for a mid-winter game might have become extinct. True, those clubs which persist with Christmas and New Year friendlies draw some big crowds - even when they know that they will be watching below-strength sides - but special circumstances apply to them. If winter consisted of an endless series of Boxing Days, that would be absolutely fine.

So everything in the summertime garden is beautiful. Well, no, not quite, because there is a definite down-side. The statistics show that Super League has brought in a new audience and the trend of attendances is steadily upwards, but the game has lost some of its continuity. A lot of the people I knew, who went every week in all weathers, have lost the habit. They have other things to do in summer and they do them. They are outnumbered by the newcomers, but the process has changed the mix at grounds, where there are less people whose attachment to the game runs really deep. People who had grown up in the game have wandered away from it; maybe they would have done so anyway, but the fracture in the game's history meant that a lot of them leaked away in the mid-to-late 90s.

There has been another cost and one which cannot easily be repaid. Far from harmonising the international game, summer rugby has dislocated it completely. Playing at the same time in the northern and southern hemispheres means that proper tours are an impossibility. Under the old regime, Great Britain would fly out in May, roughly in the middle of the Australian season. Clubs were training and playing, interest in the game was at its height and Britain's finest were back in the country in plenty of time for the start of the new (winter) season.

Consider the summer alternative. We cannot go there at the end of our season, because they have packed up for their summer. They don't want to come here for any length of time at the end of their season, because we've packed up for our winter. There is the theoretical possibility of a mid-season window, but so far all that has amounted to is one disastrous hit-and-run and embarrassing defeat in Sydney. We won't be doing that again.

When they had Sky's millions thrown at them in 1995, British clubs were not greatly interested in finding reasons not to accept them. Obviously, any thought about the subject would reveal that full-scale tours would be an inevitable casualty of summer rugby, but there were soothing voices to placate anyone worried about that.

The then chief executive of the Rugby League, Maurice Lindsay, admitted to me then that traditional tours would no longer fit into the calendar. But they had been on their way out in any event, he said. You could cite what has since happened to cricket and rugby union tours - now mere, brief shadows of their old selves - as evidence that full-monty rugby league tours were doomed.

Well, not as far as the thousands of British fans who had booked to travel on the tour that never took place, they weren't. Proper Lions tours still had a great appeal to them. So did they as far as the broader constituency for the game in Australia was concerned. The senior clubs in what was then the Winfield Cup might have been growing lukewarm about incoming tours in mid-season, but it was never their show. Nobody who had been, within the previous few years, to the country towns in Queensland and New South Wales which hosted Lions' games would have detected any waning of enthusiasm.

Most of all, I feel sorry for the players who have missed out on what should have been the defining experiences of their careers. Take Andy Farrell, for instance - oops, rugby union already has done; he played rugby league for his country for over a decade without touring Australia, although he did play in Papua New Guinea and New Zealand - neither of which we have toured since 1996. A whole generation of players has missed out on what should have been a highlight of their lives. I wouldn't attempt to blame summer rugby in itself for the drip-drip of defections to union, but when has one of our lads ever crossed the divide without declaring, in some form of words, that he was attracted by the rah-rahs' international dimension?

That might not be the problem it has turned out to be if the game had lived up to Lindsay's promise that old-fashioned tours would be replaced by "something much better." What has that been? Well, on one level, the World Club Championship in 1997 was quite fun in a "how much worse can this get?" sort of way, but, as Chris Caisley observed, came several years too early to have any hopes of being a genuine contest. Since then, we have had short tours in this direction, one Tri-Nations in the southern hemisphere, to which the same remarks about being a genuine contest apply, followed by one over here (and another one by the time you read this). The Tri-Nations produced some compelling action in 2004 and will no doubt do so again, but the problems it raises over player availability at the end of a demanding season in both hemispheres show that it is no easy answer to the lack of sufficient international competition.

Anyway, it will never be a replacement for a full-scale tour. It is hit-and-run, designed for television and not geared to giving spectators outside the main centres the experience of seeing great players in the flesh. A lot of the Australians coaching in Britain now are of an age where their most vivid memories of rugby league - the ones that have tied them to the game ever since - concern watching tour teams. Many of those who follow the game most enthusiastically in this country trace it back to watching teams like the 1982 and 1986 Kangaroos - live. Those are the sort of opportunities that are not coming back under the present arrangements.

There were other fears at the time that summer rugby was first mooted. One theory was that pitches would suffer from having matches played on them throughout the months when their grass was growing. Dire pictures were painted of rugby league being played on dustbowls, with sandstorms blinding spectators when the harsh, dry wind blew in the wrong direction. You look now at how much better the average playing surface is and wonder what all the fuss was about, but perhaps the game was fortunate that the switch to summer came at a time when pitch technology was moving forward rapidly.

Another thing that worried players - especially big forwards approaching the back ends of their careers, as I recall - was that it would simply be too hot to play rugby and that pitches would be littered with dehydrated bodies. I think global warming was mentioned. There have been one or two cases of heat exhaustion; maybe, if Widnes' experience at Toulouse in the Challenge Cup this year is any guide, there will be some more when Les Catalans are playing in mid-summer. So far, however, you could hardly call it an epidemic.

Summer rugby has created work for extra water-carriers. Despite what some old-timers might say, players do need to take on more fluid; the techniques for making sure they do that now seem more than adequate. All the same, summer rugby might not have worked very well under the old, two substitute rule. Once the decision was made to play in the summer, it was inevitable that the interchange rules would be liberalised. There was even an international lobby for unlimited replacements at one time, but the consensus has settled on 12 changes from a four-man bench. That takes something away from the game as well as adding something.

What is lost is the element of attrition, of wearing down and outlasting the opposition. Provided they haven't messed up their substitutions - and God knows there have been a few instances of that - they always have relatively fresh legs ready to come into the game. You could argue that that means the spectator is seeing a better contest. In a sense, though, that argument is redundant; summer rugby means that the game will inevitably be one of multiple comings and goings, for better or worse. As soon as players in an old-style, 15-man format - or, think about this, straight 13-a-side - started keeling over, it would be a health and safety issue.

So summer rugby has brought with it things that we now regard as standard - the rotation of props and the second hooker on the bench to name just two. It has placed a greater emphasis on pace in all positions, because players rarely or never play in conditions where everyone is slowed down to the same speed. It has made players sprinters rather than cross-country runners and those who were at their best in the mud are now best suited to the North-West Counties or Pennine League.

There were things about winter rugby I still miss. There was that tantalising uncertainty about whether games would be played, or whether they might be frozen, fogged or flooded off - or all three at once at Odsal - followed by the huddling in the warmth of the bar until two minutes before kick-off. There was the steam rising off the packs, the seeking out of the more crowded areas of the terrace, because it would be warmer there.

A couple of minutes after the final hooter, you were out of there, to the dressing room or the pub. No hanging around to watch the dancing girls; you were in and out of the place in an hour and a half. It was a purer experience, not topped and tailed with all manner of irrelevances; the game, the whole game and nothing but the game. I loved it. It was enough for me and always would have been.

I can see now, though, that it had to change and that it isn't ever changing back. We are all southern softies now; we are creatures of the summer and we wouldn't survive a decent December and January. Yet I still say there is a down-side, a removal from normal life that is forced on those of us who have to be at the game in the summer.

It is perhaps best articulated by something Tommy Martyn said to me the day he was shunted out of his coaching job at Leigh and decided that he was finished with rugby league and was going driving a lorry instead. I'd call Tommy the epitome of the summer rugby league player - all top-of-the ground, attacking brilliance, played on firm surfaces with the sun shining - but there is a price to be paid. "For once in my life, I'm going to put my family first," he said, as he packed up his gear at The Colliseum - try calling it that in the sleet. "We're sick of going on holiday and finding everything shut up."

I can empathise with that. If you play or watch rugby league for a living, you can't really be a normal, functioning member of society any more. All that proves is that my instinctive wariness towards summer rugby 10 years ago was essentially selfish. I wanted it both ways; I wanted to be at every possible game and to sit on dry-stone walls and watch the grass grow for a few months every year. Well, you can't have it all; there aren't enough months on the calendar.

What you can have, however, is a very different game which has made a pretty good fist of a difficult transition. You can keep all the peripherals for me, if the game is still recognisable as rugby league. Just occasionally at Odsal, I get nostalgic for a bit of a nip in the air, for a hint of fog rolling in off Rooley Avenue.

And so far, I've resisted the temptation to walk down a few rows of the stand and say: "You were right, Mr Caisley."

● *Dave Hadfield has been the rugby league correspondent for The Independent and the Independent on Sunday for longer than he can remember. He broadcasts regularly for Sky and the BBC and has written or edited four books about the game: "Playing Away"; "XIII Winters"; "XIII Worlds" and, most recently, "Up and Over – A Trek Through Rugby League Land". He played what he expects to be his last game of rugby league at the age of 53 and would have set up a try if anyone could have been bothered backing-up his break.*

2. Pies, Sky & Press Gangs

Christopher Irvine

April 5th 1995, 7pm. It was an unremarkable midweek night. Doncaster were sacrificial lambs for a Wigan side who needed 32 points to exceed the record 941 points scored in their runaway Championship of 1987.

A reasonable line for us there then. Failing that, there was a meeting of club chairmen at Headingley. They were discussing some fanciful idea about switching the season to summer. Yet another rugby league gimmick. Half an hour before kick-off, I squeezed into my favourite spot in the old wooden Central Park press box, conscious of some talk from behind me by the BBC's Dave Woods about revolution.

What? The general consensus was to tell Woodsy to put a sock in it, stuff his daft revolution and carry on preparing for the game. But eventually his persistence got our attention. Something about a mad dash by Maurice Lindsay to London the day before for talks with BSkyB ... an approach by Rupert Murdoch's News Ltd for a European Super League ... a summer season from 1996 ... £5million on the table, maybe more.

Hang on, forget the match, get hold of Lindsay, the Rugby Football League, anyone. While Wigan dutifully put bottom-placed Doncaster to the sword, pandemonium raged among the assembled media. Murdoch's millions kept ratcheting up ... a £10m deal, £20m, £25m.

At one point, *The Sun*'s Phil Thomas was on his hands and knees crawling to get to another landline, having demolished his own phone, screaming something to the sports desk about a £50million windfall and teams in London, Cardiff, Manchester and Paris ("you heard me, Paris"). The only "Murdock" interesting the crowd at that stage was Craig Murdock who, together with Sean Long, were tying poor Donny in knots. The Wigan supporters were as blissfully unaware of events as my own sports desk in Wapping, apparently. Confirmation of rugby league's instant revolution had not yet reached that corner of the Murdoch empire. Write everything you know was the instruction. Er, right.

When we at last got hold of Lindsay, he was breathless in his excitement. Maurice is never one to shrink from bold statements, but when he spoke of Murdoch and News Corporation "sharing our vision of taking rugby league to the world," it appeared peculiarly at odds with Wigan's still unfolding demolition of Doncaster. Watching Kris Radlinski poach his second try of the night, I wrote a pay off-line to the effect that if a Super League started, Wigan would probably dominate that, too.

Nothing in the intervening decade has quite compared with the media storm that engulfed rugby league in April 1995, although Ian Millward might argue otherwise after his mad May of 2005. The day after the night before and everyone was on to the story. Ken Cowley, Murdoch's number two, upped the ante in Sydney, talking about a done deal with the RFL, now that Super League had broken away from the Australian Rugby League. The split in Australia, the biggest sports story there since the introduction of World Series Cricket in 1977, had reverberated 11,000 miles. From cloth cap and begging bowl to sun hats and untold riches. All the clichés were there.

A sport afflicted by debt, inertia and parochialism in this country after 100 years, suddenly glimpsed a second century laden with commercial and expansionist possibilities. In his talks with Sam Chisholm, BSkyB's chief executive, Lindsay had somehow got the figure up to a staggering £77m over five years. It was a case of take it or leave it; Sky in those days were not ones for drawn-out negotiation. Acutely aware of league's parlous finances and the threat posed by rugby union going professional, Lindsay's only concern was his sales patter to the clubs. From Sky's perspective, rugby league was there for them in the early days, filling in the odd hour between big truck racing and log chopping. Eddie and Stevo were up and running. The tie-up was a natural progression.

There had been hints of course.

Indeed, *Open Rugby* magazine had set out in its January issue a 10-team Super League designed to go head to head with a rival Australian competition, but somehow all the preamble about a so-called Premier League, months talking about switching to summer and the "Framing the Future" document looked like hot air and waste paper. Overnight, all that changed, and a new phrase about rugby league took on a life of its own: "The sport that sold its soul to Rupert Murdoch." Up to a point, Lord Copper.

The fatally-flawed first Super League draft, the result of a meeting of club chairmen in Wigan on April 8th that managed to supersede the Grand National in the sporting conscience that day, embraced Sky's expansionist agenda but so disregarded the views of supporters as to be laughable. The press had a field day with the misguided series of proposed mergers and the fan power that had them overturned three weeks later. They burnt effigies of Lindsay, carried a coffin at Halifax, while Featherstone became the epicentre of the northern uprising. "These are truly dramatic times. We can only hope that our game is not sacrificed along the way," Harry Edgar wrote in *Open Rugby*.

Naturally, the outside view was not so much a new and glorious future but a sport seemingly tearing itself apart, while noting that the new money was being poured into the pockets of players as "loyalty" contracts to prevent them signing with the Australian Rugby League. Unlike Australia, the perception that those of us working for News Corporation's British newspapers were somehow beholden to Murdoch's grand plan was at odds with my experience. I tentatively enquired with my sports desk whether we should toe a particular line, to be told to write the story as I saw it. "Super League hatred rife on the terraces" was a headline on my report from what was cast as the last Castleford-Wakefield derby.

All roads led to a meeting of clubs at the Hilton Hotel, Huddersfield, on April 30th - the day after a Challenge Cup final between Wigan and Leeds overshadowed by whispered conversations with player's agents - and closure, of sorts, to the most dramatic month since the original 1895 split. Widnes were omitted and took out an injunction, but a 12-team Super League, incorporating London and Paris, a return to three divisions and withdrawal of merger proposals realised a final sum of £87m. Not bad for rugby league's sale after a century, for all the moral high tone adopted in certain quarters over the deal.

The general view remained sceptical. Laura Thompson wrote in *The Independent*: "As it is now, rugby league is an anachronism because its strengths still come from a source that no longer figures in the world of sport: the communities to which it belongs. Now in order to thrive it must find strength elsewhere, in the marketplace. Will it be able to do so?"

In the run-up to Super League's launch, the scare stories refused to abate. Paris Saint-Germain were declared a "French farce" in a prescient piece by the *Sunday Telegraph*, 10 weeks before the season began. Paris were derided for having only a short time to build a team from scratch to match opposition who had been at it for 100 years. Lindsay was quoted as saying that Australian players might have to be drafted in. "To strengthen Paris," he said. "I'd go anywhere in the world." That is precisely what happened, to the club's ultimate cost.

Despite insistence by British administrators that they retained full autonomy over the running of the sport, a leaked player "loyalty" contract purported to show that News Corporation had power of veto over any transfers. As Wigan had collared that particular market as the only fully-professional outfit in the pre-summer era, it looked an area ripe for reform anyway. As it transpired, News Corporation's overriding intent was simply to keep adding to a portfolio on Sky Sports transformed by the advent of football's Premier League in 1992.

Rugby league was in the vanguard of satellite, multi-channel sports broadcasting, but was anyone actually watching? In the early days, 40,000 represented a good audience for Friday night matches. The figure is around five times that now.

One sacrifice News Corporation had insisted on was Great Britain only playing Super League opposition at international level on Sky, so it was farewell to the BBC on that score after the surprisingly successful 1995 World Cup. There was a brief coming together of the two broadcasters for live coverage of the World Cup in 2000, although the less said about that shambolic tournament the better. The BBC certainly will never live down the opening match between Ireland and Samoa at a crumbling, threequarters-empty Windsor Park, Belfast.

With the Regal Trophy kicked into touch, the Beeb was left clutching the Challenge Cup, which looked for all the world like a pre-season trinket. The 1995-96 centenary season ended on January 21st 1996. The following season's cup kicked off seven days later - try selling that crazed bit of fixture planning to a London newspaper office - with the fourth, fifth, sixth rounds and semi-finals shoehorned in before the start of Super League. Pure madness, but with a defining moment, when Salford memorably ended Wigan's 43-match winning cup run. The world really did change that February afternoon at the Willows.

The media battle to be won at the opening Super League match in Paris on March 29th 1996 was hardly helped by the flight from Leeds-Bradford being cancelled. Journalists embarked on a mad Planes, Trains and Automobiles dash for the evening kick-off - Charlety Stadium or bust. Some, worse for wear after a Channel Tunnel junket, failed to make it. Another, glass in hand, fell down the concrete steps of the press box. Free plonk was one way of winning hearts and minds. Those who did see the game fully focused had some of the questions over whether summer rugby was a masterstroke or a ghastly mistake answered by a near 18,000 crowd and an unforgettable victory for the Paris new boys over Sheffield. The big screen, fireworks, music all worked. Vive la difference!

Ian Chadband was effusive in *The Sunday Times*: "There, in the scrum of back-slappers, was the man who has had to endure an unfair share of ridicule and abuse this past year. 'I'm just happy, not smug,' Maurice Lindsay promised, but after all the setbacks and doubts which still hover over his brave new world, he could for one night at least afford to feel both emotions. Eleven tries, excellent entertainment, good TV, big crowd; the ideal advert for his grand designs."

Down to earth at Oldham less than 24 hours later, we were treated to simply the worst Tina Turner lookalike and a more familiar routine of Wigan in overdrive. The Oldham bear mascot appeared a particularly sorry beast, more Paddington than grizzly. The following day it snowed at Odsal and Leeds heralded the summer era with a pre-match display so flawed and cringe-worthy that they were forced to issue a public apology and sack their cheerleaders. The slickness of today and the outbreak of opera singers across the M62 was a long way off, but Bradford doubled their gate, 54,000 people for the six matches represented the most popular start to a season for 23 years and, apart from a disputed Martin Offiah try for Wigan, the video official enjoyed a relatively trouble-free introduction.

The early verdicts were favourable - "Summer off to a Super start," *The Guardian* reckoned, even Alex Murphy was quoted as saying that Super League had given the game a new lift - but the summer counter-attractions were some way off. And, besides, the battle still raging around Super League in Australia, confusion among spectators and the worst preparation possible were cracks again papered over by players managing to stamp their credibility on the radical restructuring.

The key battleground remained June and July. Here the media needed much more convincing. Bradford v St Helens up against the men's final at Wimbledon, Sheffield v Leeds competing with the British Grand Prix, St Helens v London going head-to-head with the Lords Test. Could Central Park, Headingley and Knowsley Road really join Henley, Royal Ascot and SW19 as the places to be seen that first summer?

As one who gently whiled away the warmer months covering the grass court tennis season, the odd cricket match and an eclectic mix from water skiing and canoe water polo to jungle rallying and, God forbid, early season football matches, a summer of rugby league took some readjustment. To warm things up, we had the two-part freak show of Wigan playing Bath. It deservedly won Wigan some good publicity but set rugby union's tortoises in pursuit of a couple of hares in Jason Robinson and Henry Paul. June arrived, and whereas Bradford had doubled their attendances to 9,000, Wigan's crowds were down nearly 20 per cent and at Leeds by 25 per cent.

Alex Murphy, who else, was on the case in *The Mirror*: "Nobody should be afraid to alter course. I bet the captain of the Titanic would have changed his route if he knew he was steaming towards an iceberg." The author Geoffrey Moorhouse said that there were those in the game as nervous as the horses before the great 1906 San Francisco earthquake, yet the overall impression was not so doom-laden. By the end of that first season, Murphy was back in there fighting, his Warrington side standing between St Helens and getting their hands on the ugly but no less distinctive Super League trophy.

For those new readers of *The Times*, who had armfuls of free vouchers pressed into their hands to follow the newspaper's "rugby league team" - a team of one, I might add - column inches for the game had expanded, even through the dreaded Wimbledon fortnight, when all available space tends to get saturated. Not that the first Super League season felt appreciably different to what had gone before - the JJB, KC and Halliwell Jones Stadiums were distant mirages and the Grand Final just a daft means of deciding the Australian champions - but the difference between the haves and have-not was already startling.

The dozen leading clubs were about to form themselves into the semi-autonomous Super League Europe Ltd, prompting the first talk of breakaways. But while the club scene, for all its fault lines, was strengthening at the top level, the nadir of Super League's international scene was reached a few weeks later in New Zealand. Great Britain's results were bad on tour but the financial losses were far worse, resulting in nine players being brought home early. The saving was said to be all of £5,000. A far higher price was the sight in Christchurch on a news bulletin of the nine boozing it up in an Auckland hotel room.

A decade on, the Tri-Nations concept has helped restore some of the international game's reputation and there is a World Cup to look forward to in Australia (at last!) in 2008. It's not the same as it was pre-1996. Long tours were consigned to history when our season was brought into line with Australia, but enough carping on that score.

What we've got in terms of Great Britain is a darn sight better than we had for the first five years of Super League, and approaching 2006 and the summer competition's second decade, the wider perception is of a cutting-edge sport that is not afraid to question itself or try out new things.

When the Football Association was going through one of its bouts of self-flaggelation in 2005, the RFL was cited by several newspapers as a model governing body, one that under Richard Lewis has transformed its financial position after the disastrous 2000 World Cup. A former tennis player, who once went eyeball-to-eyeball with Jimmy Connors on Centre Court and so was not going to be fazed by the Rugby League Council, did have his wobbly moments negotiating Sky's present contract but has proved himself the steady hand at the tiller necessary.

He set his tone early in an interview with *The Times* in 2002: "I'd like to see more than one London team. It's important to be recognised as a national sport. Let's be honest, even though the game's played in every county in the country, without more than one top team outside the northern heartland, it's difficult to say we're a national sport. It's tried to expand too quickly and on too grand a scale. That's a trap I'd like to avoid."

There has been no more enthusiastic proponent of Super League XI's French newcomers, Les Catalans, than Lewis, for which he could be accused of pushing the boat out too far. That would be unfair. No new club has been so carefully nurse-maided through its pre-Super League infancy, in contrast with the lack of foundations dug at Paris. Lindsay talked in the formative years of clubs in Milan and Barcelona. With a couple of games pencilled in for across the French border, Super League's tentacles will finally reach Spain. Too grand? We'll see.

The advent of Les Catalans and Harlequins (née London Broncos) is the innovative, forward-thinking for which rugby league is more generally portrayed nowadays. Whippets and flat vowels are occasionally dragged out and some of us still have to live down having to translate Eddie Waring's catchphrases into French to accompany a feature from Perpignan, but for a few years now the game has largely been spared those Home Counties soothsayers who foresaw the worst based on a few high-profile switches to rugby union.

It is interesting that Andy Farrell's move elicited none of the same criticisms - in fact the reverse, with union seen as once more having to return to the league well - that accompanied those who crossed over in 2001. "It is utterly inconceivable that rugby in 2031 will be anything other than a single code," Frank Keating wrote in *The Guardian*. "Did I say 2031? Make that 2006, more like, and alas for league."

Sorry, Frank, still here, and more popular than ever. One notorious "colour" writer who accompanied me to Wembley in 1997 was predicting the end for the game even then - "a villa on the slopes of an active volcano," he described it. It's easier to bash, but in terms of knocking league as a has-been sport, that is now a pretty mined-out seam. Stephen Jones, in *The Sunday Times*, often lives up to his reputation as league's arch media critic, whose gripes with the code's lack of global appeal are thoroughly documented, but whose admiration, often privately and occasionally in print, cannot be denied. Of St Helens in the 2004 Challenge Cup final in Cardiff, he wrote: "This was the best rugby seen on the ground by any team playing in red for some years."

There is every reason for league folk to feel chippy when it comes to what some people have written about the sport and a history of it being run down in certain quarters, but there is a tendency also to overlook the positive vibes and search for underlying negatives. The fact is that Robinson, Paul, Farrell and Iestyn Harris, together with coaches such as Phil Larder, Mike Ford, Shaun Edwards and Joe Lydon, have stood as bastions of excellence in the union game for their former code.

In *The Sunday Times*, former England union fly-half Stuart Barnes wrote: "England, by training with Leeds Rhinos, are tacitly admitting that league has won the battle for skills, or at least the positive skills ... England won the World Cup through a combination of mauling, scrambling, destructive defence and sheer cussed force of personality. League fans would not have drooled at the performance as I did when I first saw Wally Lewis and the 1982 Kangaroos."

Rugby league's presence in the red-tops and middle-market

tabloids is a shadow of what it was in the days when most national newspapers had big northern staffs. The London-centric nature of today's press is partly to blame for declining column inches in those publications. Ignorance, as opposed to conspiracy, is at the heart of the problem. That and an insane appetite for football, so bloated now that it has wiped out other sports coverage, the effect similar to a big supermarket on a corner shop's takings.

The so-called "heavies" have prospered more in the Super League era. What can never be denied in league is the propensity for good stories or colourful and, more importantly, accessible characters. Sports desks recognise that of league, even if you have sometimes to explain to them, as politely as possible, that a play-the-ball is unrelated to ruck and maul. It was not always the case in the pre-Super League dawn, but mention Paul Sculthorpe, Adrian Morley, Sean Long, Lesley Vainikolo, Keiron Cunningham, Robbie Paul, Brian Carney, Kevin Sinfield, Jamie Peacock, Danny McGuire and several others to the sports news editor of the day and you can just about guarantee some space.

In my own newspaper, *The Times*, there is no getting away from the fact that union holds sway. Its greater international dimension and participation demands it - a lesson for league there - coupled with the diverse nature of its competitions and the perception, rightly or wrongly, that with two-thirds of circulation inside the M25 orbital, league generally comes second to union as code of choice for our readers.

The trend in newspapers is to throw vast resources at big events, Olympics, football World Cup, Wimbledon, Ashes cricket, Open golf, to just about the exclusion of everything else. When you're scrapping for a few paragraphs, it can be agonisingly frustrating, but no different than for many reporters trying to promote their sport. As a freelance for *The Times* in 1992, I was something of a rarity, but now every rugby league staff job has disappeared in the across-the-board cost-cutting and slimming-down forced on every national newspaper.

Far from depleting our numbers, the ranks of freelances dedicated to the code's cause has grown, especially with the explosion in the number of commercial radio stations, internet sites and extensive Press Association service. Rugby league's grip on the admirable local and regional press is as tight as it ever was, a fact rarely taken into account by the knocking brigade. The service by BBC local radio remains second to none, while Five Live, albeit fitfully on occasions, at least treats the sport seriously and regards it favourably.

There is no doubt, too, that BBC Television, whose idea of league in the old days was as a filler on Grandstand between the motocross and the 3.00 from Newmarket, has learnt from Sky's multi-angled, multi-featured coverage. The 2005 Challenge Cup final in August was a high point of the Beeb's rugby league renaissance, the only pity being that it packed up its bag of tricks until the start of the cup again in April 2006. We get the play-offs and Tri-Nations highlights on Sunday Grandstand and the Super League Show in the north, but the terrestrial/satellite balance is still overwhelmingly in favour of Sky, a reminder also about who pays the piper and calls the tune.

As custodians of the game on our television screens, Sky's technical mastery is beyond question. A dedicated rugby league team has honed and perfected the sport's coverage. What haven't changed are Eddie and Stevo, a light-entertainment partnership as established as Little and Large or Cannon and Ball, whose hyperbole turns out not to be the unashamed hard-sell everyone thought in the early days - the delights of Oldham v Paris really was stretching the imagination - but a part of the act. There they are, fronting the show, commentating, doing the half-time analysis, before nipping back to the microphones for the second half, then wrapping the programme up.

"One is reminded of one of those remote Scottish villages where the man who runs the post office is also the landlord of the pub and tends the local petrol pump, as well as delivering the newspapers," Giles Smith wrote in *The Times*. "It may not be the cosy message Super League wants to send while attempting to establish itself as a globe-girdling colossus, but it's impressive anyway and a lesson to other, lazier areas of sports broadcasting."

There are times when a bit more gravitas and analysis certainly wouldn't go amiss - the midweek *Boots 'n' All* programme regularly misses both opportunities - but Sky and Super League have become synonymous with Friday and Saturday nights. For those of us with deadlines that demand we write pieces for early Saturday editions to "hold" space for a match report that has to be delivered in chunks at half-time and on the final whistle, in order to squeeze it in to later editions, matches ending at nearly 10pm are far from ideal.

Bradford reverting to Friday nights for the 2006 season and joining Leeds, Wigan, St Helens and Salford is bad news for those of us trying to cram reports into Saturday's papers, although I recall one official of a club moving to Friday night kick-offs saying: "I couldn't give a stuff what the press think. It doesn't matter to us if they're here or not."

Fortunately, such short-sightedness is a throwback in a sport that has gained an unprecedented level of media credibility in the past 10 years, despite what the sceptics suspect.

And by the way, whatever did happen to Wigan?

● *Christopher Irvine has followed rugby league since starting as a cub reporter on the Warrington Guardian in 1981. He then became crime correspondent on the Coventry Evening Telegraph before joining the Yorkshire Post in 1986, covering politics and as senior reporter. After heading up a news investigations unit on Scotland on Sunday in Edinburgh for two years, and reporting on the 1991 Gulf War, he returned to Leeds to pursue a freelance career and became a News producer at Yorkshire Television. He joined The Times as rugby league and northern rugby union correspondent in 1992.*

3. Deep Throat, Deeper Pockets

Malcolm Andrews

Back in the 1950s, a respected Australian political correspondent, Alan Reid, coined a name for the power-brokers who ran the Australian Labor Party. He called them the Faceless Men.

It was a name that was to haunt the socialists for years to come - and helped them lose election after election. The faceless men, mainly from the trade union movement, told the elected members of parliament from the left how to vote, and in doing so kept Labor in opposition for 23 years.

In the mid-1990s, rugby league had its own version of the faceless men. They were the scheming backroom boys who plotted to take over the game in the three countries where it was a force - Australia, Great Britain and New Zealand. They cloaked their machinations behind a word of their own: vision. They had a vision of a world stretching from Cardiff to Capetown, Melbourne to Manchuria, Bulgaria to Buenos Aires, in which rugby league would rival football. "It's a whole new ball game" was their slogan. They were living in a dream world.

But in November 1994, Super League was spawned. The faceless men managed to get a quick foothold in Britain through the power of the cheque book. Sponsorship of £87m bought a lot of support. And, in March 1996, the European Super League kicked off. In Australia, however, their efforts resulted in all-out warfare, the fall-out from which crippled the game for almost a decade. There were bitter court battles where the only winners were the raft of lawyers who made tens of thousands of dollars while the battle raged. Lifetime friendships were shattered. Legends of the game were slandered and the scars are still there today. The hostility has made Super League a product that is greeted by a large percentage of fans down under with, if not outright disgust, at least derision.

That Super League is now a way of life in Britain and that, a decade on, rugby league in Australia is enjoying record popularity is a tribute to the excitement generated by the sport that we like to call 'The Greatest Game of All.' As celebrated Australian coach Jack Gibson once noted: "Rugby league is such a great game that it has succeeded despite the efforts of its officials." And the efforts of the faceless men!

I first heard of this fanciful scheme to take over rugby league worldwide in the middle of the 1994 Australian season, from a contact at the Brisbane Broncos. I had written a lot of stories for the Broncos' monthly magazine and the club's officials trusted me. I used jokingly to call my contact 'Deep Throat' - although league's rebellion was hardly on a par with America's 1970s Watergate scandal.

At first I laughed at his suggestions, until I realised that the faceless men were deadly serious. The Broncos had found an ally in Rupert Murdoch's News Ltd. This was largely thanks to the Murdoch chiefs getting the cold shoulder from the ARL when they wanted Ansett Airlines, part-owned by News, to take over from Winfield as the major sponsor of rugby league in Australia, after Federal Government legislation outlawed the sponsorship of sporting events by tobacco companies. And, of course, the Broncos reckoned the Sydney clubs were conspiring against them. Paranoia? Maybe so. But the all-powerful Sydney numbers men had, after all, worked a deal that resulted in Broncos chief executive John Ribot being eased out of any decision-making roles.

There were rumours in the media of the plans - but only vague gossip. And nothing was mentioned about Britain until my source at the Broncos told me that there was to be a major upheaval in Old Blighty. In return for Murdoch's multi-million pound rescue package, the RFL would be forced to completely change the way the game was organised. The RFL would have to toe the News Ltd line.

It was obvious to me right from the start that, as Australian correspondent for Britain's *League Express*, I was being used by the faceless men to fly their kites. They would tell me their plans, I would report them, and if there was too much flak they would gently fine-tune the proposals before making everything official. I didn't mind being the conduit. I was getting exclusives - and history shows how most of the ideas eventually came to fruition.

In November 1994, as the touring Kangaroos prepared for the Third Test against Great Britain in Leeds, the Australian media began to predict a major walkout of top Australian clubs. My source was on the phone for one of our now regular twice-weekly chats.

"What would you say if I told you that we're going to swap the British season to the summer?" he asked. "I'd say that you and your mates are certifiable," was my reply. "No, no. You don't understand. Murdoch's got the television rights to English soccer. Rugby league can't compete with that over there. And he's also got the rah rahs. They can fill in the gaps between soccer games but, come summer, it's only the cricket. No one really cares about that. So the idea is to make league a major summer sport. The long English twilights mean it can be played in the cool of the evening. The whole family can come along. Quite frankly, would you rather watch the game on a balmy summer's evening or in the fog, rain and sleet of an English midwinter." He had a point.

But now there was no stopping my 'Deep Throat'. "The English club bosses don't know yet - but here's what is going to happen," he said. "Just a handful of the most famous clubs will remain as separate entities ... Wigan, St Helens and Leeds spring to mind ... then there will be London and Paris ... and finally merged sides will make up a Super League of 10 or 12. Local sides like Castleford, Featherstone and Wakefield will merge for the Super League competition. Salford and Oldham will go under the banner of Manchester. The old village teams will remain in a lesser fringe competition as feeder clubs.

"The Australian and British Super League competitions will be run in parallel, with their respective Grand Finals on the same day. A Super Sunday for Murdoch's PayTV networks on each side of the world. The Australian Super League Grand Final would be played on Sunday night and after all the presentations and post mortem the focus would switch to England for an afternoon Grand Final over there. About 12 hours straight of rugby league. A television bonanza.

"Then there will be a World Club Championship play-off between the top four sides in each hemisphere. The second and fourth-placed sides in Britain will fly to Australia to play the first and third teams and vice versa. The venue for the Grand Final in November will be auctioned off to the highest bidder. It may be Hong Kong or Dubai or wherever. Money talks in any language."

I explained that the fans of clubs like Leigh, Salford, Halifax and Oldham would never countenance supporting a merged side. This would especially be the case with Hull and Hull KR. The faceless men saw them as a single entity on Humberside. "Mate, it would be like trying to merge Liverpool and Everton soccer sides - or, worse still, Celtic and Rangers," I told him. "There is no chance of it coming off."

And what about one of the merged clubs names - Calder? "Come again? Calder? What sort of name is that?" Like most Australians, I didn't know it was a river that winds through West Yorkshire and that the area was known locally as Calder Valley.

My story about summer rugby league in England appeared in *League Express* on November 11th 1994. Talk about the 'you-know-what' hitting the fan! Traditionalists wanted to keep their game in the winter. "There is nothing else to do," they moaned. As I'd explained to my source, mergers were anathema to almost every last fan. Officially, the plans were not put forward until the following year.

Of course, history shows how rugby league in summer became a way of life but the idea of mergers died a quick death in England, although some were forced on Australian clubs. Western Suburbs Magpies and Balmain Tigers became Wests Tigers and St George Dragons and Illawarra Steelers became St George Illawarra Dragons. Eventually both proved to be successful. On the other hand, a marriage from hell was consummated when Manly Sea Eagles and North Sydney Bears became the Northern Eagles, playing half their games out of Brookvale and the other half out of Gosford on the NSW Central Coast. The Northern Eagles lasted just three seasons (2000-03) before the inevitable annulment.

How ironic was it that the faceless men chose 1995 to go public. It was the centenary of rugby league, celebrating the events of 1895 when the clubs of northern England rebelled against the old school tie regime. And 1995 was when the game down under embarked on an audacious expansion plan. Four new teams were admitted to the big league: a second Brisbane side in South Queensland Crushers; North Queensland Cowboys from that state's tropical north; across the continent in Perth, the Western Reds, named after Australia's biggest and toughest breed of kangaroo; and over the Tasman Sea - dubbed "the big ditch" - the Auckland Warriors.

For the opening round of the 1995 season, the ARL had chartered an Ansett aircraft to take media and officials on a latter-day Cooks Tour of league's new bailiwick. On the Friday morning we assembled at Sydney Airport ready to welcome the new era in rugby league. Little did we know what a very different era it would be.

That night in Auckland we watched a spine-tingler in which the Warriors very nearly overcame the Brisbane Broncos. Then, up before dawn, we flew to Brisbane to see Canberra Raiders easily account for the Crushers. There was then a police motor-cycle escort to Brisbane Airport for a flight to Townsville where, in cloying humidity, the Sydney Bulldogs gave the Cowboys a rugby league lesson the same evening. In the morning, as we waited to board our plane for the flight to the Western Australian capital, members of the ARL hierarchy, especially boss Ken Arthurson, were grim-faced. The *Sydney Sun-Herald* newspaper carried a report that nine of the 20 Premiership clubs were to defect to a new Super League, starting in 1996. They included the Western Reds who, later that afternoon, became the first of the new teams to win, beating St George 28-16.

By the time our Ansett jet arrived back in Sydney just before 11pm (after a journey the equivalent of travelling from Sydney to Cairo) the battle lines were drawn, although the ARL chiefs were still in the dark after questioning club bosses. "Somebody is either not telling the truth or living in fantasyland," said chief executive John Quayle. Within days Arthurson met with Murdoch's top man in Australia, Ken Cowley, and Arko told the press: "Any Super League proposals will be directed through me." Oh, really?

A fortnight later and the rebels launched their blitzkrieg. The irony of the news breaking on April Fool's Day was not lost on either party. What followed was 18 months of bitter uncertainty, coupled with rampant inflation as both sides threw ridiculous amounts of money at players in return for their "loyalty". Unknown reserve-grade journeymen were handed $100,000 - tenfold what they would have expected for a season's struggle. It would be revealed in court at a later date that Test stars Laurie Daley, Bradley Clyde and Ricky Stuart topped the Super League lists with a $100,000 signing-on fee and $600,000 per season. Paul "The Chief" Harragon was top earner in the ARL ranks with a $650,000 sign-on fee and $350,000 per season. No wonder he persuaded his beloved Newcastle Knights to reject Super League overtures, members of the media mused.

Five days into the battle Super League played what it believed to be its trump card when, at a media conference in a swanky Sydney hotel, it announced that Great Britain and New Zealand had switched camps - just as my source had predicted five months earlier. British supremo Maurice Lindsay was lavish in his praise of the new order. The move enraged Arthurson and the ARL which quickly took the battle to Britain. The Lions coach Ellery Hanley accepted a reported $950,000 to switch camps, and another $11.5million was spent on nine British players including Gary Connolly, Jason Robinson, Lee Jackson and Jonathan Davies. Leeds' Craig Innes also took ARL cash.

Most of the British had to finish their existing contracts before the ARL could hope to use them in Australia. But the ARL saw their signing as a PR victory over Super League and they would eventually force several of them to fly down under to play for the Rest-of-the-World in so-called 'Tests' against Australia. The first victims were the players from the Australian clubs aligned with Super League. Despite a public denial that they were discriminated against, the ARL chose only players from 'loyal' clubs for the 1995 State of Origin series. When he realised this was going to happen, Queensland coach Wayne Bennett quit, noting: "I don't want to be part of a farce."

The same criteria applied when it came to choosing Test sides for the Trans-Tasman Series against the Kiwis (most of whose players were aligned with Super League) and the squad for the Centenary World Cup in Britain. The top Australian referees Bill Harrigan and Graham Annesley, both with Test experience, were ignored because they had agreed to join Super League. Among those missing from the Australian side that had won the Ashes in England the previous year were Mal Meninga, Brett Mullins, Wendell Sailor, Andrew Ettingshausen, Steve Renouf, Laurie Daley, Allan Langer, Ricky Stuart, Glenn Lazarus, Bradley Clyde and David Furner. At official functions the antagonism was evident, with ARL officials and the Australian team pushed out of the limelight. But the Australians did have the last laugh when the relatively inexperienced team captained by Brad Fittler beat Great Britain 16-8 in the final at Wembley.

The topsy-turvy legal battle in Australia meant that, unlike in England, the Super League could not get underway in 1996. The ARL had a stunning court victory, announced as Super League's World Nines were being played in Fiji. ARL lawyer Mark O'Brien described the court ruling as akin to a rugby league side posting a 100-nil win. Justice James Burchett ruled that rebel clubs were bound by loyalty agreements and the judge banned Super League from starting its competition - which was to have included Auckland Warriors, Brisbane Broncos, Canberra Raiders, Canterbury Bulldogs, Cronulla Sharks, North Queensland Cowboys, Penrith Panthers, Western Reds and two new sides Adelaide Rams and Hunter Mariners - until 2000.

Enter the white knight - Maurice Lindsay. Two days before the ARL Premiership was supposed to kick off, with the eight so-called Super League teams that had played in 1995 involved, Lindsay tried to launch yet another rebel competition in Australia. It was to be called Global League and would include all the players previously allied to Super League but playing for new teams with new colours and new strip. Despite Mo floating the Canberra Vikings, Cronulla Dolphins, Penrith Cats *et al* before the Australian public, the court ruled against his proposal and after forfeiting their first-round matches the rebel clubs returned to the ARL.

They stayed there for just one season. Upon appeal, Super League was able to go ahead in Australia the following year and the two organisations embarked on parallel competitions in 1997. Super League's rebel players were rewarded by a decision to have an expanded World Club Championship now involving every last side in both Britain and Australasia - giving fringe players who could never hope to make an overseas tour a chance to see the world. It was an embarrassing failure, recalled in greater depth elsewhere in this book.

Even before that ill-fated adventure, it was obvious to everyone involved in the sport that the battle in Australia, if continued, would probably kill the game. In Britain, rugby league was thriving. In Australia it was in crisis, with attendances affected, a dramatic slump in marketing income and the newly-professional rugby union keen to take advantage. Peace was eventually negotiated by ARL chief executive Neil Whittaker and Super League boss Ian Frykberg but there were losers. The Western Reds, Adelaide Rams, Hunter Mariners and South Queensland Crushers ceased to exist. The Gold Coast followed a year later and South Sydney Rabbitohs were kicked out at the end of 1999 until a concerted public campaign and court action saw them return in 2002. A decade after the war, the game on both sides of the world is booming. There are record attendances and potential sponsors are falling over themselves to jump on the bandwagon. In Britain, the Super League banner flies high. The contrast down under will be forever noticeable.

In my wardrobe is a Super League T-shirt given to me by a PR man in the first euphoria of the 1995 breakaway. It has never been worn. For me to have walked down the street in those days wearing such an item of clothing would have been foolish in the extreme. Without a doubt, angry supporters of the ARL would have tried to pick a fight. Today there wouldn't be fisticuffs. But I would most certainly have to endure nasty taunts.

The T-shirt is destined to remain in my wardrobe as a silent testimony to a revolution that succeeded in one country and failed in another. Paradoxically, it was a success in the place alien to the faceless men who planned it. In their own country, they failed because they looked at rugby league as a business rather than in the way the fans looked at it (and still do).

As a way of life.

● Malcolm Andrews is a respected Australian journalist and author with more than 40 years of experience with such media organisations as the London Daily Express, Sydney Daily Telegraph (with which he was a daily columnist for much of the 1980s), The Australian, Australia's Nine Television Network and the US State Department's Radio Free Europe. He watched his first game of rugby league in Sydney in 1953 and in Britain in 1967. Five of his 26 books have been about rugby league. He has been Australian correspondent for League Publications for the past 15 years.

4. Fouroux the Bell Tolls

Mike Rylance

Towards the end of the first Super League season, in August 1996, Maurice Lindsay called Paris Saint-Germain "a dazzling success". For the RFL's chief executive, the new French club was what rugby league of the future was all about. "It represents my dream for rugby league," he said.

Lindsay was by no means the first and will certainly not be the last to be seduced by the City of Light. The ideal of one of the world's great capitals playing host to high-level rugby league was shared by outward-looking supporters of the game. More than London, Paris symbolised a new era in which rugby league in the northern hemisphere at last moved out of its provincial, industrial landscape and into the metropolis.

The new-look architecture of the Charléty stadium, on the southern fringe of the city, pointed the way ahead for the many English clubs still holed up in their antiquated grounds. Against this backdrop, the broadcast-quality presentation and pre-match entertainment created an ambience which reduced other efforts to the level of pub karaoke. It provided a fine setting for sometimes heroic performances, given the circumstances, from a team which showed that French players can survive and flourish at the top level. Lindsay would claim that rugby league had become the second biggest spectator sport in the city behind soccer. It was a ringing endorsement of the so-called product. Those blasé Parisians had proved that rugby league really was the greatest game.

Paris represented the Super League vision and more besides. The classic jerseys, with the broad red central stripe piped with white set against the blue, were the haute couture of the Championship while the oh so sophisticated name gave the lie to the need for cheap, bolted-on nicknames dreamed up under the heading of "marketing".

The alluring combination of a world-famous sporting brand and the controversial figure of Jacques Fouroux ensured huge media interest when rugby league first joined Paris Saint-Germain Omnisports, an organisation which already embraced several other sports. Fouroux, the enfant terrible of French rugby union, the former captain and coach of the national team and vice-president of the governing body, had caused a sensation when, some 18 months earlier, he announced his conversion to the 13-a-side game.

While in Australia in the summer of 1994, Fouroux had been greatly impressed by the rugby league on show there and made contact with French Rugby League Federation president Jean-Paul Ferré, who was accompanying the France team on tour down under. With moves towards full-time professionalism in rugby union already taking place, Fouroux had a vision of blazing a trail in a different direction. "Rugby league has a hundred years' start on rugby union as a professional sport," he declared. "It is in an ideal position to become the rugby of tomorrow because its rules do not need to be improved. It already has the right mixture."

The former international scrum-half had been at loggerheads with rugby union's leaders and, after being invited as a guest to the Wembley Test match between Great Britain and Australia in the November, he became an evangelist for his adopted code. It wasn't long before he launched what he hoped would be a blueprint for the future, organising a summer competition in which regional teams played matches divided into four quarters, enhanced by a festive atmosphere.

As Super League plans unfolded, Maurice Lindsay laid claim to having "thought up the idea of rugby league in Paris". Certainly PSG fitted perfectly with the notion of a big city league, even if Jean Galia had had more success, 60 years earlier, in sowing the seeds which would lead to clubs in Bordeaux, Lyon, Toulouse, Marseille and, of course, Paris. Fouroux made equal claim to conceiving the Parisian project, convinced that no other European city offered the same potential. He disowned another proposal, current at the time, of having a second French club in Super League, to be based in Toulouse. For their part, the French Federation were happy to go along with the project, seeing Paris as a rallying point with which no traditional rugby league city, such as Toulouse or Perpignan, could compete, in view of the mixed loyalties within the game's heartlands. The first foreign club ever to enter the British Championship, Paris was the means by which Super League spread its European wings, at exactly the same time that rugby union had created its own European Cup. Equally it was intended to give impetus to the game across the Channel, which had been falling behind international standards for too long. For this, Fouroux, with his aura of the great rugbyman and widely-connected businessman, opened the doors.

As for the practicalities, an invaluable role was played by Tas Baitieri, without whom the club could barely have functioned. Long experience in France as a player and coach, and as a development officer in both hemispheres, gave Baitieri unequalled knowledge of the territory. But that undoubted competence could hardly have prepared him for the combined roles of chief executive, team manager, media relations officer and various other duties which included coaching and making travel reservations. Fluent in French, Baitieri would be the essential intermediary between the disparate strands of Super League, the Fouroux organisation and the French Federation.

Not the least of his responsibilities was to put a team and coaching staff together, drawn from the existing resources of the Federation. Just three months before the competition was due to start, Michel Mazaré, who had briefly been in charge of the France team some five years earlier, was named as coach after Joe Lydon and Andy Goodway had turned the opportunity down, with Villeneuve coach Dave Ellis being appointed as assistant. A squad of players was drawn up from the domestic Championship, which was in full flow. It is hard to believe now that a supposedly full-time professional outfit could depend on a squad of players who had never played at this level and who would continue to play for their own clubs, situated at the other end of the country, at the same time. As scrum-half Patrick Entat said when excusing himself from the captaincy, which was given to Pierre Chamorin: "It's one thing to launch a new rugby league club, but when it's also in Paris, it takes on different proportions altogether."

With unprecedented media interest for a club match in France, with three television channels and the national newspapers, both British and French, covering the game, it was vital to make a positive first impression. On that Friday evening, March 29th 1996, the Paris Saint-Germain team, consisting of 10 Frenchmen, three Australians, a New Zealander, a Tongan, a Pole and a Moldovan, pulled away from Sheffield Eagles in the last quarter of an unforgettable Super League opener to win 30-24 in front of 17,873 elated spectators. "We had to win tonight," said scrum-half Todd Brown. "Everything depended on this game." Brown's St Estève team-mate and captain, Chamorin, was even more upbeat. "It's like a dream. It's as if rugby league has arisen from the ashes," he said. The brilliantly-staged event and its hugely significant outcome led national coaching director Louis Bonnery to comment: "Paris has rediscovered rugby league tonight."

But, like all major capitals, Paris is a city of contrasts and contradictions and Paris Saint-Germain Rugby League was built in its image. That record crowd was based on large numbers of free tickets, which meant that the club would have very little, if any, income from gate receipts. Outside the playing and coaching staff, the club had almost no structure, hence the dependence on an overworked but uncomplaining Baitieri. Even the players did not belong fully to PSG. Two days after that momentous victory over Sheffield, almost all team members split up again to join their club sides in the south-west, for whom they turned out in the domestic competition. After that, they switched jerseys again to play two Super League matches over the Easter weekend. It would be unthinkable, a decade on, to place players under such pressure. "We are making a lot of sacrifices," explained Baitieri. "But the players know it's now or never."

Respectable performances during April were succeeded by trying times in May and June. After many players had taken part in either French Championship quarter-finals or cup semi-finals, they faced a journey to Wigan which ended in the team's first heavy defeat. For some, it was their fourth match in a week and resulted in a 76-6 rout, which prompted Wigan coach Graeme West to take up their case. "The League should ensure that they can concentrate on Super League," he said. "They are playing at a higher level and need the time to adjust. If they keep playing two or three times a week, their Super League form will nosedive."

And it did. "To play Wigan at Wigan, then play a rigorous semi-final on the Wednesday, before going up to Paris to play Leeds on the Friday was physically impossible," said Dave Ellis. "Straight after the semi, five Villeneuve players and three from XIII Catalan had to jump into cars to get to Toulouse airport to fly up to Paris. It's been very difficult."

Defeats at the hands of Wigan and Leeds were compounded by the loss, immediately before the 60-32 hammering at Bradford, of the Polish forward Greg Kacala. The former union player, brought into league by Fouroux, had been making great strides and playing consistently well. He was lured back to union not only by a generous offer but also by the threat of being banned from ever playing the 15-a-side code again by rugby union authorities who were desperate to contain the sudden threat posed by the PSG upstarts. In the following week, Chamorin and front-rower Darren Adams would also be approached. All of that had an unsettling effect, with Baitieri scouting around for a replacement for Kacala the day before the team travelled to Bradford.

St Helens, Castleford and Sheffield all racked up over 50 points against PSG in successive weeks, but Baitieri defended his men, saying: "You must remember that when Canberra Raiders and Brisbane Broncos first started up, they got similar floggings. It took them five years to get where they are now and in five years Paris will be in the same position." Comparisons with Australian rugby league were regularly made, with PSG expected to follow the model of the Auckland Warriors. But in fact the PSG venture in no way resembled the well-funded, well-organised projects of the Australian competition. One of several crucial differences was that television had opened up a pathway for a New Zealand club side to join the Australians, whereas Canal Plus, who were said to be supporting the Paris initiative, showed little more than highlights of the opening match, saying that the public was not interested in watching a losing side.

No one was actually saying so, but PSG was close to crisis. Only Workington lay below them in the table and relegation loomed. The players were being pulled in three directions all at once, as their duties towards PSG and their domestic teams were added to by international responsibilities. France's 73-6 thrashing by England at Gateshead prompted Lindsay, who said he was "very angry" with the French, to call on the French Federation and their president Jean-Paul Ferré to take some decisive action.

Stakeholders in the club were blaming one another: a sure sign of the predicament. Only the week before, Fouroux had slammed some of his players for what he thought was a lack of loyalty to the cause. Villeneuve had won their first French Championship final for 16 years, beating St Estève 27-26, and, as title winners do, had celebrated that Saturday night. In doing so, they failed to make the trip back up to Paris for the match against Halifax on the Monday, incurring the displeasure of the chairman, who called it "completely crazy" that four players and the assistant coach should party in Villeneuve rather than fulfil their Super League commitments.

Lindsay sent national coaching director John Kear to Paris to give the team some direction and a week later a small contingent of Australians arrived to bolster the squad. Set against that, the fragile structure of the club was weakened when its mainstay, Tas Baitieri, was recalled to Australia to work at the New South Wales Academy. Curiously, the ARL, who had allowed him leave to help develop the game in France, had only just noticed that, by aiding PSG and being paid by the British, he was, in the heat of the Super League war, working for "the opposition".

A usually diplomatic Baitieri admitted: "I'd like to think that I've brought something to the code in France but because of the poor administrative set-up nobody has benefited, because it's all been a crash course, fast-rolled into action without the necessary staff."

At almost the same time, the chairman himself resigned, although his decision did not become widely known until weeks later. Fouroux had realised that "the beautiful adventure", as he called it, was not the commercial success he had hoped for.

"We have run PSG like amateurs because we are in effect unpaid volunteers," he reflected. "We now have to set up a professional structure in Paris. The powers that be must ensure that we have big clubs in the big capitals. Rugby league already has the good fortune to have succeeded in London in playing terms and in Paris in promotional terms. The success of the concept is obvious."

The team did enough to ensure survival, thanks largely to a 24-18 victory over London, which ended a run of 11 defeats, in front of almost 10,000 spectators on July 13th, the eve of the national holiday. That win, and the failure of Workington, kept the French presence alive in Super League.

It had been a close-run thing. But the second Super League season saw the already tense relations between British and French strained to breaking-point. If Fouroux thought that Paris Saint-Germain had lacked credibility by the end of the first season, the French flagship met increasingly stormy conditions in 1997. Not that Fouroux's views counted any more. The RFL had declined to employ the club's former chairman as a kind of European development officer and he returned whence he came, to rugby union.

Fouroux was succeeded by his deputy, Jacques Larrose, while Maurice Lindsay and Harry Jepson made up a British presence on the PSG board. In the second season, and despite the involvement of Federation president Jean-Paul Ferré and secretary Philippe Dallongeville, the club took on an even greater Anglo-Saxon identity. Two RFL employees were seconded to Paris to run the club, while Australian Peter Mulholland, formerly in charge at another outpost, Perth Western Reds, was appointed as coach. The idea of issuing central contracts to French players failed to materialise, as Pascal Bomati, the club's top try-scorer in the first season, and winger Arnaud Cervello crossed over to rugby union. The French clubs refused to release their players for a second year and insisted on keeping them until the end of the domestic season, which, however, had been brought forward to its earliest ever date at the end of March. With the Challenge Cup looming in early February and Super League starting in mid-March, Mulholland recruited as best he could. With only around £400,000 to spend, he assembled a squad of Australians who, like himself, would live in a hotel on the outskirts of the city.

Still the club had almost no income from gate receipts and no takings from the bars, which were run independently. Nor was there access to merchandising rights from PSG Omnisports. The Canal Plus television channel, which had no connection with Sky TV but did enjoy close boardroom links with the PSG parent company, was still not showing much enthusiasm for broadcasting matches. In addition, the stadium hire was a major item of expenditure.

By the time PSG competed for the first time in the Challenge Cup, in which they won at Batley and lost at Salford, the squad consisted of over 20 Australians or New Zealanders but no Frenchmen. During the whole of the second season, only Pierre Chamorin and Fabien Devecchi, among the home-bred players, played more than a couple of matches. It had been Mulholland's intention gradually to integrate more French players into the squad but, constrained by the smallest budget in Super League and increasingly conscious of the need to stay clear of relegation, the coach came to depend more and more on his Aussie troopers.

Expectations had been naively high before the beginning of the season, with Ferré expressing the hope that a top-four place would be within PSG's reach. After just two months and a string of eight defeats, Mulholland became the sixth Super League coach to be relieved of his duties and was replaced by Wigan old boy Andy Goodway, who had turned down the chance to join PSG at the beginning but who had now left Oldham.

While Mulholland became involved in a feud over payment, chief executive Rob Elstone, who had been seconded to the club from England, left the RFL saying, "Rugby league is still dogged by self-interest and short-termism. If the sport is to make any kind of progress, it has to start thinking long-term." Elstone was exactly right. Improvised decision-making - the result of inadequate planning at the top level - simply led the club from one problem to another.

Michel Mazaré, PSG's first coach, now working as a national

development officer, also expressed his regret that so little was being achieved. "For us, Paris is the ideal to aspire to and all our work is orientated in that direction," he said. "It's vital that harmony is achieved in the administration of the club. We don't have that at the moment because everyone is pulling in a different direction. The great strength we had last year is that we had little in terms of resources but we all had the same aim and we pooled our strengths."

The divisions within the club were by now ingrained and departure followed departure, with chairman Jacques Larrose also coming to the end of his tether at seeing his position undermined. He reflected: "The club was being run by the decisions of other people. It wasn't me who appointed Peter Mulholland; it wasn't me who brought the Australians over; it wasn't me who sacked the coach; and it wasn't me who appointed Andy Goodway. I now feel the club is doomed to failure. Every other Super League club has various sources of income but Paris only has the Murdoch money. We were told that business partners would be brought in and that the club would develop along the lines of the Auckland Warriors. Instead the club lives by the generosity of Maurice Lindsay."

Despite its many difficulties and numerous crises, still the feeling remained that PSG represented a turning-point and had helped build a bold new image of the game. British fans, perhaps because the capital was such an exceptional away venue, did not appear to kick against the idea of a *nouveau-venu* in their midst, except to lament, as with London, the high proportion of Australian players there.

One such player, Tony Priddle, observed: "If everything was going well, Paris would be the best place in the world to be." Indeed, when Paris beat Perth in the World Club Championship, it seemed, for a moment, that the Super League dream had come true. Big city teams from opposite sides of the globe playing against each other gave glamour and star quality to the game, because this was the kind of thing that happened in major world sports. No matter that the Paris team was made up largely of Aussies, some of whom were playing against former team-mates. As Jean-Paul Ferré later remarked, when the PSG basketball team, made up of foreigners, played the Chicago Bulls in front of 15,000 spectators, no-one seemed too concerned.

Once more, however, the club was besieged by controversy. A dispute with the parent company meant that the team had to send for the France national side's jerseys to wear instead of their PSG kit. An "official" attendance of 959 for the Perth match appeared at odds with estimates of around 4,000, Lindsay later accusing the company in charge of promoting the club, old friends of Fouroux, with announcing false figures. A British national newspaper, which had been tipped off, alleged that a police inquiry might be held into why players had been playing on tourist visas rather than work permits. All was eventually resolved but it seemed almost as if the club had less in common with the European Super League than with Euro Disney, such was its roller-coaster season. Amazingly, new heights were scaled with a 30-28 home victory over Wigan, which led the third club chairman, Jean-Paul Ferré, to declare: "This is undoubtedly the best ever night for the sport of rugby league in Paris and the best win in the club's history. In fact it is incredible after the week we have endured."

Following two on-the-road matches in August, a victory over Halifax in front of 8,000 spectators at Narbonne and a defeat by Warrington watched by 1,500 at the strangely-chosen venue of Bayonne, relegation was still never far from the coach's mind. Goodway drafted in a number of untried French players for a match he must have regarded as unwinnable at Bradford. The 68-0 thrashing - the first time PSG had been nilled - proved him right, while allowing rested players to pick themselves up for the relegation decider, three days later, against his former club Oldham. PSG's 23-12 win ensured their own survival, sent Oldham down and saw Goodway on the verge of being appointed Great Britain coach.

For the second season in a row Paris Saint-Germain had earned the right to remain in Super League. But the future of the French presence was called into question that autumn, because, said Lindsay, "we believe we should not be running a side which is made up of Australians and which is not an authentic French team." There were simple reasons for that, as Lindsay must have known. One of the many ironies associated with PSG is that, once the French were out of Super League, the next innovation was the suspension of automatic relegation. John Kear who coached the side in the second half of the first season, pointed out that if there had been no relegation, they could have persevered with a basically French squad, who had made quick progress.

The British clubs apparently expressed "an overwhelming desire" to see PSG stay in their midst, but only if the French would pay their own way. The French half of the board objected to being held responsible for debts, reckoned to amount to almost half a million pounds, which they claimed had been accumulated by British decision-making. And so Paris Saint-Germain was consigned to what was famously called a sabbatical year which, as we now know, became eight (and counting...).

Tas Baitieri knew all about the club's shortcomings and their causes. As he left for Australia in June of the first season, he observed: "People have misjudged the enormous difficulties that a team out of Paris was going to present. When new teams are accepted into the competition in Australia they're given three years' notice in which to organise all the many aspects involved in building a new club. All of that has been lacking here because Paris has been fast-tracked."

Apart from the wrangle over the club's debts, there was no good reason why PSG could not have relocated to become Toulouse Olympique or XIII Catalan in a third season. Neither would have had the cachet of Paris Saint-Germain, but a Super League club in the south-west would certainly have gained the support of genuine treizistes. That would have provided income from gate receipts, merchandising and bar sales as well as greatly reducing the costs of travel, accommodation and stadium hire. Instead all that effort and money went to waste, giving the quinzistes the opportunity to step in.

Fouroux had been pleased regularly to invite his rugby union chums to the VIP lounge at Charléty, where they could see for themselves how "rugby" could be promoted to a previously indifferent public. The PSG chairman had expected many more members of his coterie to follow him into league, but it didn't happen and must privately have given him another reason to resign. While he himself now coaches at club level in Italy, the Stade Français club has made itself into one of the most powerful rugby union outfits in

France, with the backing of one of Fouroux's rich friends who had seen what was on offer at Charléty. Fouroux talks philosophically now about his innovatory ideas of attracting big crowds with live music and initially free, or very low-cost admission. "So much time has passed, but so much is relevant today," he muses. He was correct, too, to pick up on the modern trend of wanting to be part of an event and to be associated with success, as the "I was there" factor of that first match against Sheffield showed. That, more than the allegiance to a particular sport, is a recent phenomenon which has touched other parts of Super League.

On their own initiative, genuine clubs picked up the baton which Paris had dropped. Toulouse, who had wanted to enter Super League as early as 2000, made all the early running, followed by Villeneuve and then, at a late stage, the Catalans. If any one of those had originally been selected instead of Paris, the French venture would have had a far stronger chance of long-term survival. Though the eventual decision to select the Catalans ahead of Toulouse caused some surprise, the Perpignan team was rightly given three years to prepare their way. Once again there will be a significant Anglo-Australian presence at the club, and officials will have the heavy responsibility of ensuring that past mistakes are not repeated.

Commenting on the demise of Paris Saint-Germain, Jean-Paul Ferré, made what we might think a typically French observation. "Paris was like a beautiful woman," he said. "Very attractive but making increasing demands the more time you spent with her." It must be hoped that Perpignan's relationship with Super League is a more fruitful and longer-lasting one.

● *Mike Rylance was the founding editor of League Express, for which he continues to write about French rugby league. He has contributed to numerous other publications, both in Britain and France, and is the author of best-selling books "International Stars of Rugby League" and "The Forbidden Game". The latter has since been up-dated for a second edition. He is currently researching the history of Wakefield Trinity.*

5. Refs, Tries & Videotape

John Ledger

Like all defining moments in your life, it's something you'll never forget. For instance, the day I realised I was no longer a kid will stay with me forever. There I was, innocently having fun with my pals on the swings and roundabouts. "Oi, you lot, gerroff them swings and bugger off, you're too old to be in here," yelled the park keeper, his gruff words cruelly bringing down the curtain on my childhood.

He was right, of course: 23 is not an age when you should be hogging the rides in the local playground. And then there was the occasion when I knew beyond a shadow of doubt that I had completed the journey from adolescence into manhood. I was at the bar in the Graziers pub near Wakefield's Belle Vue ground before a match and had ordered three pints of hand-pulled Tetley's only to be told by the uncaring landlord: "That'll be £3.90 please." For the first time, ever, he'd not asked if I was 18. That I was actually 30, already balding and looked nearer 40 didn't matter; nor did the fact that I hadn't been in the Graziers for 13 years; or that going to the bar has never been my forte (I am a Yorkshireman, after all). It was the principle.

But the most epiphanic day in my professional career came on Sunday June 23rd, 1996. I had to look that up, of course, remembering dates is never easy when you get to my age. It was sunny. I do remember that, though, because I was at Odsal and I wasn't wearing a coat. And there haven't been many days when it's been warm enough to do that since 1895. Bradford were playing Sheffield, the old versus the nearly new. The Bulls had lost to Castleford only the week before (oh happy days) and all was well with the world. And then the match kicked off.

Just 18 minutes later the score was 18-all and my outlook on life had changed forever. I had started the match as an ardent enthusiast, a progressive observer of the game who was keen to champion the summer rugby cause in the pages of the *Yorkshire Post* but by the time the final hooter blew to signal the end of a fixture the Bulls won 64-22, my new-found status as a rugby league dinosaur was confirmed: 86 points in a match between two of the sport's elite teams! What was going on?

Although that was Bradford's highest score of the inaugural Super League season, matches with similar outcomes were suddenly becoming the norm. Wigan scored 68 against a sorry Leeds team, who a week later put the same total past an even sorrier Workington; Oldham even managed to top 30 points on more than one occasion, most teams reached a half-century against Paris and London ended their season with a 56-0 defeat of Castleford.

As a youngster, I hated it when Ray French described a free-scoring game on *Grandstand* as being "just like basketball," because rugby league clearly never was. But this was even worse. In basketball, the sequence usually went "you score, we score, you score, we score, ad infinitum" but, suddenly, rugby league had become the "you score, we score, we score, we score again, and again, and again" sport. Never mind "it's just not cricket," more pertinently "it's just not rugby league."

Wasn't one of the reasons the game in this country had spent so much time looking to Australia the supposed need to learn defensive techniques from our Down Under country cousins? So why had players stopped tackling? Could it be, given the switch to summer, that the sun was always in their eyes?

After all, every club had embraced the new formula which, rumour had it, was part of the game's £87m broadcast contract with News Ltd. The deal was this: until such time as the Sky people had got their heads around the technicalities of the summer phenomenon, worked out where to put their cameras and come up with insightful catchphrases, Uncle Rupert would much prefer it if coaches kept it simple.

Forget fancy runaround moves, switch passes, dummy runs, sidesteps and the like: five drives and a kick would do. All a team had to do was keep possession for five tackles, hoist the ball into the sun (or, when in Cumbria, the area of sky which was the lightest shade of grey) and a try was assured. It worked for St Helens in the Challenge Cup final at Wembley that year, when Sky were thanking their lucky stars that it was the BBC boys who had to try and keep a camera on that clever clogs Robbie Paul, and it worked again and again over the next few seasons. Endlessly.

So much so that by the time Sky had positioned a camera in all the best vantage points, read the rule book and abandoned any notion of inventing insightful catchphrases, many of the old traditional skills had either been forgotten or dismissed out of hand as antiquated. But not in Australia. While some Super League coaches were busy censuring half-backs for not carrying the ball enough and dropping wingers who dared to try and beat an opponent on the outside, the Aussies were developing a new breed of intelligent, creative players whose style was redolent of a different era.

One of the main reasons followers of the game in this country took so readily to the exciting play of the likes of Andrew Johns, Brett Kimmorley, Wendell Sailor, Darren Lockyer and Gorden Tallis was that they reminded us of how our heroes used to play rugby league. Sure, the advent of Super League has certainly made players fitter and better prepared but are they really any smarter? If all the time spent on the training field as a result of full-time professionalism really has created a new breed of super-intelligent player, why do coaches feel it necessary to have a 14th man - the conditioner or trainer, usually - running behind the line, water bottle in hand, organising them over the course of a match?

Players such as Garry Schofield, Alex Murphy, Alan Hardisty, Roger Millward, Steve Norton, Billy Boston and Neil Fox would have been stars in any era and all would have benefited greatly were they afforded the same advantages granted the average Super League player, but might their natural talent have been dulled by modern coaching methods?

Fortunately, 10 years on, a new philosophy has begun to creep into Super League with many coaches now acknowledging that genius is an inherently fragile gift which cannot be instilled into a player but one that can be damaged by careless guidance. The days when someone like Leeds stand-off Danny McGuire was omitted from the national team because of his limitations - the then Great Britain coach David Waite was of the view that a player whose greatest asset was scoring tries and winning matches had no place in his plans - are thankfully over.

Unfortunately, the preponderance of high-scoring non-events continues to blight Super League and from recent experience it is clear that the blame does not lie with the coaches or the players but with the administrators. The 2005 Challenge Cup final proved to be a veritable classic with eight tries equally shared between Leeds and Hull, who won through by virtue of a drop-goal by the player with the dodgiest mullet in Super League, Danny Brough. Hull's performance that day, just as it had been in their semi-final victory over St Helens, was flawless - unlike their scrum-half's hair - and as impressive as anything seen at any time in the modern game. Yet, just four weeks later, the very same players who had completed one of the finest victories in the history of the Challenge Cup were humiliated 71-0 in a Super League play-off match at Bradford.

As well as the Bulls played that day, and in spite of the dismissal of Stephen Kearney for a high tackle on Stuart Fielden, Hull did not deserve to lose by such a scoreline. The comment afterwards by their coach, John Kear, that Hull had "cascaded into indifference" was succinct if rather harsh, for the Challenge Cup holders had merely become the latest victims of a set of rules which are threatening to turn rugby league into a real-life computer game.

Perhaps the most virulent rule is the one that dictates teams be kept 10-metres apart at the play-the-ball, creating a space which is downright dangerous to those who play the game, has a suffocating effect on some of the sport's more sublime skills and which engenders a pattern of scoring that is, quite frankly, boring. The 10m rule, allied to the bizarre situation where a team which has just conceded a try has to give the ball straight back to their opponents at the restart, allows such an irresistible level of momentum to be gained by the dominant side that matches with silly scores are inevitable.

Now that players have become such fine physical specimens from all their long hours in the gym and scientifically engineered diets, the speed and ferocity of their collisions is indeed spectacularly brutal. Big hits - or crash tackles as we dinosaurs still like to think of them - make for great television and are guaranteed to crank up the atmosphere on the terraces, but at what cost? A quick pass from the play-the-ball by the hooker to a second row forward can set in motion a chain of events which causes lasting damage to either the ball carrier or those whose job it is to stop a 17-stone hard-as-rock leviathan who has been running at terminal velocity for 15 metres.

One of the attractions of rugby league is its gladiatorial combat but the frequency of season-ending injuries, snapped ligaments and broken bones surely has to be a cause for concern. No-one wants to see a return to the days when corpulent old forwards were able to trundle around the field, launching their beer bellies at defenders who would find themselves suffocated beneath an arsenal of adipose tissue, well into their late 30s. But is it right that 30 has almost become the cut-off point, the age at which players are usually deemed to be in such a physically irreparable state that retirement becomes a medical necessity? Somehow I don't think it is.

Rugby league has not just become a sport exclusively played by the young and chiefly appreciated by the Playstation generation, it is also refereed and controlled by a new breed of match officials. Some of the most famous whistle blowers became household names by virtue of both their notoriety and their longevity with Robin Whitfield, Fred Lindop, Gerry Kershaw and John Holdsworth all remaining as men in black until their 50th birthdays.

"There is absolutely no way that a referee could referee in Super League at 50 now," says Stuart Cummings, the Rugby Football League's match officials director. "People like Fred and Robin would have gone on longer were it not for the fact that 50 was the compulsory retirement age for a referee. We don't have a compulsory retirement age any more because we don't need one. The referees' list is now decided by the fitness testing all the officials have to go through. I can't image there coming a time when any referee can sustain the level of fitness needed to referee in Super League past 45.

"The intensity of the game is far greater now than it was even 10 years ago. I refereed the first ever Super League match between Paris Saint-Germain and Sheffield Eagles at the Charlety Stadium in 1996 and looking back it was played in a real carnival atmosphere. The pace of the game nowadays is just incredible. There's rarely a break in play and the referee is always having to make judgment calls. When I started refereeing, I had a lot more time to think but it's so technical now that referees have to act on instinct and instilling that instinct is a long and difficult process."

Cummings was 42 when he called time on his refereeing career to take a desk job at Red Hall - "I could have done a couple of years more but opportunities like the one I had don't come along that often" - and he has no regrets about stepping down when he did. "The referees still get a great deal of enjoyment from what they do but they have to work very hard to stay at the top of their game," he says. "We ask a whole lot more of them than we did pre-Super League. The main reason it has become so demanding is that they are still part-time while the players are all full-time. That is something the game urgently needs to address."

Cummings has long championed the cause of professional referees and can see a situation whereby all referees and touch-judges will be employed on a full-time basis, as they are in Australia's National Rugby League, within the next decade. The opportunity for aspiring match officials to plot a career path through the grades will certainly assist with recruitment, which remains a demanding area for the game, even though the RFL have, according to Cummings, added an extra 200 referees to their active list between 2001 and 2005.

"Finding new referees has always been tough," adds Cummings. "The profile of the referee has increased somewhat because of Super League and many of the new officials have come on board for that reason. It's my belief that 50 per cent of the people who watch rugby league regularly could referee a game if they put their minds to it.

The difficulty comes in persuading them that there is a positive side to refereeing and that it's not all about having the crowd, the coaches and the commentators on your back."

With Sky having a camera covering most of the important angles, referees are under more scrutiny than ever before and Cummings insists that is predominantly a healthy situation, except perhaps when TV pundits mischievously criticise officials knowing they are in the right just to "sex up" their coverage.

"Criticism is never good, especially when it's blatantly ill-informed, but on the other hand the coverage the game gets on television allows us to assess and analyse a referee's performance in a way we could never have dreamed about not too long ago," he says. "The super camera work that Sky do has benefited us immensely because it allows us to dissect every key incident in a game. The tapes of matches screened by Sky are an invaluable training aid for us."

Super League officials in recent years have benefited from a highly-visible sponsorship deal with Powergen, whose logo is so prevalent that matchdays often resemble an electricians' convention. It used to be said that refereeing was the loneliest job in sport but now, with touch-judges, in-goal judges, a match commissioner, interchange official, video referee, refereeing coach and physiotherapist in tow, the man in the middle often has more support than the away team. The presence of a video referee at just two Super League fixtures per round remains unsatisfactory but until such time as the technology becomes more affordable, the competition will continue to be run under two sets of rules.

While the overwhelming majority of the decisions made by video referees during the Super League era are incontrovertibly correct, errors are occasionally made, as Bradford have discovered more than once to their cost in Grand Finals. As welcome as the technology is, its value is undermined when a system designed to minimise human error merely introduces another human capable of making errors. Video referees are neither seen nor heard while the Super League referee remains a visible yet largely silent figure who invariably keeps his opinions and outlook on life to himself. Cummings is naturally protective of his charges but the senior referees' perceived lack of accountability is the source of some serious disquiet among the Super League coaches and the former schoolteacher faces a huge test of character in sorting it out.

It could be, of course, that referees want to speak out but are unable to on health grounds. After all, with so many tries to award in Super League matches, all that pointing to the floor and blowing of the whistle must leave them quite breathless and suffering from repetitive strain injury. That Super League has been a force for the good in terms of refereeing is not in doubt for Cummings, whose words ought to serve as a salutary warning to all those who would take the game back to the dark days of winter rugby.

"I spent the last six years of my career refereeing the summer game and I would never, ever go back to winter," he said. "There is no comparison. I have refereed matches when I was so cold I couldn't straighten my finger to point to a try. There were times when I lost track of the score because I was too cold, or it was too wet, to write down the scorers.

"The game may be more technical now, faster and more furious but it's clean, comfortable and the players usually leave the field in the same colour as they went on it. There is nothing romantic about mud, snow, cold, rain and frost. Give me sunshine any day."

And a return to five metres. Now wouldn't that be a wonderful way to start Super League's second decade?

● *John Ledger joined the Yorkshire Post in 1990 and five years later became the newspaper's fifth rugby league correspondent since the split of 1895. In 1998 he was named UK regional sports writer of the year for a series of articles exposing financial irregularities at the Rugby Football League. He lives in Ackworth near Pontefract and is not averse to people standing him a pint in the Junction Inn, Featherstone.*

6. Capital Gains, Capital Losses

David Lawrenson

If the first 10 years of Super League have been something of a roller-coaster ride then there's no doubt that the London Broncos have been in the front seat. No club has experienced more ups and downs than the capital's only fully-professional rugby league side, from their controversial inclusion in the new 12-team competition in 1995 to survival by the skin of their teeth in 2005.

There has never been a dull moment. London have probably used more players, played on more grounds and certainly travelled more miles than any other outfit in Super League. It's a quarter of a century since the latest attempt to establish a professional rugby league team in London saw Fulham beat Wigan in their inaugural game at Craven Cottage. And 25 years to the day their successors, London Broncos, beat Widnes Vikings at Brentford in their final game before moving to the Stoop and becoming Harlequins RL.

Most people in the north can't comprehend the significance of that game in September 1980 to rugby league's southern exiles. Imagine living in London with your nearest club 200 miles away. The only time you get to see the great game is on rare visits, usually at Easter or Christmas.

I first came to London to college in 1970 and rather than play union I opted to play football. I wasn't aware of any opportunities to play the game, let alone watch it. Mind you, it was handy for Challenge Cup finals, but one game a year wasn't really satisfactory so the emergence of Fulham was fantastic. Sadly the dream didn't last long and although I made occasional trips to places like Crystal Palace, Chiswick Polytechnic and Barnet Copthall, it just wasn't the same.

Rugby league clubs thrive on being part of the community and having players you can identify with. But with Fulham, who later became the London Crusaders, not only did you need the big version of the A to Z to keep up with them on their ground hopping, the players seemed to change on a weekly basis. Half the time the side seemed to be made up of Aussie backpackers. Thanks to some incredibly dedicated people the club was kept alive, and just before the advent of Super League the Brisbane Broncos got involved, which meant another change of name and hopefully some stability and rugby league nous.

Barry Maranta, the chairman, was often quoted as saying how he had helped to establish the Broncos in Brisbane and would do the same in London. However, London ain't Brisbane, as he soon found out. Just to illustrate the problems the club had, in that last season before Super League the Broncos played their home games at four different venues in the capital, Brentford's Griffin Park, the Valley at Charlton, Barnet Copthall and the Stoop Memorial Ground, home of Harlequins rugby union club. They only got into Super League by luck, having been in the old Second Division when the Murdoch people came up with their plans to revolutionise the game. They insisted on a London team, much to the chagrin of clubs like Widnes and Keighley.

The Valley was to become London's home in that first season of summer rugby. I had actually been to the ground once before, in 1974, but in very different circumstances. Along with about 80,000 others, I was there to see The Who play one of their great concerts, and later discovered that it was in the *Guinness Book of Records* as the biggest gig in Britain up to that time. But it was a very different place when I returned to see the Broncos for that first Super League season in 1996. They had a new coach, Tony Currie, who had taken over from Gary Grienke, and the squad boasted players who were to become Broncos legends: Russell Bawden, Peter Gill, Tony Martin, Terry Matterson, Tony Mestrov, Tony Rea and Tulsen Tollett. Towards the end of the season they also signed London's greatest ever rugby league player, Martin Offiah.

That season also saw some of the biggest attendances since the Craven Cottage days, with over 10,000 for the game against Wigan. The club finished in a very respectable fourth place and even helped St Helens end Wigan's seven-year dominance of the Championship. Saints finished the season just one point ahead of their great rivals and no doubt Wigan reflected on their match against the Broncos at Central Park earlier in the year. The 'Pie Eaters' had a comfortable 18-4 lead going into the second half, but a fantastic goal from the touchline by Terry Matterson late on forced an 18-18 draw and cost them what turned out to be a vital point.

In what was to become an all-too familiar pattern the club upped sticks the following season and moved across London to the Stoop. However, 1997 proved to be London's most successful Super League campaign. They finished runners-up to Bradford Bulls in the Super League and recorded some great victories, notably over Wigan and Canberra Raiders, the latter being one of those seminal moments in London league history. It was a good time for the club, with league legend Shaun Edwards joining his mate Offiah in a strong squad.

Listeners to Virgin Radio around that time became used to one of their breakfast dee-jays, Jono Coleman, extolling the virtues of the Broncos - amazing, considering that all other references to sport on the station consisted of football, football and more football. It was through Coleman that Richard Branson became interested, bought a 15 per cent share in February and ended the season as majority shareholder and chairman. Now, at last, surely there would be a big push to promote the club and the sport. After all, weren't Virgin all about publicity and promoting the brand? Sadly, it proved not to be the case.

There was little or no publicity, no innovative marketing ideas. All I personally remember was one big poster featuring Offiah and, I think, Mark Carroll but it seemed entirely the wrong approach. That area of south-east London is very much commuter-land. Every weekday morning, thousands of people pass through the Richmond,

Twickenham and Kingston stations on their way up to central London. I could never understand why they didn't stick some posters up there, saying something like: "See the Londoners take on the northerners at their own game."

After the on-field highs of that season, 1998 was desperately disappointing with the team finishing in seventh place. It did, though, mark the debut of one of the club's most loyal servants: Steele Retchless. Great name, great bloke, Steele was a tackling machine of a second rower. When the Broncos played Bradford Bulls in Edinburgh that July, he made a world record 66 tackles to help the team to a 22-8 win. Even the guy who compiled the stats found it hard to believe, so he reviewed the game again the following day before confirming the figure. Steele was one of the great Broncos and certainly had one of the more unusual names. He sounded like a villain from a Barbara Cartland bodice-ripper. At the time I was working on *The Sunday Times* and a colleague who wrote the Sport on TV column was so taken by Steele's name that he used to try and crowbar some mention of him into his copy whenever he could. I remember talking to Steele and asking him about the origin of his name, but I can't really remember the reply so it can't have been that memorable.

After that disappointing season Tony Currie departed to be replaced by Dan Stains. A committed Christian, Stains must have had a word with the man upstairs because in 1999 London made their one and so far only appearance in the Challenge Cup final; an historic occasion as it was the last to be staged at the old Wembley. However, they very nearly didn't make it when Castleford looked to be taking control of their semi-final at Headingley. In a pulsating finish, a Peter Gill try and Brett Warton conversion dragged the Broncos back into it, but extra-time looked a certainty after Danny Orr brought the scores level with a drop-goal. Then, in the dying seconds, a certain second-rower suddenly saw a gap open up in front of him and he had the line at his mercy.

Now, Steele Retchless wasn't used to wide open spaces and looked around for someone to tackle, before eventually deciding that he'd better head for the line. Steele seemed to realise that this crucial moment would be shown on national television and would need more than a discreet touching down of the ball. So he tried an elegant swallow dive which, in fact, turned out to be more like a dying swan. Definitely nul points for style but it did the job and took the club on its first trip down Wembley Way. "I just thank God that we got the job done," said Stains. Thankfully, worries about playing in a half-full stadium proved unfounded as the great rugby league supporting public turned up in their thousands. Richard Branson ignored cup final sartorial convention and led the team out in jeans, but the day will mainly be remembered for the record four tries Leroy Rivett scored in Leeds' 52-16 victory.

After Wembley, it all started to go horribly wrong again. Coach Stains, who hadn't endeared himself to the fans by banning Shaun Edwards from the club, departed after the team were hammered 74-12 at Bradford in June. His assistant, Les Kiss, and Tony Rea took over. The pair ensured London ended the season in eighth place before Kiss departed to be succeeded by John Monie.

The new millennium saw the Broncos leave The Stoop after three seasons and return to The Valley at Charlton. Now I have to admit that I'm a west London boy (well, since leaving St Helens anyway) but I always felt that west London was the spiritual home of professional rugby league in the capital. Of course, you've got to go where you're wanted but I wasn't happy going back to The Valley. Moving to the other side of London is like suddenly telling Wigan or Saints fans that they will have to travel over to Castleford to watch their team.

It's a hell of a journey by car or public transport and the area has no rugby background whatsoever. Stand-off Karle Hammond cited the move to south east London as one reason for their poor showing that season, saying that it had upset their preparations. They also made one of their worst signings in winger Frank Napoli. He arrived from an Australian team called the Burleigh Bears, who are presumably the Australian equivalent of the Paddington Bears. Things didn't go too well for Frank or his new club all year, although there were some notable events with the Broncos going on the road to play their 'home game' against Warrington Wolves at Newport. The match against Castleford at the Valley was brilliant thanks to the Tigers' sponsor, Jungle.com, hiring coaches to bring thousands of supporters down the M1 and giving the club their biggest home gate of the season. But at the end of it all, with the team sitting second from bottom with three games remaining, John Monie was sacked to be replaced by chief executive Tony Rea.

The 2001 season promised much with a host of exciting signings. Dennis Moran joined a squad that included New Zealand full-back Richie Barnett and Aussie stars Jim Dymock and Jason Hetherington. Off the field, the Broncos appointed Lionel Hurst as Rea's replacement. Lionel had been the driving force behind the national summer conference, already well on its way to becoming one of the great success stories of rugby league expansion. However, my memories of him at The Valley revolve around a radio programme that he was due to take part in after one of the Broncos home games.

The radio guys had set up their equipment in the press box, which is high up in one of the stands. Unfortunately, Lionel didn't have a head for heights and couldn't stomach the long climb up. When the match was over, myself and the journalists took our usual route down to the bowels of the stand to the room where the after-match press conferences were always held, only to be turned away at the door. Apparently, the new chief executive had insisted on doing his radio piece in there, so we all had to troop down several corridors to find an alternative room while Lionel was left to do his stuff - hope he wasn't agoraphobic.

The team put up a good showing that season and finished sixth, with local boy Dominic Peters selected to represent Lancashire in the Origin game. But there was trouble on the horizon. Disastrously, or so it seemed, Virgin announced that they were pulling out and the club appeared to be on the verge of folding. Just how close they came to doing that was revealed by Tony Rea's programme notes for their penultimate game at Griffin Park in 2005. Businessman David Hughes had become involved in the club at the start of Super League in 1996, but when Virgin came on board they decided they wanted to own the whole thing lock, stock and barrel, including Hughes' 20 per cent. David decided to hold on but that meant putting more money into the pot, which is what he did. When Virgin later decided to cut their ties with the club, he thought about taking on the whole thing himself. Around this time, Tony and David decided to go for a meal in Brick Lane, the London curry capital. It turned out to be the most expensive meal David has ever eaten.

Tony pointed out that if Richard Branson couldn't make a go of it, what chance was there of him doing it. At the end of the meal they had reached the sad conclusion that there was no point in him throwing good money after bad. David agreed to call Virgin the following morning - effectively signalling the end of the club. But when Tony rang him the following day he was astounded to learn that David had indeed rung Virgin but told them he was willing to take the club on himself. A stunned Rea asked about their discussion the previous evening and the conclusion they had both seemingly agreed upon. "Yes I know," Hughes replied. "But I just woke up this morning and thought bugger that." Although Virgin continued with a sponsorship package over the next few years, without David Hughes, the Broncos would have been sunk.

Almost inevitably there was soon another move, this time back to west London for what was to be the Broncos' final home: Griffin Park. Brentford is an interesting place, a solid working class district for much of its history until it suddenly became, in one of those phrases beloved of Hull fans Kirstie Allsopp and Phil Spencer on Channel 4's "*Location, Location, Location*", an up-and-coming area. Hotels and upmarket residential developments began springing up all over the place. To the outsider, the area still looks slightly down-at-heel with terraced houses surrounding the ground and, most notably, a pub on every corner. I remember one of my colleagues commenting on the downmarket surroundings as we walked to the ground but he was stunned when I told him that you couldn't buy one of those terraced houses for less than a quarter of a million pounds.

The Broncos didn't get off to too good a start at their new home. After their first four fixtures they were without a Super League win, but all changed when St Helens came to town. Saints were hammered 40-6, which was not only the Broncos first win in Super League and their first at Griffin Park but also their first ever win over their illustrious visitors.

The biggest bugbear surrounding the new venue was the need to vacate the premises in the middle of the season, for up to seven weeks at a time, so that work could be done on the pitch. In 2002, this meant playing Warrington in the south of France, at Carcassonne. Inconsistency meant that London again missed out on the play-offs, finishing eighth. Things looked good for 2003, until Dom Peters, one of the few genuinely talented local lads to come through into Super League, was banned by the RFL for 12 months for taking an illegal substance and the Broncos subsequently terminated his contract.

Winning at Brentford was a real problem but winning away wasn't. One of London's greatest away victories came at Odsal on June 1st. Livewire scrum-half Dennis Moran, who had scored a hat-trick in a win at Wakefield the previous week, had flown back to Australia due to a family bereavement. He had promised to return the following weekend for the match at Bradford, although few thought that realistic. Nevertheless, he landed at Heathrow on the morning of the game and managed to get a connecting flight to Leeds-Bradford airport before arriving, as promised, just a couple of hours before kick-off. Jet lag? What jet lag? Instead, Dennis scored three tries in a dazzling display, to help London to a stunning 22-12 victory. It was one of those *Boy's Own* stories that you get once in a while as a journalist and which you can't wait to write.

The Broncos still hadn't managed a home victory by the time they had to vacate Griffin Park and take on Widnes at Aberavon. They won that one but had to wait until late July to register their first win at Brentford. By finishing fifth they made the play-offs for the first time, but lost to St Helens in the Elimination Play-Off.

In an all-too familiar pattern, after one decent season the Broncos struggled the following year and a 12-match run without a win saw them next to bottom of the table. The question asked by some northern league fans was: "Will the RFL allow the Broncos to be relegated?". In rugby union's Premiership, they said the same about Harlequins but, when they finished bottom in 2005, down they went. I'm sure the same would apply in Super League; it would have to if the competition is to have any credibility. Thankfully, four consecutive wins in August eased those relegation worries.

Once again, though, there was uncertainty in the air, with David Hughes rumoured to be in talks with Eric Watson, owner of the New

Zealand Warriors, about a takeover. It was also a big shock to see Dennis Moran signing for Wigan in the close season. I assume he got fed up of virtually carrying the Broncos team single-handedly and who could blame him? Moran was by far and away the brightest spark in an essentially workmanlike side but, rather than bemoaning the loss of his star player, Tony Rea set about revitalising his squad for 2005. In doing so, he signed not one half-back but three, all with pace, skill and a positive approach. Enter Mark McLinden, Luke Dorn and Thomas Leuluai who, together with the likes of Solomon Haumono and Mark Tookey, promised a great Super League X.

The London crowd enjoy larger-than-life characters. When Fulham kicked off back in 1980, Ian van Bellen, a giant of a forward, became a folk hero. Since signing from Castleford in September 2004, Tookey, a former South Queensland Crushers team-mate of Steele Retchless and Mat Toshack, has assumed that mantle. As ever though, and you should be getting used to this by now, there was a crisis looming. The Broncos were once again on the verge of going down the tubes after running up debts of an estimated £3million. A plan to write it all off by forming a new company had to be agreed with their fellow Super League clubs if they were to survive. Some clubs, with an eye on their own survival or the possibility of picking up some of the London players, voted against them. Fortunately, enough - just - were persuaded to see things another way.

It was a close-run thing. Rugby Football League executive chairman, Richard Lewis, flew back from holiday to join his financial controller, Nigel Wood, in seeking to convince the clubs of London's worth, while reportedly suggesting in the meeting that a "no" vote would have to be interpreted as a vote of no confidence in him. That, plus a thinly-veiled suggestion that London weren't the only club in a bit of financial strife, seemed to do the trick. In the event, Wakefield and Widnes abstained, while Leeds, Hull, St Helens, Huddersfield and Warrington backed the Broncos and Wigan, Salford, Leigh and Bradford voted to have them punished, if not kicked out completely. Once again, all the old chestnuts came out regarding favouritism, the need to concentrate on the heartlands etc etc. Yet if rugby league voted out all those clubs with poor financial management, there wouldn't be a team left in the sport. Ironically, given their stance on the issue, Bradford did exactly the same as the Broncos in the 1960s and nobody batted an eyelid. In fact, they rallied around to help.

On the other side of the argument, it's not very good for business or rugby league when something like this happens and the Broncos were ordered to sort themselves out once and for all, with rumours rife of more major changes in the air. Having survived off the field, London began to play their rugby with real pace and verve on it, although they might have won one or two more matches had they been able to control games a little better. Again, however, they were forced to vacate Griffin Park for seven weeks, a situation which has hardly done the team or their supporters any favours. The Broncos took another game to south Wales, the round-19 clash with Hull in Bridgend, where one of the more interesting moments came when the announcer read out the London side. It was hysterical as he tried to get to grips with Nick Bradley-Qalilawa, Filimone Lolohea and Feleti Mateo. You were just waiting to hear which name he would mangle next.

Having said that, some of my colleagues who still dictate copy over the telephone rather than use a laptop computer, have been known to curse when, on tight deadlines, they have had to spell out some of the more difficult names to a copy taker, a trade whose knowledge of rugby rarely extends beyond Jonny Wilkinson. David Burke, for example, a freelance writer for whom doing six match reports on one game is a stroll in the park, tempted fate during one London match at St Helens. When Bradley-Qalilawa's name was announced, David joked: "Blimey, we don't want him scoring!". Needless to say, he did, and in fact finished the 2005 season as one of the engage Super League's top scorers with 19 tries. Keep your mouth shut next time, Dave!

The big news, however, was just around the corner. Not only was there to be another change of name, but a change of ground and ownership. In July 2005, it was announced that the Broncos were to become Harlequins RL and play at the newly-named Twickenham Stoop from 2006. "We have the opportunity in the coming years to build Harlequins into a powerhouse in both codes," said Quins chief executive Mark Evans. "While this is not a merger or takeover in either direction it does represent the most exciting coming together of rugby union and rugby league ever," added new Wigan-born Broncos chairman Ian Lenagan, fresh from taking over from David Hughes, although London's former saviour remains on the board. "We feel sure it is a very, very strong future for rugby league in the capital."

This latest move in a never less than bumpy journey does indeed represent the best chance yet. Harlequins RL get to play in an excellent stadium with great facilities and adopt one of the most recognisable rugby brands in the world. There is no crippling ground rent. There are great corporate hospitality facilities and the club gets to tap into the Harlequins marketing and promotional expertise. While Quins have always had a reputation of being supported by City types, the club realised a few years ago that if it was to be viable it would need to tap into the local community. The result is that, even after relegation, season ticket sales and attendances were hardly affected. The news didn't do London's on-field results any harm either. Despite injuries to key players, in what was now going to be their final season as the Broncos, the club made the play-offs for the second time and left Brentford with a comprehensive 68-10 win over an already-relegated Widnes Vikings.

What is now on offer is exactly what a rugby league club in London needs; a good local base from which to draw supporters who identify with the club and who will follow them through thick and thin. Anyone who spouts rubbish about this being a union plot to take over league wants his or her head testing. The rugby league club seem to be getting far more out of the deal than their rugby union partners. Let's face it, even after 10 years of the London Broncos, some people in the capital still think they are a basketball team. At least, as Harlequins, the first thing the London public will think about is rugby. In the week of the announcement, I was asked to write big pieces for both *The Guardian* and *The Observer* on the venture. I doubt whether any other story concerning the Broncos would have been given a paragraph. It was working already.

A look back at 10 years of the Broncos in Super League wouldn't be complete without a special mention for Tony Rea. He has been there every step of the way, first as a player, then as chief executive and now, probably finally, as head coach. Tony's taciturn performances in press conferences may not appeal to those looking for snappy quotes or controversial views but I can't imagine the club without him. He can't call on a vast pool of local talent but must instead persuade players from the north of England and the southern hemisphere to sign up to the London cause. He has gone through all the upheavals and close shaves seemingly without batting an eyelid. He takes everything in his stride. I just hope he doesn't go home and take it all out on his wife!

So why do we need a London club in Super League? Well, like it or not, London is the capital of the country and dwarves every other city in terms of its importance. Rugby league needs to break out of its heartlands otherwise it will remain a northern parochial oddity. What's wrong with that, you may say? Well, try selling priceless sponsorships and advertising to a major international company when the sport is only played at top level along the the M62 corridor.

One of these days, London will produce another Martin Offiah. And this time, he won't have to move 200 miles to pull on his boots.

● *David Lawrenson is a St Helens-born journalist whose career began on the St Helens Reporter and Rugby Leaguer. After leaving for London, he wrote about rock music before returning to rugby journalism. While working on and editing a number of rugby union magazines he began writing on rugby league for The Sunday Times. He became rugby league correspondent of The Observer in 2004 and now also contributes to The Times and The Guardian. He has written two books on Martin Offiah and one with Scott Gibbs. Most recently, he worked with Iestyn Harris on his autobiography.*

7. Front Row Ticket

Paul Rowley

I am one of the dwindling number of players who played top-flight rugby league before the advent of Super League and who was still playing in 2005. It just goes to show what a short playing career you have. At the age of 20 you think you will play forever, but not that many play much beyond 30 these days.

Those two years I had at Hilton Park in the early 1990s gave me enough experiences to last a lifetime. I was an apprentice plumber, earning £60 a week, and training at night with Leigh. I got my chance as a 17-year-old when the club's Australian coach, Steve Simms, threw in all the young kids. With the club's growing financial predicament, Steve had no choice but he was a brilliant coach of young players, so I was lucky to be around at that time.

In my first full season, in 1993/94, Leigh got relegated from the old division one. We won only two games but strangely, looking back, that was one of the most enjoyable seasons I had. As a teenager you don't feel the pressure and at one stage we had a full team of bachelors.

One thing Simmsy promoted was a good team spirit and we turned out regularly together as a group of mates. We didn't have any fear of losing - the next game was soon upon us. I felt I fitted in pretty well. It was like a natural progression for me and I didn't find the step-up as massive as I thought I would. The big thing was nerves and once I got over those I was alright.

Looking at the first division then to Super League in 2005, the main difference is the size of the players. Now with all the years of full-time training and conditioning they are all so much fitter and stronger. I used to do my own stuff in the gym as well as training two nights a week and Saturday mornings with the team. I was only young and knew I had to build up my physique and I was lucky that the club had some good weights coaches, especially Kevin Prescott.

Simmsy was big on analysis. In fact, I'd say our preparation was more in-depth then than in the last few years. He was great about giving new knowledge about your opponents and would make sure that you studied the stuff he gave you. The following night at training he would question you on things to ensure you'd done your homework properly.

In 1994, I was fortunate enough to go with the Great Britain Academy team to Australia. John Kear was the coach and, like Simmsy, was excellent with young players. Most of the players who went on that tour were or became regular first-teamers with their respective clubs, like Iestyn Harris, Mark Hilton, Francis Cummins and Sean Long. Though we had so many good players I don't think we quite expected the quality of sides that we played.

It was obvious then that the Australians were a lot more advanced than us and it made me even more determined to work harder at my game. We were also treated very poorly by the Australians. We stayed in hostels or in low-grade hotels where they squeezed extra beds in the rooms. At one place we were put up in an army camp. The itinerary also left a lot to be desired. I remember arriving at Perth and having to play the following day. The Aussie players seemed to do things a lot more naturally than us and had so much quality about them. They seemed two steps ahead of us at everything.

I also played against the Junior Kiwis at Wembley which is a cherished memory. Not many players get the opportunity to play there but before the game we had to change in a hut, which seemed a bit shoddy. Leigh, meanwhile, were in division two and that was a big culture shock to me. I thought I was climbing the ladder and it was a bit demoralising not to be playing in the top flight. One day the administrator called in three of us - Sid (Simon) Baldwin, Scott Martin and myself. He said that the club had offers for us and if we didn't go they would go down the Swannee. That put a lot of pressure on us but I was fortunate that Simmsy had gone to Halifax and he always promised that he would take Sid and me with him wherever he went. I looked at the Halifax team and felt it was a move that could only further my career.

Suddenly, in 1995, Super League came upon us. Everything happened so quickly as the pace of events gathered speed. One day I got a 'phone call from the club saying they were going to offer me a new deal to sign full-time and if I signed that day I would get a £20,000 Super League bonus. The Halifax directors had been paid some money by Super League to make sure the players were loyal to that organisation in the war against the Australian Rugby League. I got over there pretty smartish and signed on the dotted line. I know that some of the players got a lot more than me - John Schuster was said to have got £60,000. But I wasn't bothered. I knew that we were at the dawn of a whole new exciting era for the game and I was in at the start of it. I couldn't give up my job quickly enough.

Looking back, a lot of clubs struggled to cope with that sudden move to full-time regimes and they got a lot of their sums wrong. It was a good earning time for players. On the whole I thought Halifax coped quite well until we had a fantastic year in 1998 and finished third. Unfortunately, our success crippled the club. As we had done far better than had been expected we cleaned up on winning pay. The season after, Halifax, like most of the other clubs, abandoned winning pay and just paid out a bonus at the end of the season based on prize money they had received on their final league placing.

I remember Halifax's first game in Super League at Thrum Hall, against London. There were a few more fancy things going on around the game like dancing girls and a bit of razzmatazz but other than that it just seemed like a normal game. But our whole regime had changed as, instead of training in the evenings, we'd arrive at the club at 10am and train for a couple of hours. Then, after having our dinner in the cricket club, we'd train a bit in the afternoon. It was great to do what you love doing all day. I was still good mates with everyone at Leigh so I used to go back home and train with Leigh in the evening as well. I worked on the theory that if you are training while other people are sleeping you are getting an advantage.

Simmsy left Halifax and I was sad to see him go but there was a silver lining. John Pendlebury came in alongside David Hobbs. I had played with John at Leigh where he was well respected. As a senior player coming towards the end of his career he had proved a terrific influence on the young players and he carried on in the same mould at Halifax. One of his strengths was the way he instilled discipline and didn't take any messing from anyone.

In 1997, the World Club Championship was introduced in a bid to extend the boundaries of Super League. At Halifax we had as tough a draw as anyone and we had to play the best three teams in Australia in Brisbane Broncos, Canterbury and Canberra. We went over to Australia first with a bit of a weakened side and on a bit of a losing run, so the whole atmosphere of the tour was on "a downer" from the start. The Australians treated us really well this time, certainly a lot better than when I had gone over with the Academy team. I remember there was an advertising poster at Canterbury showing Jason Robinson, who was going to play there for Wigan. It had a caption that said "extra lean" under his picture. When Halifax played there they had a poster of our prop, Karl Harrison, that read "extra chunky". It was all in good humour and we had a bit of a laugh about it.

Though we got absolutely hammered, as many of the English teams did, conceding 204 points in the three games and scoring just 12, the short tour really had a big impact on the thinking of many players. It began to dawn upon them that full-time professionalism was about preparing properly and being absolutely dedicated to the sport. It was no longer a pastime to fit in around another job. The professionalism of the Australian players and the way they had adapted to full-time football was an object lesson to us. Looking at the results of that season there was obviously a big gulf between most of the Australian clubs and their counterparts in England but I feel that in the intervening years that gap has closed considerably. If a World Club Championship was introduced again, I feel sure the English clubs would equip themselves far more respectably.

That short tour was a real test of character for the players but most of them adapted well and never gave up the fight. It was definitely good for the game as a whole and I could never understand why the competition was not followed up. I remembered that last winter season playing from top to tail in mud and in freezing cold conditions at places like Workington and Wakefield and thinking how things had changed in such a short space of time. When the Australians came over to Thrum Hall for the return legs, a lot of them just simply couldn't believe what they were seeing. Our old, decaying and decrepit ground might have been home from home for us but to them it was a throwback to the Victorian age. I remember one of the Brisbane players looking open-mouthed at the sloping pitch, the crumbling terraces and the old stands and then walking into the pavilion with its, shall we say, rudimentary changing facilities. He said he now understood what it was like to have played rugby league in 1895 when the game was founded.

By the second leg of the tournament a lot of the interest had gone because of all the hammerings that the English teams had taken. I remember the Brisbane game attracting just over 3,000 to Thrum Hall, which is amazing when you think back that the best team in the world playing in Halifax could attract such a small crowd. We got more for our next game, against Oldham, when we ended a losing run of 13 games.

After the difficulties of 1997 our success in the following year took a lot of people by surprise, but not me. I have a favourite saying: "What would you rather have? A champion team, or a team of champions?" That year we certainly had the latter which was shown when 16 of the players went on an end-of-season trip to Tenerife. That was the year when we left Thrum Hall and moved in at the Shay. The players really developed their skills under the full-time training and the coaching staff broke down all aspects of the game and spent a lot of time working on core skills. By that I mean things like tackling technique and catching, passing and holding the ball, as well as concentrating on how you gripped the ball and held it in two hands.

Halifax had big neighbours in Bradford and Leeds but were at the forefront of Super League. Travelling into Calderdale there was a lot of Bradford Bulls hitting you in the face but we had some good results against them at the time and that was a lovely feeling. We were the poor neighbours but we thrived off the challenge and developed a bit of a siege mentality. In many ways, we over-achieved that year but it was one of those great seasons where everything just clicked.

I loved Thrum Hall to bits and was worried that we would lose that atmosphere when we moved to the Shay. But that season we did succeed in recreating the atmosphere of the old ground and making the Shay an intimidating place for opponents. It was a great shame that Halifax never built on that season. They got rid of a few players in trying to improve the squad but never succeeded in really doing that and John Pendlebury left as coach, which was a massive blow. The success of '98 was built around the characters in the side and everyone accepted them for what they were, as long as they did their business on the field.

I had been at Halifax a while by then and enjoyed my time with them, but Wigan were showing interest and made three bids for me. After the third one I asked to move but the club was not willing to release me. I found that frustrating as I felt I'd given my all for Halifax and hadn't been overpaid. If I'd had the opportunity to move to Wigan at that time I feel my game would have developed further and I might then have been in a position to push for Great Britain honours. But it wasn't to be.

Looking back, things then began to turn sour for me at Halifax and the way the Wigan bid was interpreted by some people went against me. I had always enjoyed a good rapport with the fans and everyone at the club and up until finally leaving Halifax I gave my all for them. I remember, in Australia, John Pendlebury asking me in front of the players: "Are you with us?" I found that particularly upsetting because I won three man-of-the-match awards over there and felt my performances were worth more than words.

Halifax put me on the list at £250,000. That was a world record fee for a hooker and effectively blocked me from moving on. I had been offered a three-year deal with Halifax but, after they turned down a bid from Leeds and I then missed out from Wigan, they offered me a new contract at about half the money. If that is not a reason to fall out with them I don't know what is. Fortunately for me, the chairman, Chris Whiteley, was a man of dignity and morals and eventually sorted something out.

As well as the Australian trip, Super League was spreading its wings elsewhere and I remember playing an "on the road" game at Northampton against Sheffield in 1998. In the week before, I had gone down to do some promotion with John Bentley and it was good trying to spread the word in a new area. We played Paris away a couple of times as well which was an excuse for a lot of the players to go on a massive piss-up after the game. I remember one particular game when the players hijacked a wedding party and had too much red wine. Some of the players ended up vomiting all over the hotel. One newspaper suggested that instead of being called Halifax Blue Sox we should be renamed 'Halifax Spew Sox'. Ironically, one of the national press reporters who had joined in the condemnation had been involved in the drinking session and had been drunker and more badly-behaved than any of the players. I still see him about these days and often remind him of the incident.

Being away from home could also cause some rifts between the players as there were plenty of strong characters about. I remember the time that John Bentley shaved off John Schuster's eyebrows while he was asleep and that caused a huge rift, especially with Mike Umaga. Schuster was a chief to the Samoans and Umaga was supposed to look after him. Bentley and Umaga ended up having a fight over the incident and probably as a result of that the tension calmed down. But later that night, Bentley and me crept into Umaga's room and shaved off his eyebrows as well.

John Kear had coached me with the Academy side and had always rated me as a player. So when the World Cup came along in 2000, John, who was then England coach, picked me for the squad. I was the only one from Halifax to be selected for England. I thought that I had not been playing particularly well compared to some of my previous seasons, but the selection gave me a fantastic boost and it was a real honour to be involved. I played for England against Australia at Twickenham in the opening game of the tournament and then won the man-of-the-match award against Russia at St Helens. But after beating Ireland in the quarter-final I was then dropped for the semi-final against New Zealand at Bolton. That came as a real blow to me especially as, at the time, I was living in Bolton and had desperately wanted to play at the Reebok Stadium. For whatever reason, John preferred Tony Smith to me at hooker and the game proved to be a massive disappointment as the Kiwis ran out winners by 49-6. After the World Cup was over, John wrote me a letter that stated I had been a credit to myself and my family with my approach throughout the tournament and that, in hindsight, he would have done things differently for that semi-final. I really respected him for that as he didn't need to write the letter. But that was John all over - a man of integrity and great character. It came as no surprise to me when he coached Hull to their Challenge Cup win in 2005 because he is one of the best coaches and man managers around. I still see him regularly nowadays and we always have a good chat.

My days at Halifax ended when I joined Huddersfield in 2001. The move came as a breath of fresh air to me and I got to know Tony Smith, who was the Giants coach. Before I went I had heard nothing but good things about Tony, and the professional way in which the club was run created a great environment for full-time players. Under Tony I can honestly say I learnt something new every day and my game and the way I thought about the game changed dramatically. Tony had that ability to breed confidence in players and was not only a brilliant coach before the game but after the game as well. In my experience, there are plenty of coaches that build up players for games but then ignore them afterwards. But Tony had that knack of making you feel good about yourself with the way he spoke to you when the game was over. Tony was very much a performance-based coach and worked on the theory that if the players and the team had improved from the previous week the results would eventually look after themselves. But as a player, if you came off the field and had not had a good result, you felt worse for him than yourself. You felt you had let him down personally. Tony backed his players to the hilt and was rewarded with their full support in return.

Huddersfield lost 15 games on the run and then suddenly clicked after adding Brandon Costin and Troy Stone from Australia. They gave us that little bit of know-how and experience we had been lacking and as the results turned around the players' confidence grew. The first thing Tony did when he took over as coach was make the players come up with a victory song. He flogged us in training until we got one. Richard Marshall, Martin Gleeson and me wrote the song and whenever we see one another we sing it to this day.

In the second half of the season we sang that song a few times but we ended up being relegated on the last day of the campaign. Knowing we had been relegated was just about the worst feeling I have ever experienced. With Tony there, team spirit had been absolutely fantastic and there was never once any bickering between any of the players. It was the best 12 months of my whole career but the relegation meant my days with the Giants were over. I had signed a two-year deal with them but the contract was scrapped when they lost their Super League place and the revised offer would hardly have covered my travelling expenses across the Pennines.

I felt sorry to be dropping out of Super League and knew that, as a player, it was too soon for me. But Leigh came in with a good offer to play in the Northern Ford Premiership and I felt really excited about playing again for my home town club. After that year with Tony, I was really enjoying my rugby again and had a new spring in my step. I carried that on into my time at Leigh. There were a lot of adjustments to make from Super League and the Northern Ford Premiership was certainly a lot more physical with many more grubby and gritty things going on. In the years since I had last played at that level the standard, though, had moved on unbelievably and there were some fantastic players around. There were no easy games at all.

There was a great expectancy at Leigh that they would get into Super League but for a few years we were always the "nearly men." The fans were so passionate and desperately wanted success but for a four or five-year period Leigh were the bridesmaids and that was so frustrating. In my first year there, we were unlucky to come up against Huddersfield, who had stayed full-time and had Tony Smith as coach. They beat us convincingly to regain their Super League place. In the following year, Salford also stayed full-time and we were once again the underdogs. Although we again got to the Grand Final, we didn't really get close to them.

Finally, in 2004, we got a level playing field in that none of the teams were full-time and we finally achieved our goal. The victory over Whitehaven came after a nerve-wracking game that went into extra-time but we just pipped them in the end. As well as playing, I became involved with doing development work in the schools and around the town for the club and was training in the evenings. It was a big change from being a full-time player and training all day but I felt that I adjusted pretty well.

Many people ask me how I kept the drive to keep on playing professional rugby league. The answer is an easy one - it is the fear of the alternative, having to work every day for a living. It is a privilege to be paid for playing rugby league and to keep fit and have the banter with your team-mates. For the big games, in particular, the adrenalin that runs through your body is quite incredible and as you got older your stomach seems to churn over more and more. There was that realisation that it might be the last big game that you ever played in so you wanted to give your best-ever performance. When you are younger you think your career will never end but I found that the more I played the game the more I appreciated it and the privileges that came with it.

In 2005, I played once again in Super League with Leigh. After a four-year gap from playing at that level the improvements in the general standard of play and the way that players, coaches and back-room staff approach each game were obvious. Looking back to 2001 as a comparison, the improvement in all teams was absolutely incredible.

Without a shadow of a doubt, rugby league is the toughest team sport in the world and the size and physical presence of the players is quite awe-inspiring. You have giant men who can run incredibly fast and players who display great bravery, skills and sportsmanship despite the punishing nature of the game. I have always felt that I could hold myself up to any player fitness-wise throughout my career. I have always liked a challenge and have striven to be the best I can be. But I realised in 2005 that it was very hard to compete against some of the players around the 21 to 22-years age group who are at the peak of physical fitness and have been in full-time training for six years.

Leigh were unlucky in so many games that went against us and we did pick up a couple of good wins as well as a draw. But the longer our losing run went on it did become a bit demoralising especially at the end of the season. That is the time when you find out about the character of your team-mates, whether they are resilient and rise to the challenge or not. We had some great characters and that enabled us to keep on going and try and reward our loyal fans who had waited so long to see their team back in the top flight.

Super League in 2005 was far removed from when it started in 1996. In those days, every team had at least three or four players that you could target. That is not the case any more. Even the so-called smaller players are big, hard so-and-so's. These days there are hardly any weak links. The players are incredibly fit, motivated and dedicated and their skills are incredible. The standards of coaching, conditioning and training have risen through the roof as have the way teams prepare for games with their analysis and statistics.

What are the down-sides? In my opinion, there are too many overseas players in Super League and that is stopping the development of young British players. We have some fantastic youth set-ups at all the clubs but too many players, having come up through the ranks, have been denied an opportunity at first-team level. Having had so much investment poured into their development as players, too many become disillusioned and drift away from the game.

The life-span of a player's career is also getting shorter and shorter. These days 17-year-old kids do not look out of place in a Super League team whereas 10 years ago it was very much the exception. But a lot of players are finding it harder to carry on after reaching the age of about 27 or 28. It is like having a car with so many miles on the engine. After 300 games at the top level your body has so many knocks, bumps and bruises that it gets increasingly hard to keep passing your MOT.

I think we have also slipped up on the international scene and failed to build on the positives of that World Club Championship and the World Cup of 2000. Rugby union has got an enviable international set-up and hopefully we can emulate them one day. The Tri-Nations tournament is definitely a positive step and hopefully will build-up our international credibility.

But above all, rugby league is about players and too many will have been full-time professionals since leaving school and suddenly facing the prospect of going out into the labour market at the age of 30 with no trade or education behind them. Every player knows they are only a piece of meat but, as a young player, you never think that your career will one day be over. We need to spend more time on after-care for players and looking at avenues for when their playing days are over and they are suddenly surplus to requirements.

Would I do it all again? You bet I would. I feel I've had a great career and have played alongside and against some great players and characters and had the benefit of working under some fantastic coaches. It is only through being back in Super League in 2005 that I fully came to realise just what skills and dedication the players at the top level need to show. I admire any player who plays in Super League and respect them for what they have achieved.

From a player's perspective, the introduction of Super League was a wonderful thing and, 10 years from now, I feel sure we shall be saying that the standards have risen even more.

● *Paul Rowley, 30, has played in over 150 Super League games for Halifax Blue Sox, Huddersfield Giants and Leigh Centurions, and represented England in the 2000 World Cup. In 1998 he earned national media attention after rescuing a young girl from drowning in a swollen river near his Bolton home and later that day winning the Man of the Match award for a star performance in Halifax's victory over London Broncos in a Sky televised game at The Shay, capped by an outstanding individual try.*

ABOVE: Bobbie Goulding kicks off at Knowsley Road - as St Helens prepare to become the most successful British club of the Super League era.

LEFT: RFL boss Maurice Lindsay & Australian legend Mal Meninga launch the competition at Headingley, Leeds

RIGHT: The banners in the photos say it all. The initial reaction to the Super League mergers, as reported in the 17th April 1995 edition of *League Express*

BELOW: Laurie Daley and Andy Farrell lead Australia and Great Britain out for the first Super League Test at Wembley Stadium in 1997. Australia won the game 38-14 and the series 2-1

ABOVE: The future of Sky's Super League commentary, Mike "Stevo" Stephenson & Eddie Hemmings

RIGHT: Patrick Entat & Paris got Super League off to a flying start but ground to a halt after just two seasons

RIGHT: New boss Gary Hetherington re-branded Leeds RLFC as the Rhinos

BELOW: Oldham lasted two seasons

BOTTOM: Shaun McRae coached St Helens to their first Super League Championship

ABOVE: Halifax go down to London in round one
BELOW: Leeds winger Jim Fallon faces Warrington

BOTTOM RIGHT: Paul Newlove

RIGHT: Club captains line up as the Australian Super League finally prepares to kick-off in 1997. They all competed for the Telstra Cup

ABOVE: Laurie Daley, Andrew Ettingshausen, Noel Goldthorpe and referee Bill Harrigan promote Super League in an Australian television advertisement. BELOW: British sprinter Linford Christie and Euro Super League pair Paul Sculthorpe and Robbie Paul join Aussie Super League-affiliated players to announce the 1997 season draw

LEFT: Bradford Bulls unveil a special gold shirt to be worn in the 1997 Challenge Cup final at Wembley, a game they lost to St Helens

BELOW: Bulls coach Matthew Eliott leads the celebrations & takes a drenching as his team become Super League's last Championship winners under a first-past-the-post system

Two of the men behind the Odsal revolution
ABOVE: Gary Tasker
BELOW: Peter Deakin

BOTTOM: Wigan's Va'aiga Tuigamala

BELOW: Peter Edwards & Salford enjoyed a best-ever Super League finish - sixth - in 1997. RIGHT: One young fan with divided loyalties

ABOVE: A packed stand at the Charlety Stadium in Paris, 1996

LEFT: The view from the Boulevard, Hull

Super League grounds we have known. ABOVE: The most famous rugby league ground in the world - Wigan's Central Park, which closed for business in 1999. Wigan beat old rivals St Helens, 28-20, in the final match

BELOW LEFT: Oldham's Watersheddings was hardly the most glamorous of venues as Super League kicked off

ABOVE: The Hulme brothers - Paul & David - at Wilderspool. Warrington moved out in 2003, to take up residence at the Halliwell Jones Stadium

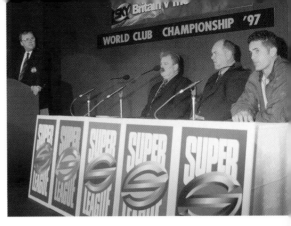

Scenes from the 1997 World Club Championship. ABOVE: (Clockwise) Castleford's Richard Gay fails to halt the Hunter Mariners; a pre-tournament press conference at Huddersfield; Denis Betts on the charge for the Auckland Warriors; the captains of Bradford, Warrington, Castleford, Sheffield, Perth, Auckland & St Helens BELOW: Fereti Tuilagi gets some future hairdressing tips from Asa Amone as Halifax lose to Canterbury

ABOVE: Odsal Stadium in 1997, as soon-to-be European champions Bradford face Penrith. RIGHT: Matt Adamson leads the Panthers out at Odsal's popular side

LEFT: Paul Sterling's wonderful length-of-field try against Adelaide at Headingley. Ronnie the Rhino is in hot pursuit. BELOW: Iestyn Harris

BELOW: Tawera Nikau in action for Cronulla Sharks against the Bulls

ABOVE: Mascots swiftly became a familiar feature
RIGHT: Alan Hunte in action for Hull Sharks

ABOVE: Adrian Morley is red-carded by Stuart Cummings for Leeds v Sheffield

RIGHT: Mark Aston helps the Eagles beat Wigan at Wembley

ABOVE: Jason Robinson shows off the Super League trophy after the first-ever Grand Final in 1998

RIGHT: A champagne moment for Wigan skipper Andy Farrell & his coach John Monie at Old Trafford

8. Build It, They Will Come

Mike Latham

There is nothing quite like the heart-fluttering sense of anticipation that accompanies a visit to a rugby league ground. That sense of excitement on arrival, the pulse quickening on first sight of the stands and floodlights and the elation felt on going through the turnstiles will be familiar to all followers of the greatest game of all.

The winds of change that have blown through rugby league since the advent of Super League a decade ago have affected all areas of the sport, not least the arenas on which the game is played. Watching and playing Super League in 2005 was, in most cases, a vastly different experience for spectator and player than it was in 1996.

At the onset of Super League, rugby league grounds had undergone their most intense period of change since the 1890s. The legislation introduced following the terrible tragedies of Valley Parade, Hillsborough and the Heysel Stadium in the 1980s was swift and wide-ranging. Rugby league was tarred with the same brush as soccer in having to accept stringent new ground safety regulations as a local registration scheme for sports grounds was introduced.

At the time of the Valley Parade fire, rugby league instinctively sought to distance itself from the round ball game but that was only possible up to a point. With four of the 12 Super League clubs of 2005 ground-sharing with Football League clubs, the two games are linked as closely together as ever, particularly as major soccer grounds, with their generally superior facilities and seating capacities, are invariably hired for internationals and finals.

Nevertheless, rugby league supporters continue to value highly the rights of freedom of movement, no segregation and no fencing at grounds and simply would not accept some of the draconian stewarding and treatment of soccer supporters, particularly those following the away team. The Taylor Report had recommended that by 1999 all rugby league grounds should be all-seated. Fortunately, intense lobbying by the Rugby Football League and the Rugby League All-Party Parliamentary Group convinced the Home Office that this was neither necessary nor desirable. But the implementation of minimum standards for Super League grounds and less stringent and wide-ranging ones for clubs in what are now known as the National Leagues changed the face of watching rugby league.

If the skills, bravery, dedication and accessibility of its players are rugby league's greatest asset, the fans are its lifeblood, without whom there would simply be no game. Far too often in the past, the aspirations of the ordinary spectator have largely been ignored, with clubs taking it for granted that the fans would turn up and support the game while enduring the most rudimentary facilities. The post Second World War years were a particular boom-time for the sport, but only a few enlightened clubs set about looking after their most valuable commodities - the paying spectators.

By the mid-1990s the mood was changing and Super League's sudden onset accelerated a process that was already underway, as clubs were swept along in the need to modernise outdated practices and faced up to the battle for the leisure pound. In the late 1940s and 1950s there were precious few options but, more recently, the picture has changed dramatically as people generally have far more leisure time, more money in their pockets and much more choice and competition for their patronage.

The funds available from central government for the building of new soccer stadiums, often on out-of-town sites incorporated as part of a retail development, or to redevelop existing venues and the implementation of all-seated grounds at the top levels of soccer, had far-reaching implications for rugby league. By 2005, the change was such that just five grounds remained which had staged matches in the first Northern Union season of 1895/96: Leeds, St Helens, Wakefield and Widnes in Super League and Batley in National League One.

The first decade of Super League saw long-established grounds disappear from the scene, with the closure of Wigan's beloved Central Park - perhaps the world's most instantly recognisable - arguably the most poignant. Of the 12 clubs that competed in the 10th Super League season Wigan, Warrington, Huddersfield and Hull were playing in new stadiums that had been in existence for 12 years or less; Bradford, Leeds and Widnes had developed their existing grounds considerably while Leigh, Salford and St Helens were considering moves to new grounds within the next few years and London Broncos were not only re-branding themselves as part of a link-up with Harlequins rugby union club but also moving to the Stoop for 2006, a ground that has been re-developed extensively in recent years and certainly so since they last played there. Wakefield, whose Belle Vue ground had changed little on three sides, accepted that they would have to move to a new ground or vastly redevelop their existing ground to stay the pace long-term in Super League.

In 1995, it was possible to visit some of the top-flight grounds and readily imagine just what it had been like to watch rugby football in that first season after the split from rugby union in 1895. Halifax's Thrum Hall and Oldham's Watersheddings were vast, atmospheric arenas, undoubtedly full of character and echoing to the ghosts of the past but with inappropriate facilities for a game soon to enter the 21st century. Situated in densely-populated areas and with roots back to Victorian times, both grounds were old and decrepit, their crumbling terraces, ageing stands, basic toilet and refreshment facilities and sloping pitches hardly conducive to the modern age.

The changing face of sport elsewhere, with soccer emerging from the hooligan-dogged doldrums of the 1980s following the advent of the Premier League in 1992, with its wall-to-wall coverage on satellite television and sudden adoption by the middle classes, coupled with rugby union's headlong rush towards full professionalism in 1995, had vast ramifications for rugby league. Many of its member clubs were insolvent and had ageing grounds that ate up cash for maintenance just to retain the status quo. The facts had to be faced that a predominantly winter sport with a nine-month season played predominantly along the M62 corridor in Lancashire and Yorkshire had major problems.

Then Rupert Murdoch came along with an offer of £87million that would change the sport forever. Seven months after the game celebrated its centenary, its top-flight was re-branded the summer Super League. By that time, the RFL had already produced a 51-page document that would have far-reaching implications for its member clubs. The report was entitled "Framing the Future" and stressed the need to concentrate on adherence to minimum standards.

Reaction was predictably mixed. Some clubs reacted positively and set about meeting the challenges of the report, appointing the necessary personnel and improving their facilities and, in some cases, looking towards a new ground. Others, instead of rising to the challenges, complained and sought sympathy, though some later saw the error of their ways and belatedly set about the path to progress.

Alongside improved facilities, clubs sought to present the game in a radical way and the term 'gameday experience' gathered usage. Marketing nicknames such as the Bulls, Tigers and Wolves were brought in to hype up the likes of Bradford, Castleford and Warrington and glitzy new kits and themed match-day entertainment were introduced in an effort to attract new supporters and retain existing loyalties.

The first weekend of Super League was a huge success, with over 18,000 witnessing a thrilling game between Paris and Sheffield Eagles at the Charlety Stadium. Bradford Bulls attracted over 10,000 for the visit of Castleford and introduced their innovative match-day package of entertainment. Looking back, it was the definitive birth of the successful Bulls brand, though winter was reluctant to release its icy tentacles as sprinklings of snow flickered across the vast Odsal bowl. Oldham swapped Watersheddings for the soccer club's Boundary Park (then a Premier League venue) and attracted 7,709 for Wigan's visit. Halifax attracted just 4,000 for the visit of London Broncos while Leeds, who struggled in the first summer season to embrace the new concept, defeated Warrington before 10,036. St Helens, meanwhile, served notice of what was to be a champion season when 3,500 saw their 62-0 thrashing of Workington Town at a Derwent Park stadium that would enjoy just one season in the top-flight spotlight.

In the second round, five of the remaining six grounds got their first taste of Super League. London achieved a high spot early on, attracting almost 10,000 for their game against Paris at The Valley. Saints had nearly 16,000 for the Good Friday derby against Wigan - a traditional date that, happily, survived the switch to summer. Castleford's Wheldon Road ground was filled with 7,179 for the visit of Leeds while Sheffield's Don Valley Stadium had 5,202 for the Bulls' visit and Warrington attracted only 4,500 to Wilderspool for the game against Workington. Warrington's football manager, Alex Murphy, called for better support from the townspeople. Central Park, meanwhile, had to wait until round three for its first game, 14,620 witnessing an Easter Monday derby against Warrington.

In fact, Knowsley Road and Headingley were the only grounds that continued to host Super League games on an unbroken basis throughout the decade. Saints' need for a new stadium to match their ambition and the consistent excellence of their talented team became more marked over that time. One of rugby league's great standing grounds and a fine traditional and atmospheric venue with good social facilities it may be, but Knowsley Road, opened in 1890, looked outdated and tired by 2005. Saints tried to develop a Sporting Club St Helens, linking up with Liverpool-St Helens RUFC and the local soccer club, St Helens Town FC, who sold their Hoghton Road ground to move in at Knowsley Road. But St Helens is one of the few towns in the world where rugby league is undeniably the number one sport. The union club, dropping down the divisions, and the soccer club, who struggle to attract gates of 100 for their home games in the North West Counties League, made little impact.

Leeds, meanwhile, were revitalised after Paul Caddick and Gary Hetherington joined forces, bringing about the successful redevelopment of the historic sporting arena known throughout the world for hosting top class rugby league and Test match cricket. The price that Leeds fans had to pay was rah-rah on their beloved turf, with Leeds Tykes playing in the top flight of the rugby union Premiership at Headingley. Excellent new corporate facilities and a revamp of the South Stand, home to Leeds' most vocal supporters, were at the forefront of a ground improvement programme that took full advantage of the benefits of summer rugby, while successful youth development programmes and community initiatives began to bear rich fruit. From an average of 8,581 in the first season, Leeds, who successfully developed the Rhinos brand, boasted an average of just over 17,000 in 2005 - their highest figure since the 1950s. The huge impact of the Leeds talisman, Ronnie the Rhino, showed how mascots could be used in a positive manner.

Bradford Bulls set the early standards for the summer era and were undoubtedly at the forefront of new initiatives. Their huge Odsal Stadium, a cold and unwelcoming place in the depths of winter that made attending some matches a test of endurance, was transformed, especially on warm summer evenings. With the start of Super League the club gained a tremendous momentum sparked by the vision and foresight of their chairman, Chris Caisley, and a whole new audience, based around the family, was attracted. Adopting the Bulls nickname was a marketing masterstroke and the previous drawbacks of Odsal were made into virtues overnight. While Odsal was being re-developed, the Bulls played at Valley Parade for two seasons but that ground became increasingly unpopular with their fans. The return to Odsal in 2003 saw average gates increase by nearly 4,000 to just over the 15,000 mark.

Warrington were one of the first clubs to develop an effective community programme and built a fan loyalty that is not dependent on the team's results. The Wolves brand was enthusiastically received and Wilderspool, an ageing ground that was once an intimidating place for opposing fans, developed an overwhelmingly vibrant atmosphere. Warrington also pulled something of a masterstoke in the way they planned their move to the new stadium north of the town. Developed in conjunction with supermarket giants Tesco, the club actively sought the views of their supporters in its design and build. The upshot was a new home that, uniquely for a club at the top level, retained two standing sides. The only downside was the lack of a supporters' bar like the one that was so busy and well-frequented at Wilderspool. The old ground received a dignified send-off during 2003 and was retained for use as a training centre and for the club's junior sides.

The future of Central Park, though, became a matter of great concern for Wigan fans during the late 1990s, with bitter shareholders' meetings and a fight for control of the club often obscuring the fact that, on and off the field, Wigan were falling away after their success-laden dominance of the game in the decade before the advent of Super League. Attendances fell and Central Park staged its last season in 1999, as fans bade a tearful farewell after the derby with St Helens when Wigan recorded a famous victory.

While Warrington handled their departure from Wilderspool extremely well, many Wigan fans appeared initially reluctant to follow the club to its new home. But Wigan, later than many other clubs, built up their community arm and gradually the JJB Stadium developed its own character. In 2005, a new record regular season Super League crowd of 25,004 saw the Wigan-Saints derby and Wigan fans, faced with the prospect of Wigan Athletic appearing in soccer's Premiership, responded with a terrific level of loyal support despite their club finishing in its lowest league position for 21 years. Their average attendance was just short of 14,000, 4,000 higher than 1999, the last year at Central Park.

The Willows, home to Salford since 1901, is the oldest surviving senior sports venue in the Manchester and Salford area but looks every bit its age at times. On the face of it, a redevelopment of the main stand and of the standing terrace opposite would change the face of the ground but the club are committed to relocating to Barton, convinced that a move from the existing location in an inner-city area is the only way forward. It is a risky strategy, attempting to attract a whole new audience and moving out of your traditional home, but one that Salford feel is necessary to progress.

Wakefield's Belle Vue ground is another that has plainly seen better days, though the construction of a large hospitality stand behind one end was one of the more ambitious and remarkable ground improvements of the last decade. There are compensations for spectators at Belle Vue with the freedom to walk around the ground and enjoy some of the better catering outlets in the top flight, but Wakefield face the dilemma of either having to finance considerable ground improvements or relocate to a new ground if they are to maintain their top-flight status in the years ahead.

Leigh decided upon the latter option, outlining ambitious plans for a new stadium as part of the Leigh Sports Village development to be shared with the town's soccer club. Once again the stage for some of the game's finest players, after Leigh's elevation to Super League for one brief season in 2005, Hilton Park, despite being relatively modern (constructed 1947) looked tired and with many disadvantages. Land-locked by houses, a by-pass and supermarket, Hilton Park's days are numbered and a new ground should hopefully give the club fresh impetus.

In the 1980s, Widnes had an outstanding team and one of the worst grounds in the top flight. Twenty years later the roles were reversed with an outstanding ground and a team that finished in the relegation places after four seasons in Super League. The Halton Community Stadium was developed on the site of the old Naughton Park ground in a piecemeal development, with the final of the four all-seated stands being completed towards the end of the 2005 season. With excellent conference, catering and function facilities the new ground would have been the ideal stage for some of the stars of that glorious era when Widnes were known throughout the game as the 'cup kings'. Despite some complaints that the ground still had a soulless feel to it and that there was an over-riding sense of it being council-owned, the Halton Stadium, particularly for local derby games, was a splendid viewing ground for Super League and is far too good to be staging National League fare.

Hull's departure from the Boulevard, their home since the first season of Northern Union football in 1895, was an emotional affair and the scenes before, during and after their last game there, against the touring New Zealanders, rivalled the last day at Central Park. But their move half-a-mile away to the magnificent Kingston Communications Stadium, co-sharing with Hull City FC, was an almost immediate success. City emerged from a long period in the soccer doldrums by winning back-to-back promotions and Hull FC lifted the Challenge Cup in 2005 to further their claims to joining the elite of rugby league clubs who have dominated the summer era. The Boulevard left a lot to be desired for the spectator. It was a very poor seeing ground and sight-lines by contrast at the KC Stadium are outstanding. The general view among Hull supporters - presumably even the old Threepenny Standers - is that everything about the new ground is better than the old one and such unanimity is rare.

Huddersfield was the birthplace of the game and its new stadium, initially known as the McAlpine Stadium and later re-named the Galpharm Stadium, set the standards for the others to follow. The stadium won the coveted Building of the Year award from the Royal Institute of British Architects in 1995 and the setting of its magnificent curving stands and excellent facilities made it a popular venue for big games. Though the Giants, by comparison, lagged behind their big city neighbours Bradford and Leeds in attracting support, the signs are that they are slowly succeeding in building up their fan base which had sunk to low levels during the last years at the historic old Fartown ground. As with Hull, the soccer and rugby league clubs appear to co-exist quite happily together.

Perhaps the best example of a traditional old ground being transformed, other than Odsal and Headingley, was provided by Castleford. A trip to The Jungle, as Wheldon Road was re-named, was sufficient to lift the most jaded of spirits. Awash with colour, facilities and with a great community feel, Castleford embraced the concepts of Super League and even managed to maintain the 'feel-good' factor after relegation from the top flight in 2004.

Athletics stadiums are generally thought to provide the worst spectator experiences of all for followers of soccer or rugby league but the excitement of Super League briefly transformed two such venues. Gateshead Thunder's one season in Super League in 1999 attracted a new audience of Geordies to the game at the Gateshead International Stadium (re-branded as the Thunderdome) and the atmosphere and entertainment at the games, plus the unforgettable mascot Captain Thunder, made the gameday experience one to savour. Average home crowds of almost 4,000 were a reminder of just what could have been achieved had the club not been a one-season wonder.

The Don Valley Stadium in Sheffield, specifically built for the 1991 World Student Games, was one of the least favourite venues for many groundhoppers due to the remoteness of the pitch. But on one unforgettable August evening in 1997, the place was transformed when over 10,000 saw Bradford secure the second Super League title.

It was a night when the Don Valley - so often labelled as an expensive white elephant - came alive as thousands of Bulls fans, bedecked in replica jerseys, waving flags and scarves, provided the perfect backdrop with the attendant colour, noise and excitement.

For groundhoppers, the Super League era was a boon with the early years in particular marked by 'On the Road' games intended to spread the boundaries far and wide. Seeing rugby league played in places as diverse as Heart of Midlothian FC's historic Tynecastle ground in Edinburgh and the Stade Aime Giral in Perpignan was an uplifting experience. Games at traditional old rugby union grounds in South Wales such as Newport's Rodney Parade, the Brewery Field, Bridgend and Cardiff Arms Park brought the game to an appreciative audience that marvelled at the skills on show. Leicester RUFC's Welford Road ground was another fine stage.

Looking back 10 years, it is hard not to reach the conclusion that the majority of changes to grounds at the top level have been for the better. The basic aim of the fan remains the same - to watch an entertaining game in comfort with a minimum of hassle and to be able to mix freely with friends and family and enjoy a decent level of catering and toilet facilities. The ability to achieve those desires in 2005 was markedly better than in 1996 and the level of pre-match and half-time entertainment was much improved. Though far from a cheap day-out, Super League admission prices compared favourably with those in soccer's Premier League. The make-up of the fans also seemed to have changed, and for the better. More women and children started going to games, with a 2005 survey revealing that almost 40 per cent of British rugby league fans are now female. The sort of hostile atmospheres that soured the watching environment for soccer spectators in the 1980s and early 1990s, and which also crept into rugby league at times, became virtually non-existent. Even highly-charged local derbies such as Wigan-Saints or Bradford-Leeds see opposing fans mixing freely before and after the game.

Rugby league lost some of its great traditional grounds during the decade - Central Park, Thrum Hall, Wilderspool, Watersheddings and the Boulevard - but it is far too easy to look back on those venues with rose-tinted spectacles. In reality, they were becoming quickly outdated and unacceptable for watching sport at the highest level, lacking in many cases the most basic of spectator requirements.

Throughout the Super League decade, rugby league has managed to advance without losing its traditional values - the basic sportsmanship and honesty of its spectators and players, and mutual respect for one another, however hard and unremitting the battle on the pitch. The behaviour of rugby league fans is generally excellent and the game provides a safe and exciting environment for families. The police presence at games is negligible and most clubs rely on their own stewards. The game has not lost that contact between the players and the communities they serve. You are still just as likely to see a big name player queuing for a drink in the social club or in the local supermarket as you ever were. Arrogance and self-importance are rare. The changes to the game, in particular video replays and the '40/20' kick, have added to the sense of theatre and involvement.

Many gripes, though, remain and what are seen as improvements by some are regarded as detrimental by others. Some fans would argue that catering facilities have deteriorated even though clubs would doubtless counter that they have improved. With many clubs franchising their catering operations, the products on offer are often unimaginative and expensive. Traditionalists point to days past when they would be served a cup of tea out of a pot with fresh milk; far better than being offered over-priced flavoured hot drinks that could have been made in a laboratory. Just look at the queues outside chip shops at some games as evidence that people would prefer freshly-made quality food to what is usually on offer inside the ground.

Over-zealous stewarding is another problem and rugby league fans cannot accept that they have to take the lid off their bottle of water before entering the ground. Too much stewarding still follows health and safety guidelines to extremes and fails to differentiate between the different cultures of soccer and rugby league supporters. Fans complain of stewards being thoughtless in the way they block people's views and find it unnerving when stewards stand in front of a group of supporters and stare at them throughout the game.

Multi-use stadiums have also not taken into consideration that, as the years go by, people are becoming larger and that the space between the seats is becoming less. Most annoyingly of all, spectators complain about the tannoy systems at grounds, the level of the loud speakers being set so high they are unable to communicate with the person next to them. Though some of the steps forward in pre-match and half-time entertainment have been far-reaching, supporters still have to endure ill-informed announcers they simply can't comprehend, and hide from the loud pop music that blares out uncontrollably.

Rugby league's biggest challenge in the next 10 years is to maintain its vibrant, family image and continue to attract new spectators and maintain existing loyalties to the sport, while continuing to improve facilities for the paying spectator and keep prices at affordable levels. In the long run, the clubs that continue to put investment in playing talent ahead of ground improvements as their over-riding priority will fall behind.

- In 10 years of Super League a total of 1,668 games were played (including play-offs) on 45 different grounds in the following 37 different towns and cities of England, France, Scotland and Wales: Aberavon (Talbot Athletic Ground) 1; Barnsley (Oakwell) 1; Bayonne (Garage de la Neve) 1; Bradford (Odsal Stadium, 109 and Valley Parade, 29); Bridgend (Brewery Field) 1; Carcassonne (Stade Albert Domec) 1; Cardiff (Cardiff Arms Park) 2; Castleford (Wheldon Road/ The Jungle) 118; Chesterfield (Saltergate) 1; Edinburgh (Tynecastle) 2; Gateshead (Gateshead International Stadium/ Thunderdome) 16; Halifax (Thrum Hall, 22; The Shay, 83); Huddersfield (McAlpine/ Galpharm Stadium) 94; Hull (Boulevard, 69; Kingston Communications Stadium, 43); Hyde (Ewen Fields) 1; Leeds (Headingley) 140; Leicester (Welford Road) 3; Leigh (Hilton Park) 14; Liverpool (Anfield) 2; London (Griffin Park, 51; The Stoop, 36; The Valley, 37); Manchester (Old Trafford) 8; Narbonne (Parc des sports) 1; Newport (Rodney Parade) 1; Northampton (Sixfields Stadium) 1; Oldham (Boundary Park, 13; Watersheddings, 8); Paris (Charlety Stadium) 20; Perpignan (Stade Aime Geral) 1; Salford (the Willows) 107; Sheffield (Bramall Lane, 6; Don Valley Stadium, 42); St Helens (Knowsley Road) 140; Swansea (Vetch Field) 1; Wakefield (Belle Vue) 98; Warrington (Halliwell Jones Stadium, 43; Wilderspool 90); Widnes (Halton Stadium) 56; Wigan (Central Park, 49; JJB Stadium, 95); Workington (Derwent Park) 11.

- *Mike Latham hosts a weekly rugby league show on BBC Radio Lancashire and has written for League Express since its inception in 1990, as well as for a variety of newspapers and other publications. He has written seven books on rugby league, the latest being "British Rugby League: A Groundhopper's Guide", published in October 2005. Having visited all the current English and Scottish Football League grounds and seen professional rugby league at over 100 venues, he is currently 'ticking off' non-league soccer grounds and racecourses as part of his groundhopping addiction.*

9. Seeing the Bigger Picture

Harry Edgar

There is a revealing irony, although some might prefer to dress it up as a perfect symmetry, in the fact that a glance back at news reports surrounding the creation of Super League in 1995 reveal Widnes ready to sue the Rugby Football League. A decade down the track, at the completion of the first 10 years of Super League, and once again reports suggested that Widnes were threatening to go to court against the RFL.

Nothing could illustrate more clearly the sheer desperation of clubs to be part of Super League, such is the huge gulf now created between the haves and the have-nots of English rugby league. Initially the great divide was all about money, as the prospect of getting their hands on some of Rupert Murdoch's millions had the leading clubs scrambling for position. But a decade later it has become about much more than just cash, after 10 years of the game outside Super League being steadily backed into a ghetto has taken its inevitable toll.

When the RFL confirmed shortly before this year's National League One Grand Final that both the contestants, Castleford and Whitehaven, had been deemed fit to fulfil their criteria on ground facilities for promotion, Widnes finally accepted their relegation fate. They then welcomed the two aspirants to "their" Super League place into their own home and watched them battle it out to see who would step into their shoes. Sky television, the Super League's paymasters who have been so influential in shaping the game over that decade - both good and bad - wasted little time in venting their feelings about the state-of-the-art facilities of Widnes' Halton Stadium being "lost" to the Super League next season and being replaced possibly by Whitehaven's less than luxurious ground.

But Sky need not have worried, as Whitehaven's admirable team who had finished top of the division and played some beautiful football in the process, failed to do themselves justice in that Grand Final and Castleford won comfortably to bounce straight back into Super League after what one Sky commentator described as their "year in the wilderness." It was just another example, perhaps now done unwittingly and out of habit, of Sky setting the agenda for what rugby league should be. Of course, after 10 years of them doing it, we now have a whole generation of new fans and players who have grown up to accept this as the norm, and who know no different. They would find it hard to believe that teams like Barrow or Workington or Featherstone Rovers used to play in the Cup final, or that Swinton or Dewsbury used to win the Championship, or that Great Britain used to go to Australia and win the Ashes. Believe me, it did happen.

It is impossible to over-emphasise the role Sky television has played in changing rugby league's big picture over the past decade. We all know the good things they have done, the skills of their match producer and brilliant use of new technology allowing the game to be presented as a fast-moving, brightly-coloured, televisual product that knocks stone dead the way the country had grown used to seeing the BBC portray rugby league. That, alongside the fact that Sky pushes Super League as one of their flagship sports and thus gives it a spin-off association with Sky's biggest populist creation, the great God that is Premiership soccer, has helped attract a new audience and a new generation of fans. To Super League, that is. And Sky have always emphasised the word "Super" leaving the rest of the game we know as rugby league looking on from the outside.

It is only natural that new support is automatically attracted to the elite levels of any sport and, of course, different levels of popular media coverage play a big role in adding to that snowball effect. Soccer first noticed the change when the BBC created *Match of the Day* back in the early Sixties - suddenly footballers were becoming stars of Saturday night television and it was inevitable the glamour surrounding them would attract the wider public. It was the end of smaller town clubs like Burnley, Blackpool, Wolverhampton Wanderers and Preston North End being dominant forces in the game as they couldn't compete with the money generated by the big city clubs, and the start of a culture in which people all around the country began declaring an allegiance to such as Manchester United or Liverpool rather than support their home town team in a lower division.

But, despite the Premiership's billion dollar wage bills artificially inflated by Sky's massive investment, soccer hasn't had to suffer the same demarcation treatment as the much smaller world of rugby league. Despite their wall-to-wall obsession with the Premiership, Sky still manage to regularly show soccer from the divisions below the Premiership, they even broadcast non-league football, they show Scottish football, they treat the whole game with respect and have people with enough knowledge to be able to talk about clubs in the lower divisions without patronising them. When it comes to rugby league, Sky's attitude to the game outside their own creation "Super League" is such a massive contrast. Not that British rugby league could ever complain about being patronised by a media organisation, plenty of people in the game have made a pretty good job of that themselves over the past 10 years, especially the bright sparks who not only decided that teams should have artificially-inseminated nicknames added to their club titles but should also run around with them printed on their shirt-tails.

Of course, it is up to Sky what they show because they're paying for it, and if they are comfortable about having their weekly rugby league magazine programme quite regularly fronted by a studio containing only Australian people - including a presenter who can't even pronounce the names of some of the clubs outside the higher echelons of Super League, never mind offer any kind of serious debate about them - so be it. But what is absolutely inexcusable for a company that promotes itself as "the rugby league channel" is its failure to give even the results of the professional competition below Super League; what was once the Northern Ford Premiership and is now known as National League One and Two. Sky cannot use the excuse of lack of air-time, because on their rolling sports news channel they provide an endless loop of results, plus league tables, from even the most obscure soccer competitions including non-league and games in Ireland and Wales, plus every few minutes they will remind us who the top try scorers in the Australian NRL are; but their editorial policy appears to be that rugby league in England is not to be mentioned outside the Super League. That means, in the eyes of the wider public, famous rugby league names like Hull Kingston Rovers, Oldham, Featherstone or Rochdale Hornets - and even for one year, to the accompaniment of bucket loads of crocodile tears from Sky's Super League presenters, Castleford - no longer exist.

It is a media agenda that has had repercussions on a much wider level; most national newspapers now only give the non-Super League results, if they give them at all, in the briefest manner, tucked away in the small print. BBC Radio Five Live, in its half-hourly bulletins or Sunday afternoon sports results, never mentions the National Leagues. Rugby league's bigger picture has got significantly smaller because to the casual sports follower many of those names they used to recognise are no longer there. And now that the majority of Super League clubs favour playing their games on Friday nights, often the "rugby league" results as far as the wider nation is concerned can consist of just one match at a time when the season is supposed to be in full flow. Bizarrely, this is all happening in an era when the leading clubs in Super League have significantly increased their attendances and several have become more vibrant than for many years.

The so-called Murdoch deal of 1995 was supposed to take the game we used to know as rugby league to a brave, and much bigger, new world. Instead, the game's strength has become even more polarised into the hands of a few elite clubs on either side of the M62. It took only two years for Super League to ruin and then dump Paris Saint-Germain, and in the process throw away the huge marketing opportunities offered by having access to one of Europe's most instantly recognised and prestigious sporting brands. They had already refused the chance to build a high-profile professional club in Wales following on from the impact made by the Welsh team in the 1995 World Cup, and when, a couple of years later, they opted to abandon both Gateshead and Sheffield to prop up clubs in Hull and Huddersfield, even the most optimistic dreamer had to accept that all the rhetoric we heard in April 1995 was just hot air. Perhaps all they really wanted was to have as many Lancashire and Yorkshire local derbies as possible each year to guarantee bigger crowds, Leeds play Bradford and Wigan play St Helens, and if eventually, as has happened now with Hull and Warrington in their new stadiums, another club on each side of the Pennines could get themselves up to scratch, then they could join the party.

Years ago, particularly during the second half of the 1980s when the Australians influenced the game to become so newly vibrant and self-confident, I had always dreamed of rugby league becoming a worldwide and trans-European sport. But I knew it was just a pipedream and would remain a fantasy without the backing of a huge transworld media organisation. Likewise, the creation of big city clubs in an elite full-time professional competition. Even the ability of the English game to switch to a summer season - something which had been talked about for decades since Lance Todd first banged that particular drum way back in the 1930s - was dependent on that mythical mega dose of outside help. My fears were that the only way rugby league could hope to make summer rugby work, and thus outweigh the obvious losses and downsides it was bound to suffer by opting out of what had been the accepted way of life for all the football codes for over 100 years, was if it became part of a new, high-profile, highly-financed, elite professional competition, promoted extensively by television and presented in a way vastly different to that which the British public had grown used to seeing rugby league portrayed. Come to think of it, I am sure Maurice Lindsay must have been reading my notes when he was first summoned for a meeting with Rupert Murdoch's men!

When news of the bombshell dropped in April 1995, after several months of speculation and rumour about what was afoot down under, I was immediately torn. Between excitement at what the Murdoch deal and Super League concept could do for the game in Europe, against anger and despair at what "bloody Super League" was doing to tear apart the game - the oh so vibrant game - in Australia (and by extension by that time) New Zealand.

The sacrifice of my long-time favourite Aussie club North Sydney and also, for a gut-wrenching couple of years, South Sydney, before the sheer weight of public opinion forced them to be taken back; the loss of a great name like Balmain and the waste of all the Australian Rugby League's years of development work in Perth and the Pacific islands, was a heavy and unnecessary price to pay. Just as damaging was the loss to the game of John Quayle, undoubtedly and by some distance the best rugby league administrator of modern times. Quayle, the man behind the hugely-influential Tina Turner advertising campaign and a key architect in the expansion of the Winfield Cup around Australia and to New Zealand which had seen no less than four new clubs created for entry in 1995, was as tough as he was astute and it has often been claimed that he would have liked nothing better than if the arguments between the ARL and the "suits" of Super League could have been settled by hand-to-hand combat.

He had been a no-nonsense second-rower for both Easts and Parramatta, and played for Australia in the 1975 World Championship alongside forwards like Arthur Beetson, George Piggins, Terry Randall and a certain Denis Fitzgerald. Yet I'd known tough old Johnny Quayle go all misty-eyed once when told that his former coach Jack Gibson was asking after him and had described him as "one of my boys." Quayle was far too smart for the likes of John Ribot and Lindsay, and could see straight through all those jumping on the Murdoch gravy train whilst talking of Super League's supposed "world vision." When John Quayle was sacrificed as a major part of the eventual compromise between the ARL and Super League, there's no doubt that rugby league's loss was the Olympic movement's gain. Quayle had always seen the bigger picture and now he was off to join it.

Nobody in Australia actually believed a word about the "world vision" because everybody knew the whole Super League shindig was really just about Rupert Murdoch's company getting hold of pay television rights. Ribot and the Brisbane Broncos may have been willing participants thanks to their discontent at having to play by the rules of the New South Wales Rugby League, into whose competition they had been first invited in 1988, but the biggest pawns in the game were to be the British Rugby Football League. For us in the UK, there was no need for a battle over television rights because the Murdoch-owned BSkyB already was the only channel interested in broadcasting Championship games live and they already had the rights. Our club officials, most of whom wouldn't have had a clue about what was actually going on in Australia, looked on with stunned amazement, half expecting to be told it was really an April Fool's joke, when it was put to them that somebody they were already happy to have as their mate, suddenly wanted to give them 87 million quid for the privilege.

Here was the game in Europe being given a plan, which was being backed with millions and millions of dollars and by a transworld media organisation - not just any old media organisation, but the biggest in the business - Rupert Murdoch's News Ltd. Amazingly, it seemed the dream could come true and rugby league's bigger picture fantasy could become reality. Well, not quite. It took only as long as it needed to walk from the Central Park boardroom to the car park before the seeds of discontent and rebellion were being sown among English club officials. "Hang on a minute," it dawned on many of them. "We've just voted to kill off our own clubs which we've spent so much effort, emotion and hard cash trying to keep alive for all these years."

Mergers were never going to happen in the way they were originally suggested as part of the Super League master plan, and so began the mixture of muddied thinking and internal squabbling that was to bedevil rugby league for most of the next 10 years. The Murdoch deal in 1995 should have been the saviour of the game - the whole game - in the UK; I saw it as an opportunity to rescue and rebuild the clubs in all its heartlands. A chance for all those clubs to pay off their debts and start with a clean sheet and to put into place all those repairs to dilapidated grounds that had been ignored for so long. To me, it was a chance to build a strong League of at least 24 clubs, by bringing back into the fold all those who fallen out of the elite and couldn't get off their downward spirals without financial investment that just wasn't available before. But it didn't happen like that, instead all the emphasis was put on pumping most of the money into a small elite division. Not that the clubs outside the Super League could complain initially, because for the first few years of the deal they were all picking up hundreds of thousands of pounds as well. Very little of that money was invested with any thought of long-term growth.

So, while the Super League itself has, during its first decade, managed to build its strength as a competition with a rousing finale every October boosted hugely by the public appeal of being staged at Old Trafford - and its leading clubs have certainly built their own strength drawing bigger crowds and improving facilities just as the original blueprint intended - the bigger picture has not materialised the way the "world vision" told us it would. In fact, international football - the one sure way of building a bigger national media profile for a historically northern-based sport like rugby league - has been the biggest casualty of the Super League years. No matter how many times Maurice Lindsay tells us that the game was virtually bankrupt in 1995, the truth is that international rugby league had never been as healthy or as vibrant as it was in the five years leading up to the Murdoch deal.

Staging big international matches at Wembley had been the key to the kind of national media attention the game could only dream about in the past. Both the 1990 and 1994 Ashes series against the Australians had attracted new record attendances, both with a Wembley Test followed by sell-out crowds at major stadiums Old Trafford and Elland Road. In between, in 1992 Wembley had attracted a new record crowd in the history of the game for an international match when almost 74,000 people turned out for the World Cup final. The same year, Great Britain had gone on a full Lions tour in which all three Tests in Australia had been sell-outs, despite this being the first Ashes series down-under to be staged in the new television age which meant that all three Tests were played on Friday nights on live television. And in 1995 came the crowning glory, a fully-fledged World Cup tournament was staged in England (and Wales) which proved to be a joyous celebration of the sport. As well as a 66,000 crowd at Wembley for the final, we had 26,000 at

Wigan on a Wednesday night to see England play Fiji and a lockout crowd in Swansea to see Wales play Samoa. In subsequent years these were the kind of attendances, to say nothing of the feelgood factor, the game could only dream about for international games in the UK - and the biggest irony was that so much of that feelgood was generated by the presence of the Pacific Island nations Tonga, Samoa and Fiji, all of whom owed almost everything to the Australian Rugby League's development work and investment, the same Australian Rugby League which was being ostracised by the other nations at the 1995 World Cup in favour of jumping on the Super League bandwagon.

Since the British game switched to a summer season, starting in 1996, the international scene has been the biggest casualty. Much to the disappointment of the Australians, we are no longer able or willing to undertake a Lions tour, or even just play a three-match Test series in season in Australia. Whereas, in years gone by, a highlight of the footballing calendar would always be seeing the Australian national rugby league team playing a mid-winter Test series every four years against Great Britain, now they have to look to rugby union to fill the gap that rugby league has vacated. Just as disappointing for the Aussies is that the British game can no longer host a real Kangaroo tour - the last time the Australians came to play an Ashes series in England, in 2003, they wanted to make it a proper tour, albeit dramatically shorter than the tours of old. But a request to have another five or six fixtures against the leading clubs was turned down by the RFL, who claimed that they didn't want the Australians over here and playing any games before our Super League Grand Final because that would detract from the play-offs, and then they couldn't play any games after our Grand Final because the domestic season was officially over, so no clubs could play them either. When you think back to the last real Kangaroo tour and how successful it was, and realise that it came in 1994, just two years before summer rugby was introduced, you realise just how enormously damaging that change of season has been to the international game.

The intransigence of the Super League over the date of their Grand Final promises to cause further problems down the track for the next proposed World Cup, now scheduled to be played in Australia to celebrate the game's 100th birthday there in 2008. The only time slot available appears to be in February, which will make the World Cup effectively a pre-season tournament. Not that anything could be more disastrous for the game than its last World Cup staged in the UK (and France) in the year 2000. After four full seasons of summer rugby, Super League and full-time professionalism, its organisers confidently predicted that this was going to be better than anything we had ever seen before and was going to make at least £1million profit to be invested in the game worldwide.

I had a very uncomfortable feeling about all these bold claims long before a ball was kicked, purely because of the people who were involved in organising it and the things they were saying. As events got under way I found myself constantly being reminded of one of Jack Gibson's famous one-liners which was: "Carry a clipboard - it'll always get you in the gate." Sadly, plenty of the games could have done with several thousand clip-board bearers to put a few bodies on the almost empty terraces.

How could the game have sunk from the World Cup we enjoyed so much in 1995 to the one we endured in 2000? What had changed so much in just five short years? Maybe it was an indicator that a large number of old-fashioned rugby league supporters had become so alienated by the changes in the game - largely its change of season and a lot of the hype that surrounded Super League - that they had stopped going out to watch it. And, at the same time, the audience of new young fans attracted by the top Super League clubs had a loyalty just to those clubs and not to the wider game of rugby league. If they discovered the game via Sky television, they possibly didn't even know there was a game called rugby league, it was Super League.

By now Sky's control of the television rights to international games had matches kicking off at 6.00pm on Saturdays to fill their vacant slot in the schedules, which was something else that did not endear them to the older fans. Whilst the 2000 World Cup, far from providing that predicted profit, turned into a financial disaster which almost bankrupted the Rugby Football League, at least it provided some good news for the game in France. A wonderful Wednesday afternoon on All Saints Day in Carcassonne, in which France rescued their tournament by beating Tonga, suddenly put the French section of the World Cup on a high. The crowds were better than expected, but - I have to admit to you here and now - not quite as good as reported in the press. Tas Baitieri, seconded from Australia to organise much of the French pool in the tournament, and I would make up the figures as we went along. Most of them were pretty accurate guesses, Paris excepted where Tas let his imagination run a bit wild, but there was one joyous occasion when, driving along in the mini-bus we used to ferry essentials like post-protectors, corner flags and footballs to the games, we had already decided on the "official" attendance before we even got to the stadium. And, believe me, it was a good crowd that night!

Much of the attitude towards the international game in the era of summer rugby and Super League was most damaging to the French, who couldn't understand why the people on the other side of the channel were supposed to be the professionals, whilst they were the amateurs, yet things appeared to be so hapless. France had hoped the positive reaction to their performances in the World Cup (to say nothing of those "excellent" crowds they got!) would be a launching pad for their international revival. But instead of meaningful competition, all they got was an occasional home game against Scotland or Ireland played on a Tuesday night in July, or a trip to Dublin to play in front of just a handful of spectators. The French, as a serious rugby-playing nation, had expected something better and it was no surprise that a batch of their most talented young players from the World Cup team gave up on the game and left to cash in on their talents in rugby union.

Thankfully, things are improving on the international front. The Tri-Nations concept puts the three fully-professional nation teams into competition together and the change of season has not affected staging major Autumn internationals in England because that was always the time we would have been hosting the Australians or New Zealanders. Even for France there has been a positive spin-off in that both the Aussies and Kiwis can use their free weekend in the Tri Nations to nip over to France and give them a meaningful international. But the British Rugby Football League cannot expect the Australian and New Zealand teams to keep travelling to Europe every year. The Aussies have offered an olive branch by agreeing to stage a Tri Nations at home in 2006, out of season, and it will be interesting to see how the public respond. If it goes well, we may yet see another Lions team travelling to Australia to play for the Ashes, which is something none of the current generation of players have ever had the chance to do.

That, and a successful World Cup, could do wonders for expanding rugby league's big picture by taking the international game back to the levels it enjoyed before 1996. In the meantime, everybody in this country can enjoy the Super League - so long as they're in it. Just ask Widnes.

● *Harry Edgar founded Open Rugby magazine in 1976 and was its publisher-editor for 22 years. In that time he also wrote regularly for Rugby League Week in Australia and Treize magazine in France and authored and contributed to numerous books. He now produces Rugby League Journal, a magazine for fans who don't want to forget the game they used to know, along with the extremely popular "Rugby League Journal Annual."*

10. It Takes 1,238 To Tango

Andy Wilson

Here's your starter for Super League X. In the first decade after the big switch to summer, which coach said: "Before you ask, yes, he is that good"? And to which player was he referring? Was it Ellery Hanley in his eventful year with St Helens, looking ahead to the debut of Phil Adamson? Or perhaps the Castleford stalwart Dean Sampson, telling the lucky Leeds supporters what to expect from the former Canberra and Kangaroo full-back Brett Mullins?

Sorry to start a celebration of the 1,238 players who have featured in Super League's first 10 seasons with a couple of cheap shots, but Adamson and Mullins offer a reminder that not every Australian has matched the unforgettable impact made in September 2005 by Andrew Johns on his Warrington debut, prompting that brief eulogy from the Wolves coach Paul Cullen. Adamson made a single appearance as a substitute for Saints before finding himself in the middle of the bitter dispute between Hanley and Eric Hughes, while by the time Mullins joined Leeds in 2001 he was a shadow of the full-back who represented Australia's rebel Super League competition on their British tour four years earlier - and clashed infamously with Sampson at the Leeds Holiday Inn.

Tripping through the roll call alphabetically, from Malcolm Alker to Nick Zisti, throws up some unlikely names. Players who by

2005 seemed to belong to a distant era - Dean Bell, Frano Botica, Ikram Butt, Lee Crooks, Andy Currier, Martin Dermott, Paul Dixon, Shaun Edwards, Patrick Entat, Richie Eyres, Karl Fairbank, Paul Forber, Mark Gamson, David and Paul Hulme, Martin Ketteridge, Colin Maskill, Billy McGinty, Phil McKenzie, Paul Moriarty, Martin Offiah, Andy Platt, Garry Schofield and Kelvin Skerrett - all took the field in the early years of the summer era. Six of the head coaches in Super League's 10th season had also played in the competition - Cullen, Tony Rea, Karl Harrison, Darren Abram and two Tony Smiths.

Talking of namesakes, the two Julian O'Neills were drawn magnetically together at Widnes, although the two Paul Andersons managed to stay apart. As did all three Paul Smiths, who together with Aaron, Andy, Byron, Chris, Craig, Damien, Danny, Darren, Gary, Hudson, James, Jamie, Jason, Kris, Lee, Leigh, Mark, Michael, Peter, Richard, Tyrone and the aforementioned two Tonys had easily the most common surname in Super League's first decade, leaving the seven Joneses (not including one Jones-Buchanan) well behind. There have also been six Browns, Robinsons, Johnsons and Jacksons; five Moores, Lees and Chapmans; four Kings, Wilsons, Hills, Peters and Bells; and three Prices, Pryces and Cooks. And a Cooke.

But there was only ever going to be one Bagdad Yasa. A fine player, no doubt, but his impact on me was roughly similar to that made by Mikhail Piskunov, Philippe Ricard and Craig Menkins, who apparently also made the odd appearance in the two seasons of the Paris Saint-Germain Super League experiment. Not that it was impossible to forge a lasting impression even in a handful of matches for PSG. Nippy winger Pascal Bomati and Polish prop Gregory Kacala both showed huge promise before being lost to rugby union, and Aussie stand-off Todd Brown was excellent in the opening night win against Sheffield.

Nor can Paris claim a monopoly of unlikely Super League players. London Broncos have also contributed generously - anyone remember Wes Cotton, Bart Williams, Paul Terry or Leroy Leapai? Anderson Okiwe played once for Sheffield, Lionel Harbin likewise for Wakefield and more recently Blake Cannova made a solitary appearance for Widnes, while Craig McDowell holds the unusual distinction of figuring once as a substitute for Bradford in 2000, Warrington in 2002 and Huddersfield in 2003. And did Paul Round really come off the bench three times for Castleford in 1996?

But enough of the supporting cast. The primary purpose of this chapter is to appreciate, and attempt to evaluate, the outstanding players of Super League's first decade. Who are our main contenders?

Men of Steel seem as good a starting point as any. From Andy Farrell in 1996 to Jamie Lyon in 2005, via James Lowes, Iestyn Harris, Adrian Vowles, Sean Long, Paul Sculthorpe (twice), Jamie Peacock and Farrell again. Each was judged, by an anonymous panel of experts meeting in a darkened restaurant, to have made the greatest impact on a Super League season - and the fact that Farrell and Sculthorpe both doubled up must make them particularly strong contenders.

Were this unscientific judging process taking place at the end of Super League IX, then it would be hard to argue with Farrell as the cream of the crop. In addition to his two Man of Steel seasons, he captained Wigan to victory in the first Grand Final in 1998, and made three more Old Trafford appearances in 2000, 2001 and 2003, when on each occasion he was personally blameless in defeats by St Helens and twice by Bradford. He also lifted the Challenge Cup at Murrayfield in 2002, and led Great Britain resolutely through more bad times than good for the first nine years of Super League after being appointed the youngest ever national captain in 1996, aged 21. As a goalkicker alone, Farrell's record is phenomenal. His nine Super League seasons brought him 1026 conversions and penalties, 433 more than the next most prolific marksman, Sean Long - one of only four others who had even reached 500 by the end of 2004 (the others, incidentally, were Lee Briers, Iestyn Harris and Steve McNamara).

But of course there was so much more to his game that such accuracy usually came low down in a list of Faz's attributes. I remember filling Dave Hadfield's battered old hiking boots as Sky's man of the match judge for a Wigan-St Helens game at the JJB late in the 2004 season, and Eddie cueing me in with the suggestion that there had been quite a few candidates for the Tissot watch. But

Farrell, in that memorable spell when he was playing at prop because of Wigan's annual injury crisis, had somehow combined the traditional front-rower's duties of hitting the ball up with his more familiar role as a creative first or second receiver. He also made a number of crucial tackles as well as plenty more routine ones, broke the Saints line for the match-winning try, and banged over a couple of touchline conversions. No other player even got a mention in the press box poll.

Farrell had one other great attribute: durability. In those nine seasons, he made 230 appearances, second only to Keith Senior - more of him later. And that was despite missing the first quarter of Super League IX after a winter knee operation. In the previous eight seasons, he had hardly missed a match. Not because he was scarcely ever injured, but because of his toughness, which inspired awe even among his fellow professionals for whom playing through pain is simply part of the job - and most spectacularly illustrated in his Elephant Man moment against Leeds which secured his second Man of Steel award. Typically, Farrell did not understand what all the fuss was about until he saw the television pictures, and even then he was a little embarrassed.

But then, roughly six months later, on the eve of the 10th summer season and after being awarded the 2004 Golden Boot as the world's best player, a *Daily Express* exclusive revealed that Faz was off to rugby union. So he can't be the outstanding player of Super League's first decade. Not just because he joined the rah-rahs - honest. But because he didn't play throughout that decade.

The 20 players who did include some surprising names - Chris Chester, Mike Wainwright, Jon Wells and the unrelated Johnsons from Wigan, Andy and Paul. None of them would sit comfortably in the very top echelon of Super League players, although all have had their moments. But if Farrell is out of the running as Super League's man of the decade because he didn't last the decade, then such an exacting selection criterion also rules out the other seven Men of Steel.

Iestyn Harris, who started the decade as a youngster at Warrington having made his name with Wales in the 1995 World Cup, was also lured to union after five seasons in which he became an all-time Leeds great, and after returning north with Bradford in 2004 struggled to recapture the effortless brilliance of his Headingley pomp. Adrian Vowles' heroics in Castleford's stirring run to within one game of the 1999 Grand Final would surely earn him a place in any Tigers' Hall of Fame, but he only spent five seasons at the Jungle - although when the club needed a helping hand in regaining their Super League place late in 2005, they turned again to the bald, bandy-legged Queenslander with a masochistic willingness to tackle - or rather throw himself at - forwards who looked twice as big as him.

Jamie Lyon only played in one of Super League's first 10 seasons, the last, although the consistent brilliance of his centre play achieved the seemingly-impossible feat of justifying Ian Millward's boldness verging on blasphemy in comparing him to the Knowsley Road legend Mal Meninga. To think that such talent, which had already earned him a Kangaroo tour as a teenager in 2001, was in danger of being wasted when he became disillusioned at Parramatta and spent 2004 pig-hunting in his native Wee Waa. Millward did Saints, the Super League and the game in general a huge service when after numerous phone calls he finally tracked Lyon down in the bush, and persuaded him to follow in Meninga's huge footsteps.

The claims of Sean Long, Jamie Peacock and James Lowes all have much greater longevity, but none have quite gone the distance. Peacock didn't make his Bradford debut until 1999, after spending time in those contrasting rugby league hotbeds of Wollongong and Featherstone to smooth the rough edges Brian Noble and Matthew Elliott willingly overlooked when they first spotted a huge, tough forward playing for Stanningley "on a freezing cold hillside in Siddal", as Noble later recalled when he appointed him Great Britain captain. Long does manage to squeeze into the 20 players who have figured in each of Super League's first 10 seasons, but only courtesy of a single start for Wigan in 1996. It was after being thrown in at the deep end by St Helens for a World Club Championship match against Cronulla at Knowsley Road that the blond scrum-half really started to emerge as one of the stars of the game - Saints having snapped him up from Widnes who were probably still chuckling at Wigan's astonishing blunder in swapping Long plus cash for the Tongan prop Lee Hansen, who made 10 try-less appearances for them in 1997.

Long's subsequent career has never been far off a soap opera, with dramatic match-winning kicks in the Grand Final wins against Bradford in 1999 and 2002, and of course his part in the great betting scandal of 2004, when after an unflattering picture on the back of the *Daily Mail* had made him the face of the controversy, he won his second Lance Todd Trophy as Saints regained the Challenge Cup in Cardiff before being banned for three months. Long being Long, Ian Millward being Ian Millward, and rugby league being rugby league, he returned as Saints captain at Odsal, the venue for the Easter Monday landslide that caused all the controversy. And after playing for Britain in the Tri-Nations series at the end of the season, he was back in the headlines in 2005, first by threatening international retirement, and then as the unfortunate victim of a late hit from Terry Newton that left him with four titanium plates inserted in a badly-battered face.

Lowes shared Long's gift for polarising opinion, but very little else. It is hard to imagine Long spending the first two weeks after a Grand Final defeat tiling and grouting, as Lowes said he had been when he was given a surprise recall to the Lions squad for the last two Tests of the New Zealand series in 2002. His subsequent performances in a draw at Huddersfield and a series-saving victory in Wigan were outstanding, the combination of intelligent acting-half scheming and tough defence that made him at least a rival to Farrell as Super League's most influential figure for its first eight seasons.

The last of the old-fashioned hookers, as he was once described by Mike 'Stevo' Stephenson - himself the forerunner of a new breed of speedy hookers 30 years or so earlier - Lowes retired with one last burrowing try in Bradford's 2003 Grand Final win against Wigan, although Wakefield's marvellously combative David March battled manfully to keep his spirit alive, getting himself sin-binned twice on one particularly memorable afternoon at Widnes. Like Long, Lowes had been literally given away, in his case by Leeds to Bradford in the transitional Centenary season. Eight years later he had made 205 starting Super League appearances, more than anyone else at that stage - with Farrell on 204 and Senior on 203, discounting substitutes' appearances which would take both him and Francis Cummins to 206 - and led the Bulls to three Super League titles and two Challenge

Cups. Jimmy remains my personal favourite of Super League's first decade, just ahead of Stanley Gene, with his combination of subtlety, toughness and humour making up for the odd disciplinary aberration such as his verbal onslaught against Russell Smith after the 2002 Grand Final - just before his tiling and grouting. But, like Farrell, he can't be the player of the decade if he didn't play through the whole decade.

Paul Sculthorpe, the other dual Man of Steel winner, did, and few would argue that for the two consecutive seasons in which he picked up the game's most valued individual award, in 2001 and 2002, he was the shining star of the Super League. But at the start of the summer era he was just emerging as an outstanding young talent at Warrington, and it then took him a couple of years under Shaun McRae at Knowsley Road when he was used mostly as a grafting second-rower before he became a truly dominant force under first Ellery Hanley, then Ian Millward. Saints fans will doubtless disagree, but I'd say that Sculthorpe's finest moment so far came with his two tries in Great Britain's stirring victory over Australia at Huddersfield in the first Test of the 2001 Ashes series. But by the end of Super League X, he was still only 28, with plenty of time to burnish his reputation, and perhaps even to match Hanley's record as a three-time Man of Steel - on the assumption that the injury problems which undermined then prematurely ended his 2005 season could be overcome.

Given the number of honours collected by Chris Joynt - Sculthorpe's predecessor as St Helens captain - in his distinguished career, it is quite a surprise to reflect that he won neither the Man of Steel nor the Lance Todd. However after lifting the Super League trophy three times at Old Trafford, in 1999, 2000 and 2002, plus the Challenge Cup and World Club Challenge in 2001 to complete a famous Saints treble, Joynt will also be remembered as one of the key figures of the decade. He won the Harry Sunderland award as man of the match in the 2000 Grand Final, and was similarly recognised for his performance in the World Club victory over Brisbane Broncos three months later, giving the shellshocked Queenslanders a lesson in ignoring the icy conditions and getting on with the game. That was typical of the down to earth attitude that made the hard-working Wiganer "an unlikely icon", in the spot-on description of his coach Ian Millward, although he will probably be best remembered for scoring the most famous try of Super League's first decade, the unlikely stoppage-time match-winner in an early play-off against Bradford which gave Eddie Hemmings his finest commentary moment, caused delirium at Knowsley Road and left the Bulls coach Matthew Elliott sliding off his seat in despair.

But like Farrell and Lowes, Joynt didn't quite last the decade either, retiring at the end of 2004. So, exactly who of the 1996 summer pioneers was still standing? As well as the aforementioned quintet of unlikely stalwarts - Chester, Wells, Wainwright and the Johnsons - there were the three veterans who teamed up under Frank Endacott at struggling Widnes in 2005, after much happier times together at Wigan. Terry O'Connor had made 222 Super League appearances for the Warriors, Mick Cassidy 220 and Gary Connolly 178, with an 18-month stint at Leeds including the 2003 Lance Todd Trophy lifting his tally beyond 200, too. Their Wigan team-mates included two more of the great survivors, Kris Radlinski and Terry Newton - who, unlike Cassidy, Connolly and O'Connor, would also be involved in Super League's second decade, even if Newton was facing an enforced delay to the start of 2006 after receiving a record seven-month suspension for a couple of horrible high-shots on Long and Lee Gilmour that led to the former's fractured cheekbone.

Across the Pennines at Leeds, O'Connor's Best Man, Barrie McDermott, and his longest-serving Rhinos team-mate, Francis Cummins, also signed off in 2005 after spending Super Leagues I - X giving largely distinguished service in blue and amber, leaving only four more of the enduring 1996 originals to play on - Keith Senior at Headingley, Robbie Paul at Bradford, and Paul Anderson and Keiron Cunningham at St Helens.

A word of explanation is necessary here which also doubles as an appreciation of some more nearly men. Nick Fozzard, Paul Highton, Mark Hilton, Adam Hughes and Toa Kohe-Love add to the list of players who started in '96 and were still going in 2005. But after four years as a fringe player at first Leeds and then Huddersfield, Fozzard did not have a Super League club in 2001 following a series of arm injuries. Highton spent 2003 in the National League with Salford, just as Hughes dipped into the old Northern Ford Premiership with Wakefield in 1998. Hilton, a rare beast indeed as a prop with a Maths degree, missed the whole 2001 season with the shoulder injury that wrecked a move to Wigan, his hometown club, before a triumphant return to Warrington the following year. And Kohe-Love, who also rejoined the Wolves for their first year at the Halliwell Jones in 2004 after spending the first six Super League seasons at Wilderspool and the next two with Hull, may technically be an ever-present but only managed two appearances for Bradford in 2004 before a shoulder injury wrecked his Odsal dreams.

So now, back to the big four. Anderson certainly fits that description comfortably, a prop forward with an old-fashioned physique weighing somewhere between 17 and 19 stone depending on the fashion of the season. He only made six appearances in the first Super League summer, for Halifax, who he had joined from Leeds three years previously. That was as a result of an unusual, uncomfortable medical condition which he summed up unforgettably in a *Guardian* interview: "Basically, I had two arseholes." But Bradford's coaching team took a punt on him at the end of that 1996 season, and in the next seven years he made 178 appearances for the Bulls - 104 of them as a substitute. Obviously, size has remained Anderson's greatest attribute, but there has always been more to his game than that. I remember one remarkable pick-up off his bootlaces in a defeat by a Warrington team inspired by Alfie Langer at Wilderspool. And a move to St Helens for the 2005 season, with Ian Millward looking to bulk up his pack, allowed Anderson to reinvent himself as something like an old-fashioned ball-playing prop. He was an ever-present, scored seven tries, earned selection in the Dream Team, and a new contract for 2006 when, at 34, he would be the oldest player in the league.

Keith Senior has a similar no-nonsense Yorkshire attitude to Anderson and power has also been the key to his outstanding career, even if he has spent most of it in the centre after being blessed with a little more pace. On appearances alone, Senior has been Super League's number one player, the only man to have passed 250, and as he does not turn 30 until April 2006, with plenty of power to add. He also capitalised on Radlinski's injury problems in 2005 to overtake him as Super League's leading try scorer, and following Farrell's abrupt departure he became easily Great Britain's most experienced player. Yet, for some reason, Senior is one of those players who don't often earn headlines. Maybe it's because he spent the first four Super League seasons with unsung Sheffield Eagles, for whom his best-remembered contribution was probably the haymaker with which he floored B-J Mather in a cup quarter-final win at Castleford. He had completed a four-match suspension in time to play in Sheffield's famous Wembley win against Wigan, but was three times a cup final loser with Leeds, against Bradford in 2000 and 2002, and Hull in 2005 when he showed huge personal courage to play with a serious ankle injury, but the Rhinos' gamble backfired and he could not continue after half-time. Indeed playing at Leeds may be the main reason for Senior's surprisingly low profile, as it's easy to forget that they went five years without a Grand Final appearance until their consecutive Old Trafford appearances in 2004 and 2005. Through no fault of his own, Senior hasn't quite dominated the Super League era in the manner of the two remaining - and surely jointly-successful - candidates.

St Helens and Bradford have been the dominant clubs of Super League's first decade. Despite competition from the aforementioned Joynt, Sculthorpe, Anderson and Lowes - not forgetting Paul Newlove, Anthony Sullivan, Tommy Martyn, Paul Wellens, Stuart Fielden, Brian McDermott, Paul Deacon and Lesley Vainikolo - Keiron Cunningham and Robbie Paul have been their key players.

Cunningham is St Helens born and bred, and reflects that he could hardly have played for his local team in a more opportune era, with his emergence coinciding, far from coincidentally, with the club's escape from the huge shadow cast by the old enemy, Wigan, for most of the previous decade. First David Howes arrived as chief executive, then Shaun McRae as coach, and Cunningham says the Australian's experience from Canberra gave Saints a huge head start at the dawn of British league's full-time era. In turn, McRae realised he was lucky - like Ellery Hanley, Ian Millward and Daniel Anderson after him - to inherit pretty much the perfect modern hooker, with his powerful acting-half drives, solid defence, and instinctive feel for the game. It has not all been milk and honey, of course; there was an injection of human growth hormone in the 2002 season for which Cunningham escaped suspension, because the Rugby Football League accepted he had been the unwitting victim of a Bolton fireman masquerading as a Great Britain nutritionist. But a ban couldn't have been much worse than the turmoil Cunningham endured as he attempted to repair his reputation and self-esteem. His 2003 season was a nightmare, but after a year of steady recovery by 2005 he was back to something like his best - and, just as importantly, seemed at peace with himself again. At 29, he could have a major influence on Super League's second decade, as well.

Robbie Paul is only eight months older than Cunningham, but at the end of his decade as a Bradford Bull he was coming to terms with a less pivotal on-field role. However he will always be remembered fondly in Bradford and beyond as the symbol of the club who were the standard-bearers in Super League's difficult early years. It was the late Peter Deakin, the league-loving marketeer from Oldham who arrived at Odsal with their new Australian coach Brian Smith late in 1995, who spotted in Paul the potential to be the competition's first franchise player, one of the Americanisms he had brought with him after a stint across the Atlantic. Paul says he wasn't really aware of what was happening at the time: "I was just a naive kid from the Auckland suburbs. But I got caught up in it, and went along for the ride." His open, engaging personality made him the ideal frontman for Bradford's innovative community programmes, as well as their variety of marketing stunts. But he couldn't have carried it off without the on-field brilliance that lit up the 1996 Wembley defeat by St Helens, when Paul won the Lance Todd Trophy after becoming the first player to score a hat-trick on the losing side. There were plenty of team triumphs to make up for that collective disappointment, as Bradford's Kiwi captain lifted the Super League title in 1997, 2001 and 2003, and the Challenge Cup at Murrayfield in 2000 and the Millennium Stadium two years later. He remembers the 2003 Old Trafford demolition of Wigan most fondly: "It was the most complete team performance I've ever played in - and the last time I played in the same team as my big bro'."

Big bro' Henry was as gifted as any of the players in Super League's first decade, but like Harris, Farrell and Jason Robinson he was lured by the global profile of rugby union, although he failed to make an impact at international level, and would surely have been better off fulfilling his lifetime's goal of playing league in Australia, thereby maintaining his partnership with Robbie for New Zealand.

Robinson was far too good to receive only a passing mention, scoring 87 tries in five seasons with Wigan including the first in an Old Trafford Grand Final. But so too were - indeed are - his Wigan team-mates Radlinski, Newton, Cassidy and O'Connor; Cummins, McDermott, Darren Fleary and Adrian Morley at Leeds; Bernard Dwyer and Tevita Vaikona at Bradford; Darren Albert, Kevin Iro, Sonny Nickle and Apollo Perelini at St Helens. And the less glamorous clubs had their heroes, too. Malcolm Alker at Salford, Steele Retchless in London, David March for Wakefield, Paul Broadbent for Sheffield, Brandon Costin and Stanley Gene at Huddersfield, Paul Cooke and Richard Horne for Hull, Martin Moana for Halifax, Darren Rogers - immortalised as Harry Potter by John Ledger of the *Yorkshire Post* - and Nathan Sykes, Dale Fritz and Danny Orr at Castleford.

And what about some of the other characters? Brian Carney's remarkable journey from Wicklow to Surfers Paradise via Gateshead, Hull, Wigan, Newcastle and the GB vice-captaincy. Sid Domic, wholehearted centre and gifted Aboriginal artist. Geordie boy Chris Thorman. Jason Hetherington, with his gravelly Aussie outback drawl. Graeme "Penguin" Bradley, the only player named after a Batman villain. Freddie Tuilagi and his personalised wigs.

It sounds naff to say that it's the players who make rugby league so great - of course they do, and that's one of the reasons why a national, full-time, summer Super League offered, and hopefully still offers, the opportunity for them to finally receive the recognition they deserve as the most under-appreciated athletes in sport. But conversely, it must be a bloody great game to produce so many memorable players. Thanks to them all. Even Bagdad Yasa.

● *Andy Wilson has covered rugby league for the Guardian since the retirement of Paul Fitzpatrick in 1997, after spending the previous seven years working for League Express - initially as the Oldham correspondent - and, from 1996, the Observer. He is also a regular contributor to Rugby League World magazine and occasionally appears on BBC local and national radio when no-one else is available. For three years he did a poor imitation of James Lowes as hooker for Leeds University.*

11. On the Bosses

Ian Laybourn

"Ellery Hanley does not eat humble pie!" The words were repeated mantra-fashion as his finger prodded rapier-like at its target and his beady, penetrating eyes stared relentlessly at their prey. Hell hath no fury like a besmirched Super League coach. Or at least one who believes his reputation has been sullied.

Super League has been awash with entertaining characters throughout a decade that has seen coaches come and go like red buses through Piccadilly. It's an appropriate time to take a look at the great and the good, along with those who, quite simply, were not up to the job.

Ellery Hanley, of course, was right up there when it comes to greatness. Some might say he was the best player of his generation, nay of all time. He was also a successful coach, certainly at Super League level in his brief, but colourful spell with St Helens in 1999, and one of the game's true characters. But he was definitely not a man to cross. Asking questions at a Hanley post-match press conference was a case of lighting the blue touch paper and standing back. It was not so much an explosion that was to follow but rather a cold, calculated and often sustained personal attack on his unfortunate victim.

Hanley's initial response to any question that might contain the slightest hint of criticism inevitably began with the words: "If you had ever played the game..." Almost as entertaining as he was on the field! Here was an intimidating figure who was greeted like royalty on the streets. But, if the red carpet was rolled out for Ellery, everyone else trod on eggshells in the great man's presence.

The aura of greatness was accompanied by a definite feeling of discomfort for here was a man who appeared to have little time and absolutely no respect for the media, a simmering hatred, in fact, that went back to his early playing career when one or two news hacks intruded far too close for comfort into Hanley's private life.

The former Wigan and Great Britain captain was an unforgiving type and, when a smiling Hanley insisted at his introductory press conference that what was in the past stayed in the past, several knowing glances were exchanged between the seasoned journalists at Knowsley Road that day.

It was bound to end in tears but there was joy along the way too, as Hanley guided St Helens to the 1999 Super League Grand Final and a nail-biting victory over Bradford. Hanley was adored by players and fans alike, but his strained relationship with the media was mirrored in his dealings with the Saints board of directors, who quickly came to the conclusion that no one man was bigger than the club.

Signs that all was not well came via a telephone call from Maurice Lindsay, then managing director of Super League, who set up a meeting between Hanley and this reporter at the Birch Service Station on the M62, a famous trans-Pennine venue for the occasional cloak-and-dagger rendezvous over the years.

It was a convivial get-together - unlike our next one-on-one confrontation - which Hanley used to get the message across loud and clear that the signing of Australian forward Phil Adamson was strictly the work of the St Helens board. Mischievous rumours suggested that the directors had signed the wrong brother, having mistaken him for international second rower Matt Adamson, but whatever the explanation, Phil never started a match under Hanley.

The coach was even more outspoken a few days later when he accused the directors of being "ignorant and rude" in failing to support his efforts to strengthen the St Helens squad and it was no surprise when he was suspended from his duties. It all made wonderful copy, as is the case when rugby league clubs wash their dirty linen in public.

It was especially tasty when football manager Eric Hughes, who threatened legal action against Hanley, revealed that the coach had tried to swap Keiron Cunningham for Hunslet hooker Richard Pachniuk and stand-off Tommy Martyn for Graham Holroyd, of Halifax. It was difficult to work out which tarnished Hanley's reputation the most - his total lack of diplomacy or his staggering misjudgement of players.

It mattered little to the St Helens fans, though, and in scenes that would re-appear six years later, they staged a protest at the next match, calling for the coach to be re-instated and for the board to be sacked. Hanley duly got his job back after apologising for "any offence caused", hence the suggestion regarding "humble pie", something to which he took great offence.

With diligent investigation that would have done a journalist proud, he tracked down the author of the story and, after a series of telephone conversations failed to douse his fire, a face-to-face meeting was arranged, this time at Headingley where Saints were to play their first match since his re-instatement.

Absurdly, Hanley arrived complete with "minder", who looked much less threatening than the man himself, and proceeded to deliver his lecture with his target more or less pinned up against a wall.

Conversation was totally out of the question and, while it all ended in stalemate with Ellery needing to get to the dressing rooms ahead of kick-off, at least he was able to let off steam. It was tempting to point out to him that journalists invariably hang around longer than coaches and, of course, the end came for Hanley seven months - or 16 matches - later.

He did not help his cause by declining to attend the official launch of Super League V at Bradford's National Museum of Film & Photography and refusing to give an interview to the BBC before a Challenge Cup-tie, and was sacked a month into the 2000 season after once more criticising the St Helens club in public.

Hanley took up a new career in rugby union, working his way into the England set-up via a spell with Bristol, but re-surfaced

Messiah-like four years later in the unlikely setting of Castleford, who were in desperate need of divine intervention after finding themselves in serious danger of relegation for the first time in their history.

He was given the title of coaching consultant, working alongside newly-promoted head coach Gary Mercer, but it was a bizarre appointment and he left less than two months later after the Tigers had won just one out of seven matches. Castleford issued a statement saying the former Great Britain coach had left them a survival plan but, whatever his influence, the club were duly relegated and Hanley's reputation took another knock.

Controversial coaches are nothing new at St Helens, and Hanley was succeeded by another larger-than-life character. Eventually, the outspoken Ian Millward was also suspended and ultimately sacked but not before guiding Saints through an unprecedented period of success. Millward - or "Basil" as he is widely known - had the Midas touch from the outset, steering the club to a triumphant defence of their Super League crown and he went on to help them lift five major trophies in his five seasons.

There was never a dull moment at Knowsley Road with Millward in charge but, while Hanley came across as a cold, calculating figure, the little Australian was - and remains - a lovable rogue who knows a news angle and delights in providing a non-stop stream of wonderful copy.

Strangely, Millward's more outrageous comments usually followed a victory rather than a defeat. There was the time, for example, after a fantastic victory at Bradford, when he labelled the Bulls chairman Chris Caisley "a loose cannon". Then there was that famous occasion after a home win over Hull in 2003 when he used the "f" word 31 times in the post-match press conference to describe graphically the extent of his players' injuries. Even seasoned hacks were startled by Millward's outburst but relations were repaired at his next press conference when BBC commentator Ray French produced a cuss box and invited the Saints boss to make a hefty contribution.

Having been on the receiving end of that series of expletives, it was naturally with disbelief that reporters greeted news of Millward's suspension in May 2005, essentially for verbally abusing two media officers and swearing at a Rugby League official.

The bombshell decision naturally caused uproar in the streets and even split the Saints board with the legendary Eric Ashton, whose record six-year coaching rein Millward looked certain to break, going public to distance himself from the actions of his fellow directors. It prompted another media circus and, in a carbon-copy of the reaction to Hanley's suspension, around 2,500 fans staged a protest sit-in at Knowsley Road following a Challenge Cup-tie with York.

Bob Millward, a renowned figure in Australia's National Rugby League, made a 24,000-mile round trip to support his son and it was a strangely subdued, even emotional Millward who fronted a press conference arranged to enable him to defend himself.

Even then, Millward managed to lighten the sombre mood with a timely quip, revealing that he was unable to field potential offers for his services because St Helens had taken away his mobile phone, in addition to his company car! This time the Saints board, completely changed six years on, stood firm and sacked the most successful coach in the club's history on the grounds of gross misconduct.

But, mobile phone or not, Millward was never likely to be out of work for long. It was, in fact, just 12 days later when he was appointed by Saints' arch-rivals Wigan, who had just been booed off the pitch after slumping to a first home defeat by Huddersfield for 48 years. Millward became only the seventh coach in a century to have crossed the great divide when he was unveiled at a never-to-be-forgotten news conference at the JJB Stadium, where Dave Whelan, a down-to-earth millionaire if ever there was one, took great delight in announcing that Millward would never be sacked by his new employers for swearing! It might have been the story of the year, had Andy Farrell not decided to break from rugby league and throw in his lot with Saracens.

If life was to suddenly become livelier at the JJB Stadium, things calmed down noticeably at Knowsley Road, where new coach Daniel Anderson quickly won over the doubters with his contrasting style. Apparently, he can be quite volatile in the privacy of the dressing room, but you are more likely to catching the Pope swearing than witness Anderson blowing up in public.

The former New Zealand boss is very much in the mould of St Helens' first Super League coach, fellow countryman Shaun McRae, who until returning to Sydney in November 2004, was the only man to hold the position of head coach throughout the first nine seasons of Super League. It is difficult to think of a more calm, rational man than McRae, who was a journalist's dream - articulate, helpful and never short of a nice quote. But not all Australian coaches in Super League have been such natural communicators. Steve Anderson had a shocking time at Warrington and what about Dan Stains (has anyone noticed his surname is an anagram of Saints)?

The rather eccentric Stains will rightly be remembered for guiding London Broncos to the last Challenge Cup final at the old Wembley in 1999, but my abiding memory is of him breaking down in the middle of a press conference in the week leading up the big day. The club had just managed to get hold of then-owner Richard Branson via a telephone link from his island retreat and there was Stains blubbering uncontrollably in the middle of the top table as the emotions got the better of him. A deeply religious man, Stains was, it appeared, trying to thank his players for taking the club to Wembley but it was rather difficult to decipher his words in between the weeping and wailing.

Stains resigned shortly after the Broncos' record Cup final defeat by Leeds and, after successors Les Kiss and John Monie lasted barely 15 months between them, chief executive Tony Rea decided he would try his hand at this coaching lark.

Rea had joined the Londoners from North Sydney just before the advent of Super League and gave good service as a hooker before swapping his scrum cap for a shirt and tie. And he has proved to be the great survivor for, jointly with Bradford's Brian Noble, he holds the record as the longest-serving coach in Super League, having held the post since October 2000.

Gary Hetherington and John Harbin both went the other way, swapping the role of coach for that of chief executive. Hetherington, of course, was player, coach, director, chief cook and bottle washer with Sheffield Eagles and, as Leeds chief executive, in 2005 became the first double-glazing salesman to lead a team out in a Challenge Cup final.

The equally versatile Harbin quit as coach of Wakefield in 2001 and shortly afterwards became chief executive of first division Dewsbury. The English-born Aussie was forced to endure a difficult time as head coach at Belle Vue as the Wildcats, docked two points for breaching the salary cap, flirted with relegation but Harbin, with a style all of his own, never lost his sense of humour.

Warned off by the authorities for continually criticising match officials, Harbin once delighted his audience by claiming his father was of the opinion that the referee allowed the opposition to score a couple of tries directly from forward passes. Harbin's wonderful mannerisms brought him to the attention of former Northern Ireland international footballer Iain Dowie, who persuaded him to switch to the oval ball game with Oldham and later Crystal Palace. The amiable Harbin became something of a guru and was credited with playing a huge part in Palace's promotion to the Premiership.

If Harbin was a natural, for others coaching must have seemed like an alien occupation. Steve Anderson arrived at Warrington at the start of the 2002 season an unknown and went almost as quickly as he came and with equal anonymity.

Formerly right-hand man to Chris Anderson on the 2001 Kangaroo tour, he was in freefall at Wilderspool almost from the moment he took over from Darryl Van de Velde. Within two months he had handed over the coaching reins to his assistant, David Plange, and four weeks later quit his other role of performance director, accepting the blame for Warrington's disastrous start to the season which had seen them plunge to the foot of the table with just one win from their first eight matches. Anderson went on to work in the performance department of the Scottish Rugby Union and now holds a similar position with Ireland so he clearly had talent. It just seems he was more at home behind a desk than at the coal face.

As for ex-Hunslet coach Plange, the opportunity in Super League obviously came too soon in his fledgling career, for he lasted just four months in the Wilderspool hot seat before making way for former player Paul Cullen, a hugely popular choice among players and fans alike.

Others thrust forward before their time were Wiganers Steve McCormack and Denis Betts. McCormack, whose playing career was cruelly curtailed by injury, became the youngest coach in Super League at the age of just 28, when he was promoted from within to replace Australian John Harvey in 2001. And he was doing a reasonable job in difficult circumstances when the Reds board panicked in the face of the threat of relegation and sacked him after 10 months in charge. But the cream, as they say, rises to the top and McCormack duly re-emerged with Whitehaven, the club that also gave Cullen his big chance.

It is to be hoped that Betts can similarly bounce back. He was persuaded to hang up his boots at the age of 32 in order to help Wigan get under the salary cap and, after cutting his coaching teeth with the club's academy team, quickly found himself propelled into the front line when Mike Gregory was taken ill after the Challenge Cup final of 2004.

An horrific run of injuries, compounded by the loss of hugely-influential skipper Andy Farrell, exposed the inexperience of both Wigan's back-up players and their rookie head coach and it was no surprise when Maurice Lindsay swooped for the tried and trusted Millward. The Warriors were going through something of a crisis but nothing so irretrievable that couldn't be put right by the expertise of the 45-year-old from Wollongong, who has few rivals when it comes to hot-house coaching.

Perhaps Millward could have handed on a few tips to fellow countryman Dean Lance, who was never comfortable in the Leeds hot seat despite taking the Rhinos to the 2000 Challenge Cup final at Murrayfield. Lance had hardly covered himself in glory in the 1997 World Club Championship in which his Perth Western Reds team became the big Australian failures, losing to struggling Super League clubs Sheffield Eagles and Paris Saint-Germain.

Apart from being simply the wrong appointment, Lance had a tough, probably impossible, act to follow. Graham Murray had guided Leeds to the inaugural Super League Grand Final in 1998 and then carved himself a slice of history when he brought the Cup back to Headingley for the first time in 21 years. Murray, who first came to prominence on the British scene as coach of the Fijian team which thrilled crowds in the 1995 World Cup, was a popular figure in the Leeds dressing room. But his contract was not renewed at the end of the 1999 season and his popularity on the terraces suddenly dipped when he took one of the Headingley crown jewels, Adrian Morley, back with him Down Under.

In returning to a high-profile post in Australia's National Rugby League, Murray beat a path that has become well-worn in recent years. Brian Smith, the man in at the start of the Bradford Bulls revolution, had already left England for Parramatta and his Odsal successor Matthew Elliott subsequently jumped at the chance to take over at Canberra. Later, Stuart Raper put his experience with Castleford and Wigan to good use before landing a dream post at his old club Cronulla and, more recently, Shaun McRae finally ended his love affair with Super League to lead the revival at South Sydney. New Zealander Tony Kemp also cut his coaching teeth in England, helping steer Wakefield through one of their crises in the middle of 2000 before going on to land a plum job with New Zealand Warriors, although his tenure was cut short in September 2005 when he was handed the sack. The ability of the English system to turn out high-quality graduates reflects well on Super League, the Swiss finishing school of rugby league coaching.

Rugby union has been another beneficiary of the English game and that has become a far more worrying development. Graham Steadman, in charge of Castleford from 2001-4, and Neil Kelly, who took Widnes into Super League in 2002, have both followed former Wigan, Castleford and Great Britain scrum-half Mike Ford into Irish rugby. They are in good company, too, joining the likes of Phil Larder, Joe Lydon, Damian McGrath and, most famously of all, Shaun Edwards in the 15-man code, which has not been content to simply poach players from rugby league.

Far from pointing the finger, however, the game should look at itself and ask whether it did enough to keep some of its famous sons in rugby league. Lydon certainly felt his talents were not being harnessed sufficiently by the game's ruling body and Edwards applied for the vacancy at Warrington long before establishing himself as a leading figure in the Guinness Premiership with London Wasps.

In addition to keeping Widnes in Super League, Kelly worked

wonders with Wales, masterminding their fabulous semi-final performance against Australia in the 2000 World Cup. Kelly's achievements at club level were acknowledged when he was named Super League Coach of the Year in 2002 but that particular honour has become a poisoned chalice over the years. John Pendlebury (Halifax), Frank Endacott (Wigan) and Shane McNally (Wakefield) also landed the dreaded Coach of the Year award only lose their jobs within months. It all helps to illustrate the fact that there are just two types of coaches - those who have been sacked and those about to be sacked.

The life of a Super League coach is a perilous one, as no doubt 60 of them will testify. That's the staggering total of coaching casualties in the 10 seasons of summer rugby or, put another way, it means the departure of a coach every two months.

Wigan's drive to reclaim their former glories has made them the most ruthless club, with nine coaches in the 10 seasons of Super League. Nobody has held the job for more than 18 months and poor old Andy Goodway was in charge for just 16 matches in 1999.

Goodway has, in fact, held the position of head coach at three different Super League clubs. He had also been sacked by Oldham in April 1997 but was spared a similar fate at Paris Saint-Germain five months later when the struggling French club were removed from the League. The luckless Goodway actually lost two coaching positions in the space of a month in the autumn of 1999 for he was not retained as Great Britain boss following the disappointing Tri-Nations Series down under and he was eventually succeeded by former Kangaroo David Waite. It's no wonder, then, that he recently decided to emigrate to Australia. If you can't beat 'em...

Most of the coaches will have seen the sack coming but the unfortunate Eric Hughes had a shock when he arrived back from holiday at the end of the 1997 season to discover a note tucked under the windscreen of his car informing him of his fate. Hughes eventually turned his back on coaching and it's easy to see why. He was doing quite a reasonable job at St Helens on the eve of Super League I, when the Saints directors opted to dispense with his services and bring in a little-known Australian by the name of Shaun McRae. As it turned out, it was a shrewd move but it's difficult not to have some sympathy for Hughes, who was forced to give way to another Australian, John Monie, after just eight months in charge at Wigan.

It was Wigan, of course, who started the trend of appointing overseas coaches in the Eighties, with phenomenal success too under the Graham Lowe/John Monie dynasty. But there is little doubt that Super League clubs have had an unhealthy dependence on foreigners and it all came to a head in July 2000 when the sacking of John Kear by Huddersfield-Sheffield left Super League without a single British head coach. When Australian Tony Smith (not to be confused with Englishman Tony Smith, who in 2005 replaced Shane McNally at Wakefield) was appointed as Kear's successor a month later, the English top-flight had nine Aussies and three New Zealanders holding the key coaching positions. It got to the stage where an Antipodean accent outweighed even the most impressive Curriculum Vitae and it seemed that the answer to the first question at every press conference would always begin: "Look..."

For the record, the Kiwis were Frank Endacott (Wigan), Gary Mercer (Halifax) and Tony Kemp (Wakefield), who lined up alongside Australians Ian Millward (St Helens), Matthew Elliott (Bradford), Dean Lance (Leeds), Stuart Raper (Castleford), Darryl Van de Velde (Warrington), Shaun McRae (Hull), John Harvey (Salford), John Monie (London Broncos) and Smith.

The alarm bells were ringing loud and clear and it was only a matter of time before the Rugby Football League tightened up the regulations, restricting overseas appointments to coaches with at least two year's experience in Australia's National Rugby League.

It is a sobering statistic that, of the 72 coaches used in the 10 seasons of Super League, no fewer than 41 have been from overseas, 30 were British and there was one Frenchman, Michel Mazaré, who was the man in charge when Paris Saint-Germain entered the scene in 1996. London Broncos have never had an English coach, perhaps not surprisingly given their reliance on overseas personnel, while Sheffield Eagles' three coaches during their Super League existence were all British.

The count as Super League brought the curtain down on its first decade was six apiece but Oldham-born Steve Deakin will help tilt the balance in favour of Englishmen when he brings Les Catalans on board for 2006 at the expense of jovial Frank Endacott's relegated Widnes Vikings.

That's the way it has to be and, as fanciful as it may seem, I can't be alone in looking forward to that fine day when Super League is made up of 11 Britons and a Frenchman. Perhaps Ellery will be one of them!

● *Ian Laybourn has reported on rugby league for 31 years and celebrated his 50th birthday by covering the 2005 Powergen Challenge Cup final in Cardiff. He began his career on the Batley News in 1974 after swapping a season ticket for a press pass and spent 16 seasons following the fortunes of the Fartowners for the Huddersfield Daily Examiner before joining the Press Association in 1994. He is a qualified coach and lives with his wife Susan and family in Holmfirth.*

12. A Game of Snakes and Ladders

Gareth Walker

"Murdoch and Lindsay - murderers of rugby league." So proclaimed a banner at Cougar Park on Sunday 9th April 1995, one day after the momentous meeting that unveiled the sport's bold new Super League adventure. Another went even further: "Murdoch and Lindsay for the electric chair".

The bone of contention for the Keighley support? That their club, arguably the most progressive in rugby league at the time, had been omitted from the grandiose plan, despite the fact that the Cougars were finally set to realise their long-held dream of promotion to the top-flight. It all opened a can of worms that has been squirming ever since.

The issue of promotion and relegation is one that has stirred rugby league passions like few others during the summer era. Suggest the abolition of the gateway between divisions to any National League supporter and they will talk of destroying dreams and ripping the soul out of the sport. Ask the chief executive of a Super League club in the bottom half of the table about relegation and they cite lost livelihoods and the inability to structure long-term planning.

Not a season has passed since that Sunday afternoon in 1995 when the topic hasn't emerged as a major talking point. The Cougars were the first to challenge the establishment over their right to promotion, while Batley, who finished as runners-up to Keighley that season, soon became immersed as well. Lindsay became the target of much of their anger, following his role in the revolution as Rugby Football League chief executive.

"I have been stunned because Maurice Lindsay has been citing us as the example for all clubs trying to develop themselves," Cougars chairman Mick O'Neill lamented, on the weekend of the Super League announcement. "Yet when it came to the crunch, there was no place for us." He found a willing supporter in his Batley counterpart Stephen Ball. "Morally they can't refuse us and I believe that the first division chairmen will see the justice in our case and get behind us," he said.

Ultimately, Ball was wrong. But there was no lack of support for the two clubs on the terraces and MPs stepped forward threatening to take the RFL to the Monopolies and Mergers Commission, alleging restraint of trade. The Cougars also went public on their legal intentions, immediately rejecting an early offer of £100,000 compensation to remain in what became Division One.

Then came the Super League re-think, with a revamped Super League consisting of 12 teams, none of them including the much-maligned merged entities of the original proposal. But still Keighley and Batley were excluded, and there was even more controversy at that meeting. Only one club voted against the new proposal - Widnes - but bizarrely, the vote was taken with the Cougars officials out of the room. "Whilst Keighley was privately considering its position, a vote was taken in its absence," the club's solicitor Richard Cramer was reported as saying at the time. "It is surprising that the meeting should have proceeded to a vote in the absence of Keighley, and we are urgently requesting the details of the resolution of the meeting."

When everything eventually settled down, around a month after the initial announcement, the Cougars agreed to remain in Division One, while seeking increased compensation. They missed out on promotion to Super League in the first summer season to Salford, and have been in almost constant decline ever since. Similarly, Batley actually finished bottom of Division One in 1996 and were relegated to the bottom tier of the game, after being a whisker away from clashes with Wigan and St Helens.

The weeks of controversy also had far-reaching financial implications, particularly at Keighley where the club went into administration with reported debts of £1.5million in 1997 and bad feeling over their rejection still remains. On the day of the initial protests, 4,221 people watched their clash with Swinton. For the equivalent fixture in 2005, just 967 were at Cougar Park and that figure had almost halved for some games towards the end of the campaign.

Once Super League was actually up and running, the inaugural 1996 season was a rarity in that promotion and relegation went reasonably smoothly. Salford, under coach Andy Gregory, were comprehensive winners of Division One (ahead of the Cougars) and went on to finish sixth in their first season back in the top-flight. The only storm clouds gathered over Workington Town, who finished bottom of the first installment of Super League and then went into rapid freefall, both on and off the pitch. They encountered considerable financial problems and slumped to the bottom of Division One straight away, suffering consecutive relegations. For the first time, observers were beginning to look seriously at the implications of relegation in the game's new, professional era.

Those fears were reinforced the following year, when Oldham Bears slipped out of Super League and out of existence. After finishing three points adrift at the foot of the table, the Bears were wound up with massive debts. Not long afterwards, the then Super League chief Chris Caisley was forced to deny a report in the *Rugby Leaguer* that the Rugby Football League wanted to boot out Keighley and Workington, so bad were their troubles since their top-flight dreams had evaporated. Next came a report from KPMG accountants, which claimed that most clubs in the top two divisions were in serious financial trouble. The anti-promotion and relegation feelings were suddenly snowballing.

Oldham managed to preserve professional rugby league in the town when a new club was formed at the end of 1997, beginning life in Division Two. But the legacy of unpaid debts that the Bears left behind took some time for the new owners to overcome, particularly when seeking sponsorship.

Another club went to the wall that year, too, when French club

Paris Saint-Germain folded after just two seasons. That opened up a further place in Super League, with Hull already having been promoted to replace Oldham Bears. PSG's place went to Huddersfield Giants, who had finished second behind Hull and also beat them in the Divisional Premiership final at Old Trafford. The Giants would soon become enveloped in the promotion and relegation issue, primarily due to their constant failings in Super League. They would go on to finish bottom of the pile on four consecutive occasions before eventually dropping down a division in 2001.

Huddersfield's first saviour flew to the rescue clad in a purple superhero suit, yellow cape, and boasting a Geordie accent. With the arrival of new club Gateshead Thunder in 1999, a decision was taken to expand Super League to 14 teams but even that didn't pass without objection and some clubs in Divisions One and Two were angry at the Tyneside outfit's fast-tracking. The other extra place was taken by the newly-named Wakefield Trinity Wildcats, promoted after a touchline conversion from Australian centre Garen Casey sealed the first ever Grand Final win in this country, 24-22, over local-rivals Featherstone at the McAlpine Stadium.

With the demise of Gateshead and Sheffield, Super League returned to 12 teams in 2000, but the Giants were again saved from relegation, this time by two factors - a 'merger' with the Eagles and Hunslet Hawks becoming the first club to be denied promotion, despite winning the 1999 Northern Ford Premiership Grand Final. A late Jamie Leighton drop-goal sealed a thrilling win for the Hawks over Dewsbury Rams at Headingley, and chairman Grahame Liles immediately signalled the club's intention to push for promotion. Their main problem was the capacity of their South Leeds Stadium which, at just 2,500, was well short of Super League requirements.

Hunslet unveiled plans with Leeds City Council to develop the ground, also discussing proposals to merge with troubled Bramley as part of it. But when the independent franchise panel - remember that? - met, they refused the Hawks entry to the top-flight.

In the ensuing weeks, Hunslet even considered changing their name to South Leeds, but were faced with vehement protests from their supporters, with scores of passionate letters appearing in the local press. As with Keighley, the Super League set-back hit Hunslet hard. By the time a final decision over their future had been made, coach David Plange was well behind rival clubs in recruiting for the new season because of the uncertainty and the Hawks have struggled ever since, with their crowds dwindling below 500 at times.

In 2000, that unlikely merged entity of Huddersfield-Sheffield retained the Giants' place at the bottom, but once more they were let off the hook when NFP Grand Final winners Dewsbury Rams were denied promotion. This time the rejection caused even more of a stir.

Rams chairman Bob McDermott was not a man to do anything quietly and, immediately after his side's Grand Final win over Leigh - another one-point thriller - he said that Dewsbury would be demanding a place in Super League, warning that the game would be "thrown into total turmoil" if they were not supported by the RFL Council.

Again, the major obstacle was Dewsbury's Ram Stadium home and, again, plans were unveiled to increase the capacity. McDermott also pledged that the club would play at Sheffield's somewhat distant Don Valley Stadium while the work was being carried out. But the Council rejected the temporary stay in south Yorkshire, instead urging the Rams to prove that they could upgrade their ground to a 10,000 capacity. Tentative plans to move to Wakefield's Belle Vue were discussed, but the Rams' dreams were ended when the weekly newspaper, *Total Rugby League*, revealed that they only had planning permission to upgrade to a capacity of 5,510.

Soon after, McDermott announced that the club would remain in the Northern Ford Premiership, amid reports that the Rams owed £97,800 in unpaid VAT. "This is not an admission of failure, it is an acceptance of the fact that Super League might have come at a price we cannot afford," McDermott later explained. But, like the Hawks, Bulldogs and Cougars before them, Dewsbury found it difficult to recover from the rejection. Under Neil Kelly, the Rams had been a constant force for three years, but the following season they began to slip down the league ladder and have only recently shown genuine signs of a resurgence, both on and off the field.

Just when it appeared as though the drawbridge would be brought up permanently, in sailed a new hope: Widnes Vikings. The famous old club had enjoyed a tremendous and swift revival after recruiting the shrewd Kelly as coach in 2001 and, with their plush new Halton Stadium, were confident of getting the green light ahead of their Grand Final with Oldham, who themselves had come a long way since reforming less than four years earlier. The Vikings duly won through 24-14 at Rochdale's Spotland and, on the nod of the independent franchise committee, were granted entry into a division they had not graced since the winter era. Promotion was back.

Unfortunately for Huddersfield, that meant that relegation was back as well. Despite showing signs of significant progress under a rookie Australian coach by the name of Tony Smith, the Giants' fourth consecutive wooden spoon was confirmed on the final day of the 2001 season. Even then the matter was far from clear, with next-to-bottom Wakefield having had four points deducted mid-season for breaches of the salary cap, a punishment that was later - crucially - reduced to two.

The Giants didn't go quietly. Chief executive Ralph Rimmer was a stern opponent of the relegation system, both before and after the club's ensuing promotion campaign. Coach Smith, having come from an Australian background where relegation simply doesn't exist, was also baffled. "Business-wise it would be crazy to let a team, a backer and a club like this go," Smith mused after Huddersfield's final-day heartbreak. "They are a Super League team and it's a Super League club. It would be a very poor decision I reckon. But that's business - or is it sport?"

Still, the Giants' fall began a new era for relegated clubs - the notion of remaining full-time in order to earn an immediate return to the top table. Backed by the club's millionaire owner Ken Davy, Smith constructed a team that included Super League quality players such as Steve McNamara, Stanley Gene and Chris Thorman. But just as importantly, the Giants also brought through a host of talented youngsters; players who took a risk by accepting relatively low wages in a bid to earn a Super League contract the following year.

It worked to near perfection - Huddersfield lost just one game all season (at Doncaster in the Challenge Cup), and were richly-deserved Grand Final winners against Leigh. Winning the Buddies Cup also provided a high for their long-suffering supporters and

Smith's ploy of not simply buying a host of established NFP players paid off the following year, as the Giants produced their best Super League season, winning 11 games and finishing 10th.

Their success provided something of a blueprint for Salford, the team who dropped out of the top flight on Huddersfield's return. The Reds weren't quite as dominant as their predecessors in the now National League One but, equally, there were precious few occasions on which Karl Harrison's side looked anything other than Grand Final certainties. Scrum-half Gavin Clinch was their talisman through an excellent campaign and Leigh again played the role of bridesmaids on Grand Final night at Widnes.

Now the game was faced with a new dilemma. Would the relegated team simply be able to remain full-time and blast past their NL1 opponents every season, giving a predictability that would damage the competition at the lower level?

Halifax broke that trend before it had seriously started. They had struggled hugely in Super League VIII, after massive financial problems meant coach Tony Anderson had a minuscule playing budget compared with rival clubs in 2003. Nevertheless, they were widely expected to be the strongest side in National League One on their descent. But almost from day one, that wasn't the case. Anderson departed mid-season and only a dramatic and controversial win over York City Knights in the NL1 qualifying series final prevented them from suffering successive relegations.

At the same time, Leigh Centurions finally realised a dream that had started with Ian Millward's arrival in 1999. The club had been steadily building towards promotion since then, losing three Grand Finals in the process. But in 2004, Darren Abram's side beat Whitehaven to top spot on points difference and then defeated the Cumbrians in extra-time in a thrilling NL1 Grand Final. Castleford Tigers - a club who had previously never been relegated in their entire 78-year history, and who were widely regarded as a shining light for what a family-based summer approach could do for even the most traditional rugby league community - finished bottom of Super League and headed in the opposite direction.

Leigh's elevation and the Tigers' demotion once again opened that old can of worms.

Certainly, with the odds stacked against Abram and his staff, it was no real surprise to see Leigh struggle in Super League from the outset. After playing in the NL1 Grand Final the previous October, and with the Centurions not having had the experience that Huddersfield and Salford enjoyed, recruiting an almost entirely new team in such a short timescale proved too difficult. Abram also encountered difficulties in establishing a training regime, with many local fields and swimming pools fully booked by the time the level of competition at which Leigh would be competing was officially announced. After a long and difficult 2005 season, the Centurions recorded just five points and, predictably, the old murmurings about National League clubs not being able to compete at the higher level made a comeback.

It got messier still. If the principle of promotion was to be maintained, the entrance of French club Les Catalans into Super League from 2006 meant that two clubs would have to be relegated. The second of those, Widnes, at first refused to go gracefully. Soon after their place in the bottom two was confirmed, the Vikings indicated that they would be prepared to take legal action against the Rugby Football League should any of the NL1 clubs be given special dispensation over the minimum criteria laid down for promotion-seeking clubs.

In the event, it was a threat that they withdrew but, even so, the issue had complications. The RFL had amended the rules mid-season, stipulating that NL1 clubs must have all their ground improvements in place by August 31st. For a club like Hull Kingston Rovers, whose main concern was the size and state of their Craven Park pitch, the work was impossible to undertake during the middle of the campaign. Similarly, Whitehaven had no chance of building the new stands that would increase the seating capacity at the Recreation Ground to the level required while their stadium was in use. Even Castleford, whose homely old Wheldon Road ground had been re-christened "The Jungle" during the club's Super League days, resulting in a fun-filled atmosphere that met with universal popular acclaim, were made to jump through bureaucratic hoops and left in a state of limbo until they, like Whitehaven, were given the theoretical nod just a few days before winning the 2005 Grand Final, ironically at Widnes. It seems that promotion and relegation in rugby league will never have the clarity that it enjoys in football.

The RFL confused everyone further by announcing in mid-2005 that they intended to scrap the automatic promotion/relegation system altogether and adopt a new franchise process, starting in 2009. It is something that has been suggested at regular intervals since 1995 and is an idea that still has its supporters. But unsurprisingly, the proposals - which is all that they were, though the announcement led many to believe they were set in stone - were received with disgust by most National League supporters and a number of officials. Further complications, such as three-year immunities from relegation for certain clubs, made already muddy waters murkier still.

And that will always be the primary problem when promotion and relegation is not automatic. Whenever there are factors that can be decided as a matter of opinion away from the field, supporters will feel unsatisfied. Such uncertainty does not help anyone.

The main argument behind scrapping relegation from Super League is that it would allow clubs to plan for the long-term. It's a valid point - clubs still bring in short-term signings, more often than not from overseas, in an attempt to stave off the drop. That does little to aid the development of young British players and some sort of security would allow them to look beyond the end of the current campaign.

In addition, relegation brings a considerable downscaling in overall operations, meaning that off-field staff can lose their jobs through no fault of their own. Development and community work can be severely affected despite the presence of a helpful parachute payment, as can the marketing of the game locally.

Huddersfield's chief executive Rimmer outlined his thoughts on the issue after the Giants had won promotion back to Super League in 2002. "The system creates a waste of resources, both for the clubs and for the game itself," he argued in *Rugby Leaguer & League Express*. "I am not a fan of promotion and relegation and never have been. The Super League should be the pinnacle of the sport, and in order to have that you need 12 or 14 teams all achieving high standards both on and off the field.

"But with the uncertainty of relegation, clubs will spend with only one aim in mind - to avoid relegation. We did it ourselves, although perhaps not enough. During 2001, the Giants signed Stanley Gene and Troy Stone towards the end of the season to try to avoid the drop. This approach eventually stifles the standard of the competition, because it encourages short-termism, when clubs should be asked to invest in the development of the game in their area."

But what is actually being proposed here? A stale Super League where the same 12 teams battle it out, with little at stake for those in the lower reaches of the table? Annual confusion and uncertainty over which of two clubs has the superior catering facilities?

To deny a club promotion - or relegation - on the spurious grounds of off-field criteria constantly risks an outcry that could damage the game considerably. And would the NL1 Grand Final sell out if supporters knew that the game was meaningless in terms of their club progressing to the next level? Would over 8,000 people have attended this season's Castleford versus Hull KR league match if the carrot of Super League rugby was not dangling at the end of the campaign?

When Huddersfield finished bottom of Super League for four consecutive seasons, it did nobody any good - especially the Giants. A year in the NFP has seen them push on and develop as a club, to the extent that they now hold realistic ambitions of challenging the sport's biggest clubs. Hull started the summer era at a lower level. Had that promotion gate not been open to them, could they have progressed as a club to become Challenge Cup winners in 2005?

There is little doubt in anyone's mind that National League One clubs desperately need help in bridging the gap to Super League; in particular the short timescale they currently have to prepare needs to be amended. One idea of changing the National League seasons around, so that the Northern Rail Cup is played in the second half of the campaign, allowing the NL1 Grand Final to take place around July and give the winners several more months, appears to make the most sense.

Yes, there is a considerable financial gap between the top two flights. But the margins of error in football, for example, are much greater. Many estimate the riches of the Premiership being worth an additional £20million per year in comparison with the Championship. Year on year, soccer has clubs that rise and fall on a regular basis and several struggle to compete on the playing front. But when Sunderland embarked on a record losing run at the beginning of the 2005-06 Premiership season, were there any whispers of abolishing automatic promotion and relegation? In rugby league, the usual suspects would have been shouting that from the rooftops.

Rugby league history has shown that denying clubs promotion can be more damaging than giving them the chance of a shot at the big time. Just ask the supporters of Keighley, Batley, Hunslet or Dewsbury. How many thousands of fans have been lost to the game because off-field decisions determined their club's future? In contrast, the likes of Huddersfield and Salford dropped down a division and returned as far stronger entities.

The *Yorkshire Post* writer, Richard Sutcliffe, himself a lifelong Cougars supporter, penned a wonderful piece in April 2005 about his club's experience.

"Amid the back-slapping that invariably accompanies any anniversary of Super League, I doubt too many thoughts will be spared for Keighley Cougars," wrote Sutcliffe. "The tale of how a rugby league club from a town nestling between Bradford and the Yorkshire Dales rose from near-oblivion to national acclaim in the Nineties is one that transcends rugby league and sport in general. Re-branded in 1991 as the Cougars, the club became a beacon of hope for a town that had suffered badly due to the closure of the major textile mills and engineering firms.

"1995 was Keighley's big chance and, through no fault of our own, it was cruelly taken away. And such has been the rate of change over the past decade, I can't ever envisage being able to watch my team in the top division. It could all have been so different. A few seasons playing the likes of Wigan and Leeds would have helped cement our place in the top-flight. A side coached by the then Great Britain coach Phil Larder and led on the field by GB's first-choice stand-off Daryl Powell would surely have had more than a fighting chance of staying in the top division. The shame is we will never know."

Rugby league might be big business now, but it is still primarily a sport. The day that any club's future is decided by five men in suits sat around a table, rather than over 80 minutes on a rugby pitch, will be a sad one indeed. The Challenge Cup is decided on the field, so is the Super League Grand Final. Why should promotion and relegation be any different?

● *Gareth Walker first began writing on the greatest game for League Publications in 1996. He took up a full-time position with the company in 2001 and was staff writer for almost four years. During that time, he became the rugby league correspondent for The People, a position he has held since Grand Final night 2002. In 2005, he turned freelance and now also writes regularly on rugby league for the Guardian.*

13. This Steam Piggy Went to Market

Graham Clay

A friend of mine, a well-known senior player with a top Super League club, told me once how he dealt with a problem player at his club - a hardened old pro about to hang up his boots against a young upstart of a player who had won pretty much everything in the game whilst still a teenager. The veteran, one of the ever-decreasing players whose career straddled summer and winter, full-time and part-time, had cornered the whinging kid. Fed up of his attitude and arrogance, he delivered a statement which hit home.

"You only appreciate what you've done when you haven't done it for five years."

He went on to explain how, when you're winning everything, playing for your country, picking up awards, you can easily lose focus - even respect. You become blasé. Then, when you hit a lean stretch you remember how good things were, and wonder if those times will ever come back. It's only then that you realise what you achieved.

The young player got the message and his attitude changed over night. I tell this tale now because, in many ways, that's how I feel about the early days of Super League. Sure, today's game is faster, crowds are bigger, the Grand Final sells out, everything is more intense than back in 1996. But a lot of what we had - or thought we had - is conspicuous by its absence a decade on. Elsewhere in this book you will read about the global vision of franchises from Paris to Perth, the new teams of Gateshead and Adelaide, the one-time World Club Challenge finalists called Hunter Mariners. And remember Richard Branson? Hell, we even had an office in central London! All once part of Super League, but no longer.

As Super League dawned early in 1996, I was in Fiji for the World Sevens. A new era for the game, but one that was struck down almost immediately by red tape and legal wrangling brought about by the war erupting in Australia, where Super League's very existence was being challenged by the ARL. Players contracted to that organisation were forced to sit out the tournament, whilst the likes of Super League-aligned Laurie Daley conducted meetings via satellite phone back to Sydney. By the end of that weekend, the global dream had become a nightmare for all, apart from the lawyers of course, who looked forward to a bumper payday.

The upshot was that Super League in Australasia was shelved for 12 months, and ultimately all together.

Later that year, I spent some time with Super League Australia, studying licensing and merchandising. Ironically, I was in Sydney for the ARL Grand Final between Manly and St George en-route to New Zealand for the ill-fated Super League Great Britain tour, but I didn't really care who was in charge, ARL or Super League. As an outsider, it would have been quite amusing to witness the bickering if it hadn't been for the absolute disbelief and annoyance you felt at how much progress the game could have made had the mega-bucks involved been spent on the game and not blokes in suits speaking legalise. Here was the greatest team sport in the world hanging its dirty washing out in public, much to the amusement of other sports, in particular rugby union and Aussie Rules. Incidentally, that same year, Sydney Swans AFL made their first-ever Grand Final, and rugby league, for an awful moment, looked like being swallowed up in a red-and-white tide surging down George Street.

At Super League's Sydney base, I met a whole administration geared up to promoting the new game, but effectively treading water, holding planning meetings to decide planning meetings. Planning - that's all they could do really. But they did it well. Part of the new ethos was the coming together commercially, strength in numbers, a united front to sponsors and partners.

I spent most time with the newly-appointed Director of Licensing, a bloke who had previously worked with Nike. His ideas were mind-blowing, but simple and commonsense. Super League, as a phrase, is priceless, he argued, correctly. Forget your Premier League, World Series, Championship, Division One and every other title in every other sport; the one they all want is Super League. Creating the 'S' logo stretched into an oval to resemble a ball was a masterstroke and ultimately the only lasting symbol from Australia's pre-NRL days. It was they who forced through much of the idealism of Super League, and therefore somewhat ironic that the bitter court wrangling brought it to an end, for them at least. Even today, the very mention of Super League sparks a whole evening of heated debate in the pubs and clubs of Sydney and Brisbane. Most scoff at the doomed concept, and mock - in title at least - the existence of the competition in Britain.

Born in Sydney it might have been, but British clubs were quick to adapt the ideals of Super League. Yet the razzmatazz revolution had begun in the unlikely setting of a Yorkshire mill town, and at a club with grand ambitions but no realistic chance of being part of the new world: Keighley. The Cougars, as they became known, delivered the pre-cursor to full-on pre-match entertainment - blasts of music after tries had been scored, dancing girls, mascots in outrageous costumes - even the chairman wore a cowboy hat. It was almost a surreal dry run, a toe-in-the-water exercise unwittingly conducted on behalf of the big clubs. If it works, everybody follow their lead and claim the credit. If it fails, no-one will really notice, and lil' old Keighley will be looked upon as some freaky sideshow. It did work, and first to concede that - although not publicly - were the Cougars' big city neighbours, Bradford. "A lot of visiting teams didn't like it," the former Keighley director Mike Smith told *Rugby League World* magazine in March 2005. "I remember an official from Bradford calling the place a mad-house and like Fred Karno's."

Contrary to popular belief, however, the Odsal club became the Bulls long before Super League, and long before the man widely acknowledged as the concept's leading marketeer, Peter Deakin, arrived at the club. Bradford had campaigned for summer rugby for years, the then chairman Jack Bates lobbying the RFL as far back as the late Seventies. True, the vast and exposed Odsal micro-climate had always been a major motivating factor, so when the big switch finally happened it wasn't surprising that Bradford welcomed the new dawn more than any other.

But they had begun the extreme makeover from Steam Pigs to Raging Bulls in late-1994, with a think-tank of chairman Chris Caisley, general manager Gary Tasker and commercial manager John Hunt. It was they who planned and managed the most radical overhaul of any sporting club's image. New name, new logo, new mindset.

In my 1997 book, *"Running With The Bulls"*, Tasker recalled: "We initiated a five-year marketing-led plan. We knew something radical had to happen. We knew what we wanted, and that was an average of 20,000 people at every game watching a winning side and having a fantastic time. We set that target from day one. I walked into the boardroom with a picture of a Bull, and a few sketchings of different ideas for logos. At that time we had a boar for a mascot, which had historical links, but we needed a vibrant new image."

Underpinning the whole ethos of the revitalised club was a term that would become a byword for the game - community marketing. Never before had any club in any sport reached out into its own backyard in the way the Bulls tentacles now touched the city's youth. A whole new department was created, and Bulls-branded mini-buses carried the red, amber and black troops into schools and community centres. Deakin's arrival accelerated the programme, his boundless energy taking the ideas and knowledge he gained promoting soccer in a sceptical USA to a new audience.

He may not quite have been in at the start at Odsal, but few would deny that in those trickiest early days of Super League, Peter Deakin was one of its pivotal figures. Someone else may have had the initial Bulls idea, but it was Peter's limitless enthusiasm that really caught people's attention, made it all work and set an example for the other clubs to follow. This larger-than-life figure with the ultimate in can-do attitudes was never off his mobile phone, hectoring newspaper sports desks for more column inches or pitching an idea here, another idea there. He once even rang the then sports editor of the Bradford *Telegraph & Argus*, Peter Rowe, from inside a car wash halfway up Manchester Road. I have absolutely no idea what was said in that conversation, but do know that at least one of those two fine individuals would have been bubblier than the soap washing his windscreen.

It was so ironic that someone who was so full of life should have been taken from the world so prematurely, aged just 49. With his death from a brain tumour - bravely fought - in 2003, the world of sport, never mind sports marketing, had lost one of its most inspirational figures. Peter, at least, was inspirational to the end.

By then, of course, he had long since moved on from Odsal. When a short and unhappy stint as Super League's head marketing honcho came to a swift conclusion, this dyed-in-the-wool Oldham-born Leaguie took himself off to Watford where, from 1997, he played just as influential part in revolutionising rugby union marketing at Saracens as he had in the game he grew up in. What a pity that he didn't make that move into central Super League marketing today, when the far more professional set-up now in place - in which, ironically, his old Odsal mate Gary Tasker plays such a successful leading role - would have surely been more worthy of his talents and vision. Despite Peter's achievements at Sarries - the wearing of Fezs being just one practice he bequeathed the club - when the call again came from League, he didn't take much persuading to return. This time, though, it was to Warrington where he again had a major impact in increasing crowds, emphasising the community approach and putting in much of the groundwork for a proposed new £15m state-of-the-art stadium just up the road from ramshackle Wilderspool.

In January 2000, this book's editor, Tony Hannan, penned an interview with the man everybody knew as "Deaks" upon his return to rugby league for *League Express*. It neatly summed up the man's character and impact on everyone around him, with his 'hey, buddy!'s and 'I want you to meet...'s, as he set about turning around a club who had, as recently as 1998, been in a state of apparently terminal decline with £2.1million worth of crippling debts, bringing one of rugby league's founding members to the brink of collapse.

"The big thing which keeps me going in all this," he (Deakin) suddenly spurts, enthusiasm pumping through those veins again with missionary zeal, "is that I have absolute, total belief in the sport. I love the game of rugby league. It has a great future, and there are so many things that this sport can do for itself, if we only had people who believed in our game. There are too many disbelievers, too many people who don't quite have enough confidence in it. I know it's a cliché, but it's true. Let's all believe in rugby league."

Eventually, Deakin would head back to union again, only this time remaining in the north at Sale where, along with significantly raising the profile of that once-unfashionable club, he could remain closely in touch with his first sporting love. Ultimately, his stay there was cruelly cut short, but back across the Pennines in Bradford his influence was still being felt as the Bulls continued to lead the way both on and off the field, culminating in a fourth Grand Final win in 2005, in which a squad now coached by Great Britain boss Brian Noble came through from third place in the table to beat Leeds.

It would be nice to think that somewhere, high above Old Trafford, the man for whom the phrase "marketing guru" was surely coined was looking down through the fireworks and ticker-tape and enjoying what he saw, as the third Grand Final capacity crowd of 65,000-plus created the sort of remarkably noisy and brightly coloured family atmosphere with which the sport has become so closely associated and which "Deaks" had always dreamt of.

Back in 1996, however, all that seemed a long way off indeed. Then, it was a case of small, albeit innovative acorns. For a start, it wasn't a match anymore, it was a 'Gameday Experience'. In fact, it was a seven-day experience. Bradford city centre was awash with the club's colours. Wherever you went, you couldn't fail to be touched by the Bulls phenomenon. Deakin, targeting the youth, quickly tied up Burger King as a "partner" (not sponsor) and the city's favourite Saturday morning meeting place for teenagers was given the full-on Bulls treatment - Robbie Paul's face beaming down from oversize posters, framed shirts and signed balls setting the scene before counter-staff wearing Bulls baseball caps dished out free match tickets with every Whopper and Fries.

Full-time players with plenty of time on their hands found it wasn't just about training and playing any more - there were schools to visit, awards to present at junior clubs, charity events to open, supermarket promotions to attend. Borrowing a phrase from the United States, Deakin appointed skipper Robbie Paul as the club's 'franchise player' on whom all marketing and promotional activity would be centred.

And when the newly-converted arrived at Odsal, they were given plenty of reason to come back, whatever the result on the pitch. Funfair rides, face painting, jugglers and fire-eaters. Singers and dancers, fireworks and balloons. Even a helicopter landing on the pitch to deliver Bullman and the match-ball. It was a carnival atmosphere where the game was almost, but not quite, irrelevant. The original cheerleaders, called the Bullettes, were recognised as entertainers in their own right - professional dancers all aged 18-plus. Such was the clamour to become a Bullette, a mid-week dance school was formed with hundreds of members. In another example of Bradford's visionary marketing, the under-18 'Luvabulls', as they were known, were also invited to perform on the Odsal pitch at home games. Every kid out on the field had a mum, dad, aunt, uncle, bother, sister... one girl on the pitch meant another half dozen or so paying spectators. Cheerleading had become big business.

This sudden new interest meant rapid changes to the club's backroom operation had to be made. There was a new demand for an extensive range of merchandise, not just replica shirts sold on a matchday by enthusiastic members of the supporters club. Soon, the Bulls had a professionally-fitted city centre store, and another at the local Morrisons supermarket. From key-rings to bathrobes, everything imaginable was coloured red, amber and black and carried the Bulls logo. Deakin would often give away polo-shirts and jackets to the "right people" to create a sense of must-have as though it was the latest fashion craze.

But whilst the Bulls led the way and reaped the rewards at the turnstiles, other clubs struggled to keep up. Just a few miles down the road, Halifax were lambasted for becoming the Blue Sox and entertaining fans with scantily clad girls pillow-fighting. Oldham had arguably the best mascot of the time but little else; Wigan steadfastly refused to adopt a nickname.

Part of Super League's strategy had been the opportunity to present that united front, a coming together of commercial power to attract big-money sponsorships that, as individuals, clubs could only previously dream of. Unfortunately, the greed of some clubs and a reluctance of the "haves" to share with the "have-nots" scuppered that plan. Nike, for example, was keen to supply all 12 clubs with kit. But the deal would have meant "clean skin" jerseys, whereby designs were similar in all but colour, and no other sponsors would be allowed. Only the Super League "S" would be visible on the chest alongside the famous Nike swoosh. Of course, Nike was willing to pay big money and Super League was keen to have such an aspirational brand on board. Australia signed up to the deal, but in the UK, after much wrangling, it didn't happen, save for an eventual one-off deal with Wigan.

The loss of Nike was a blow, but in compensation clubs were attracting blue-chip sponsors like never before - brands such as Compaq, Toshiba, Virgin, Fosters and Computercenter. Yet one of the prime motivating factors behind Super League UK remained untapped. In Australia, centralised merchandising was driving big dollars into the game. As well as kit, Super League's official stamp appeared on everything, emanating a consistent message of togetherness. From Western Reds to Brisbane Broncos to Adelaide Rams, the oval 'S' branded gear could be bought in high-street stores, airports and by mail order through adverts in the national press.

In Britain, like the kit deal, clubs were too self-centred to support a gamewide programme. After all, why should a big club with 10,000-plus gates share its income with a struggling foot of the table club? Unfortunately, that shortsightedness threatened the very existence of the game. Apart from a quickly-curdled official Super League Milk, no central endorsement deals were concluded.

Another such proposal was for a game-wide matchday magazine, to replace the present-day programmes, a long-held sporting tradition in this country but otherwise an administrative pain in the neck for the clubs to produce and usually devoid of any serious reading matter despite frequently expensive cover prices. Again, in Australia there was a precedent already set by what is now the NRL's official matchday magazine, *Big League*, which is sold both at newsagents and grounds, with clubs obliged to provide accurate teams for its 'gameday' pages by the middle of the week. Programme collectors may have mourned, but the value to the sport of an actually readable and useful weekly magazine, boasting top-notch advertising and well-known columnists would have been priceless.

But setbacks in the formative years were offset by the success of the product on the field - not for the first time, the game disguised the faults and errors of its administrators to post year-on-year growth that jumped light-years in 1998 with the introduction of play-offs and an Old Trafford Grand Final. From 44,000 that year to consistent sell-outs, the once criticised system is now widely recognised as the biggest event in the domestic game.

Marketing wise, all levels of the game have staffed up massively. Centrally, the RFL and Super League (Europe) – once individual bodies suspicious of each other - now work together in harmony. In Super League's current sponsor, engage Mutual Assurance, the sport's top-flight continues to be sponsored by companies with a wholesome family appeal, thereby helping to further throw off the old stereotyped booze 'n' fags image that characterised it in earlier years. It's all about balance, of course, and there is still room for beer brands such as one-time Super League sponsors Stones and Tetley's - Wigan sports leisurewear giants JJB were the others - in the rugby league portfolio. Indeed, rugby league now has an official beer in Castlemaine XXXX - with cans and six-packs suitably branded up and taking pride of place in supermarkets up and down the country by the end of 2005.

Other levels of the game have seen an increase in corporate activity too. The National Leagues are currently sponsored by LHF Healthplan, there is a Northern Rail Cup for teams in those divisions to contest, Powergen continue to be wonderful sponsors of the still magnificent Challenge Cup - not to mention the biggest knock-out competition in the 13-a-side code's world, the Powergen Champion Schools - and at an international level, the arrival of Gillette to sponsor the Tri-Nations, amongst many other things including the game's first Heritage Centre at Huddersfield's George Hotel, has proved absolutely priceless. Clearly, blue-chip companies are once again taking note that, in rugby league, there is an opportunity to get involved with a rapidly-growing sporting brand that is clearly going places.

It may not be to everyone's taste but the fact remains that in modern-day sport, a professional, co-ordinated approach to marketing is absolutely indispensable. Put it this way, existing rugby league fans may know what a wonderful 'product' they support and enjoy throughout the summer months, but that doesn't mean everyone else in the country does. As we take our first steps into Super League's second decade and rugby league's third century, we need to shout about how great a game this is from the rooftops.

Fortunately, that's something the Rugby Football League's latest Director of Marketing and Communications, Simon Malcolm, who formerly did a similar job for Salford City Council after leaving a high-impact spell with Otto UK Homeshopping, seems to know only too well. "Everyone is subject to branding," the Widnes-born marketeer told *Rugby League World*, shortly after his arrival at Sovereign House in July 2005. "The reason why we choose our mobile phone company or the shirts we wear, or which brand of ice cream we eat. That is all branding. It is all about understanding customers and ensuring you meet the expectations of those customers.

"(Rugby league) has a huge amount to offer. On the field there is the pace, the power and the skills of the game, whilst off it things are pretty vibrant with a great family atmosphere, mascots, pre-match entertainment and the like. But there is the potential there to take all this to another level, and part of my brief is to come up with a new corporate brand for the RFL over the coming months. I am starting work on that immediately."

● *Graham Clay has worked in rugby league since 1992, as a writer, photographer and administrator. He edited Rugby League World magazine for four years and has travelled extensively in pursuit of the game. In 1999, he helped organise the World Cup Qualifying Tournament in Florida where, in 2001, he also promoted a series of exhibition games featuring Leeds, Huddersfield and Halifax. Now owner of a sports PR and publishing company, he currently manages Gillette's Tri-Nations sponsorship.*

14. The Quality
of Mersey

Ray French

"Summer afternoon - summer afternoon; to me those have always been the two most beautiful words in the English language." So wrote Edith Wharton, quoting Henry James, in her autobiography, "*A Backward Glance*", published over 70 years ago.

And how those "two most beautiful words" have been at the centre of the St Helens club's success story throughout the opening decade of Super League. Four-times Super League champions (1996, 1999, 2000 and 2002), four-times Challenge Cup winners (1996, 1997, 2001 and 2004) and a World Club crown following their 20-18 win over Brisbane Broncos in 2001. It is a record that no other club can equal and perfectly illustrates how all at Knowsley Road have welcomed the switch in seasons. It also confirms that the playing style, tactics and policies of the Saints coaches and management have become a blueprint for successful summer rugby league.

Mistakenly sentimental over the wind, hail, rain and snow which often accompanied my attendance as a youngster in the Boys Pen at Knowsley Road, and also mindful of stamping my heels as a Saints player on the frozen, rutted pitches of Oldham's Watersheddings or Workington's Derwent Park, I must admit that yours truly had initial misgivings over the move to summer. Yet few clubs have adapted to the warm, balmy days of June, July and August quite like Saints.

Historians of the 13-a-side code and observers of the team down the years must, however, realise that there has been no departure from the basic ingredients that brought success in the Fifties, Sixties, Seventies and Eighties. Only the playing season has changed. Nevertheless, it is a change which over the past 10 years has given St Helens a huge advantage. The musical extravaganzas, barbecues and pre and post-match entertainment promised by the architect of Super League in Britain, Maurice Lindsay, have not fully materialised thanks to the enclosed nature of our stadiums and the disinclination of many fans in this country to watch anything other than the rugby on the pitch. Odsal Stadium, home to Bradford Bulls and a most intimidating mid-winter venue, is perhaps the only ground which, due to its wide-open bowl shape and the walkways that surround its playing area, fulfills completely the criteria originally demanded by Super League (Europe). On the field, however, St Helens have entertained their thousands of fans and increasing numbers of corporate clients with a brand of rugby nurtured in the past but even more relevant to the demands of summer.

Throughout history, the Saints management has been at the forefront of signing the world's best players. For Mick Sullivan, Mal Meninga and Kevin Iro before, read Paul Newlove, Jamie Lyon and David Fairleigh post-Super League. Nor have they been afraid to look to rugby union. For Tom Van Vollenhoven, Kel Coslett and Cliff Watson in the Fifties and Sixties, read Scott Gibbs, Apollo Perelini and Mark Edmondson over this latest decade.

More than ever, the rules, pace and defensive line-ups of the modern game require gifted players. There are few places in which to hide journeymen if a coach wishes to win trophies. St Helens have regularly splashed out the cash on talent but they have maintained a style of play which has served them well historically and serves them even better on warm, sunny afternoons or evenings when there is an abundance of green turf beneath the players' boots and the air is crisp and fresh for handling the ball and running at speed.

Whether in days of yore or today, successful clubs have always needed a trio of world class players in midfield at hooker, loose forward and half-back, to provide the dynamo for fast, adventurous and attacking rugby, often by virtue of daring moves and spectacular handling executed at pace. Long gone are the muddy slopes and frost-hardened, snow-covered pitches with which the likes of former Saints loose forwards Vince Karalius, Kel Coslett and Harry Pinner, and halves Alex Murphy, Tommy Bishop and Jeff Heaton had to contend. But those traditions have been and still are being maintained in ideal conditions by the likes of Paul Sculthorpe, Bobbie Goulding, Sean Long and Tommy Martyn. In the hooker's role, although the strike and possession count at the scrum is no longer at a premium, powerful number nine Keiron Cunningham performs the role around the play-the-ball and scores the surprise tries that his international predecessors Bob Dagnall, Bill Sayer and Tony Karalius once did.

Yes, the midfield trio has always been the key to success and in the summer there are all the advantages of weather and conditions to prove it. They can probe for gaps in the middle, upset opposition plans with shrewd, tactical kicking and send runners speeding towards the try line with defence-splitting passes. But always there is a need to finish off that creativity with a try. Who better for that than a fast, elusive winger? Here, again, coaches in the Super League era, notably Shaun McRae and Ian Millward, have followed the pattern set by pre-Super League bosses like Jim Sullivan, Cliff Evans, Joe Coan and Eric Ashton. Where once, Stan McCormick, Steve Llewellyn, Frank Carlton, Mick Sullivan, Tom Van Vollenhoven, Len Killeen, Roy Mathias, Les Jones and company delighted the fans with their touchline activities, so in recent seasons Anthony Sullivan, Sean Hoppe, Alan Hunte, Darren Albert and Ade Gardner have had the pace and the guile to oblige. While the ingredients for success haven't changed, improved conditions determine that the skills which bring victory and trophies now have a far greater chance to flourish and prosper, meaning even more of the dramatic, last-gasp finishes for which the men in red and white are famed. And always have been.

As with Chelsea, Arsenal, Manchester United and Liverpool in soccer, so over the past 10 years of Super League has there been a quartet of clubs in rugby league's elite division who have attracted television cameras and viewers nationwide for the quality of their players and style of rugby. Leeds, Wigan and Bradford have been featured regularly by BSkyB on their Friday and Saturday night slots and many is the time the satellite TV channel's commentary team of Eddie Hemmings and Mike Stephenson have waxed lyrical over the three clubs' performances. I myself, my co-commentator Jonathan Davies and colleague Dave Woods have also added to those clubs' reputations via our Super League and Challenge Cup broadcasts on the BBC. But if one club has captured the attention of both the dedicated rugby league follower and the most casual of viewers it is St Helens, by playing a brand of rugby that has quite rightly seen them earn a reputation as "The Entertainers".

Their grandstand finishes and dramatic escapes from defeat in the final minutes of countless Super League matches and Challenge Cup ties – witness the first two games against Warrington in 2005 – really are the stuff of legend. Such has been the effect of many of their most outstanding performances that they have now passed into the category of: "I was there!".

It has always been so with St Helens. Whenever the team has contained one or two of the world's best players they have always been able to fashion a victory, however many minutes or seconds remain. Older supporters will recall a home Challenge Cup third-round tie from May 1966 which, thanks to the antics of a certain Mr Alexander Murphy and the intervention of the most famous referee of the era, Mr Eric Clay, ended with a win for the Saints over a Hull KR side equally as capable of progressing to the final.

Those antics took place at least seven minutes into injury-time, when a below-par St Helens seemed to be losing the battle. With thousands of severely critical fans streaming away from the ground and many already seated in the Black Bull, Nags Head and the Bird I'th Hand pubs nearby, up stepped the charismatic "Murph" to send us on our way to Wembley. Having lofted a huge, towering up 'n' under towards the Rovers try-line, the Great Britain scrum-half raced 30 metres to pounce on the ball before it almost (or did?) go over the dead-ball line, and score what was, according to Mr Clay, the match-winning try. Not according to Hull's tough backrower, Frank Foster, it wasn't. After the game, he disputed its legality with some vehemence in the communal bath but had to be satisfied with Alex's comment: "If you don't believe it was a try, then read it in the *Liverpool Echo* tomorrow night."

Saints' penchant for putting their followers through dramatic finales and nerve-shattering endings was never better illustrated than in the 1971 Championship final. Against great derby rivals Wigan, at Station Road, Swinton, they once again looked to be heading for certain defeat with less than 60 seconds ticking down on referee Mr Lawrenson's watch. That is, until centre Billy Benyon raced onto a mis-directed drop-goal attempt from John Walsh and touched down for a try. A well-struck conversion from skipper Kel Coslett completed proceedings and Saints had escaped yet again.

So it has been throughout Super League, an era in which armchair fans of opposing teams reach for the whisky bottle or some other such stiff drink whenever their team leads by a point or two in the closing minutes. Some of Saints' most magical and dramatic moments are already considered legendary and either captured lovingly on video or locked away as horror movies not fit for under-age viewing. Much to the despair of their fans, Bradford are usually number one victims.

"The most dramatic moment in Super League history," gasped Sky's Eddie Hemmings as, with the jubilant Bulls supporters counting down the last 10 seconds of the match, an amazing sequence of passes and kicks over 90 metres between Keiron Cunningham, Sean Long, Kevin Iro, Steve Hall, Sean Hoppe, Tim Jonkers, Dwayne West and, eventually, try-scorer Chris Joynt destroyed Bradford's hopes of reaching the 2000 Grand Final. An 11-10 lead in the Bulls' favour had been overturned with one of the most dramatic pieces of rugby in the history of the code, never mind Super League.

But what of Sean Long's thrilling drop-goal 60 seconds from the end of the Grand Final two years later, when the Bulls were again denied what they thought was rightfully theirs? Again, with the game tied at 18-18 and with a 61,138 crowd on the edge of their seats, Saints struck with deadly precision and upheld a reputation as the team nobody beats until the final whistle is blown. And let's not forget Bobbie Goulding's exploits in the 1996 Challenge Cup final against - you've guessed it - Bradford Bulls, when he inspired the greatest comeback ever seen at Wembley with Saints trailing 26-12, only 23 minutes before the presentation of the famous silver trophy. Three towering kicks towards the Bradford posts from the diminutive but pugnacious scrum-half seriously unnerved Bulls full-back Nathan Graham and resulted in three tries in the space of seven minutes from Keiron Cunningham, Simon Booth and Ian Pickavance, earning Saints a staggering 40–32 triumph.

Such incredible incidents, conjured up by some exceptional players, certainly keep commentators on their toes, often making them wish they hadn't said what they just did and reaching for the throat lozenges the next day. I confess to being no exception. And I know that I have been no exception among the ranks of the media with my exasperation whenever I have received a discreet telephone call from "a source" at Knowsley Road telling me of the latest sudden departure of a coach, however successful he has been. For, as the past decade of Super League indicates, the St Helens club has grabbed the headlines not only for the success of their coaches but also their often dramatic and acrimonious departures.

Saints, pre-Super League, attracted many of the game's finest players to take up the coaching reins when their playing days were over. The likes of former internationals Alan Prescott, Eric Ashton, Kel Coslett and Alex Murphy are only a few examples of those who built the club's reputation as one of the most famous in the world. Characters like deep-thinking Kiwi coach Mike McClennan and Great Britain and Saints wing star of the forties and fifties, Stan McCormick, both of whom regularly raised a smile with their antics, were welcomed too. Remember McClennan's tap-penalty ploy when he arranged for Saints' 6ft 7in second-rower John Harrison to head the ball over the opposition try-line prior to the scoring of a try - a sensational move which occasioned the changing of the rules? And my former team-mates of the Sixties will never forget the humour and amusing incidents surrounding McCormick, all of which helped to forge the team spirit so necessary in any trophy-winning side.

I well remember smiling one Saturday morning as I passed Stan's corner shop in the car and noticed a sign outside displaying the words: "Fresh Lobsters for Sale. Only Caught Yesterday." Indeed they had only been caught yesterday. The previous night, in fact, when I, Frankie Barrow, John Mantle and Cliff Watson had caught them on the Saints team bus on our way home from a match against Hull! Little did we know when we set out from St Helens on the Friday lunch-time what Stan had in mind. And little did we know what he intended to do with the huge, battered, brown suitcase he brought with him. Arriving early at the Boulevard, our coach raced off in a taxi to the docks and duly returned with a case full of the creatures. Neither he nor we realised that many of the lobsters were still alive until, on returning to the bus after the match, we found two or three of them crawling all over the seats and were forced to spend a frantic half-hour attempting to retrieve them.

And what an exit Stan made from the club, barely a week after guiding it to a Western Division Championship final win against Swinton in May 1964, amid yet another amusing incident, however unfortunate for him, this time at Wigan. With five minutes remaining and the score 7-7, I had the good fortune to run onto a perfectly-timed pass from my pack colleague John Tembey and race(!) 15 metres before diving over for what proved to be the winning try. Delight and celebrations abounded at the final whistle. That is, until having collected our winning medals and shaking hands with the Swinton players in the middle of the pitch, we were forced to move to one side while Stan, his face and shirt covered in blood, was carried on a stretcher from the field to receive 22 stitches in a huge cut on the top of his head. Poor fellow, in his excitement at my match-winning score, had leapt up in the air and forgotten all about the concrete roof on the coaches' dug-out at Central Park.

Famous coaches, imaginative coaches, colourful coaches and controversial coaches all set the pattern for St Helens in Super League. Shaun McRae and Ellery Hanley certainly continued the tradition for success and ultimately ruthless dismissal after the elite division kicked off in 1996. But few coaches in the history of the club have maintained those traditions like its former Australian boss, Ian Millward, who brought unprecedented glory and trophies between March 2000 and May 2005, before being dismissed for alleged misconduct and the use of abusive language. Like his predecessor, Hanley, who was also dismissed by a previous administration for breaching his contract in failing to turn up for a Super League launch ceremony, Ian had experienced the pleasure of lifting a trophy or two - a World Club Challenge trophy, two Grand Final trophies and a couple of Challenge Cups to be precise! His run-ins with authority, spats with match officials, other coaches and clubs and, especially, his incurring of the wrath of the Rugby Football League and over 15,000 Bradford fans when he fielded virtual reserve teams for games before the Challenge Cup final in 2002 and again in 2004, guaranteed Ian and his Saints team the full glare of media coverage.

The betting scandal involving Sean Long and Martin Gleeson, which erupted over the fielding of that seriously-weakened side in 2004 and was occasioned by both players placing bets with bookmakers at odds against their own team, also placed the club and their coach firmly in the spotlight for all the wrong reasons. But few can deny that, whatever the controversy, during the coaching reign of Ian Millward, St Helens played some of the most innovative, exciting and adventurous rugby ever seen. It was a style which took full advantage of the summer conditions and illustrated the value of the introduction of full-time squads capable of practicing and developing the multi-faceted skills needed to win five trophies in five years.

Remember the title of Edith Wharton's book in which the words "summer afternoon" were considered to be the two most beautiful words in the English language? If, like her, we take another backward glance, we might note the similarities between Millward and his tenure of office and that of his predecessor in the mid-Sixties, Joe Coan. Coan was a coach who displayed the same off-field approach with his players, who fashioned his own distinctive style of play, who was not afraid to court controversy regarding his selections and who won trophies with great regularity.

Above all it is interesting to note that, like Ian Millward, Joe Coan was completely untried as a coach at the highest level before assuming control. Indeed, he had never coached a rugby league club at either amateur or professional level in his life before accepting the job. But it didn't stop him from guiding the club to a historic four cup-winning campaign in season 1965-66; a feat which enabled team captain Alex Murphy to become what was then the most successful skipper in the history of St Helens.

One of Coan's controversial team selections upset Alex when, following the signing of scrum-half Tommy Bishop, he switched the little maestro to centre for the good of the team. Nor was he too concerned at leaving out players to suit the tactical occasion as when, set to play then-mighty Wakefield Trinity in the league seven days before a Challenge Cup first-round clash with the same side at Belle Vue, he "rested" three international forwards, including myself.

Like Millward, one of his greatest strengths was an ability to discuss with and consider at length the opinions of his senior players, while allowing them free rein to express themselves on the pitch. No matter, then, that when Ian Millward was appointed to the post of head coach at St Helens in March 2000, his only previous experience was as an assistant at the St George-Illawarra club in Australia and two years with then-Northern Ford Premiership side, Leigh. His infectious enthusiasm, passion for the game, enlightened thinking and, at times, novel tactical approach, plus those very qualities displayed by his predecessor three decades before, enabled Millward to take St Helens to the top. It is fascinating that his successor, the former Kiwi international coach Daniel Anderson, has already shown similar traits with his regular discussions with players, "breakfast meetings" with his skipper Paul Sculthorpe, and the setting up of social and judicial player committees. Traditions at Knowsley Road live on and continue to bring success.

The advent of summer rugby and Super League, however, was such a break from the traditions built up by the 13-a-side code over 100 years that there were many who poured scorn on the venture and confidently predicted the game's very demise. A perceived lack of crowds at matches in the summer and a serious reduction of income as rugby league was expected to compete with big national and international sporting events were at the top of the critics' lists. Yet both predictions have failed to materialise and it is a reflection on the impact made by Super League, both in the north and nationwide, that club attendances are at a record high while the 12 clubs in the premier league have increased their income significantly.

St Helens, after an initially difficult start financially, are no exception to that trend and, like all other clubs in the division, profit considerably through the sale of summer season merchandise. Where once a hand-knitted woollen scarf, bobble hat and possibly a heavy waterproof jacket were ideal terrace wear in the winter months, the move to summer has brought forth a whole range of designer clothes and replica goods, providing an opportunity to attract more revenue.

The number of T-shirts, polo shirts, replica jerseys and even designer shorts and tracksuits hanging from the racks in the club shops at the ground or in the local town or city centre, is testimony to the greater marketing opportunities.

The club is not short of marketing and business acumen at a time when, despite the rantings of the lollards who would seek to keep the game confined to its northern heritage, it is pleasing to see that Super League bosses and their equivalents at the Rugby Football League are intent on expansion. It is in this area, at least, where St Helens must break with tradition if they are to maintain their position among the competition's hierarchy and increase the vital revenue streams that are so necessary before any club can make progress.

In the 21st century, if a town council was to allow its High Streets to be populated by the same shops and buildings as operated back in 1895, while not allowing modern department stores to open alongside or instead of the ageing buildings, few would attract much trade and customers would shop elsewhere. So it is with rugby league. It is heartening that, at last, Super League does seem to be becoming a driving force for the game's promotion nationally and internationally, and that the "powers that be" are no longer listening to those who constantly call for the support of the grassroots at the expense of any development 60 miles either side of the M62. Support for the grassroots is vital but, without expansion and the raising of a national profile, there will very soon be no grassroots.

Those who decry the inclusion of the French club, Les Catalans, in Super League from 2006 must be ignored, as must those who recoil at the casting off of the name London Broncos in favour of Harlequins RL, and the club's move from Griffin Park to the Twickenham Stoop. The cynics who scoff at yet another attempt by a Welsh club, this time in Bridgend, to make their way via the National Leagues to Super League must be answered. Without such ambitious moves the very impact of Super League and its profile and attractions both in the heartlands and nationwide will stagnate and eventually decline.

It is good to hear too of the moves being made by the marketing, media and community departments of the Super League clubs to attract ever greater crowd support and maximise the revenue. But it is in this area where the continuance of any prowess on the pitch at St Helens is most vulnerable.

After taking control of a financially-ailing club, chief executive Sean McGuire and chairman Eamonn McManus have both displayed their strong business and financial backgrounds by returning the club to profitability. They have attracted major international companies as sponsors and backers of the club and have done much to increase the spectator base within the town.

However, by far their shrewdest move has been the campaign in Liverpool and its surrounds in the search for yet more financial support and an opportunity to increase the club's average attendances by welcoming scousers into the ground. Press conferences, media presentations and sponsors evenings have all been held in that soccer stronghold with considerable success. Already benefits have been noted and the 10-mile gap between town and city appears to be narrowing. More still must be done if the club is to expand on its hard core of support in St Helens and create awareness in virgin territory, albeit when that territory is barely 20 or 30 minutes away from Knowsley Road.

Knowsley Road! Therein lies the problem for the Saints management as they attempt to maintain the same high standards of rugby played in the past decade over the next 10 years. Opened as long ago as September 6th 1890, for a game against now-defunct Manchester Rangers, the old ground is, to many of us who grew up as children alongside it, rather like a favourite old overcoat. Comfortable and warm it might well be but these days it has a hole or two in the sleeves and looks a little frayed around the cuffs. It has no future, whatever the wearer's affection for it. And the same can be said for the Knowsley Road ground because, as messrs McGuire and McManus well know, for all the rebuilding, repainting, rewiring and re-roofing necessary to keep it in shape, the stadium is a tired one no longer capable of staging modern-day matches as the events they should be, and no longer able to generate the income needed to keep a St Helens team at the top of Super League.

Elsewhere, stadiums recently built in nearby Warrington, Wigan and, to a lesser extent, Widnes have shown just what extra income can be raised and how crowds, attracted by luxurious surroundings, lounge and dining facilities and the comfort of seats, can be increased. Sponsors and major backers have shown that, given hospitality suites and function rooms in which to entertain their clients, they are prepared to invest heavily in a club. Classrooms, lecture theatres and private business facilities at the JJB, Halliwell Jones and Halton Community stadiums are evidence that there is a demand from local and national businesses to pay for their use during the day in midweek. In short, a modern stadium is a new beginning and a chance to attract new supporters from other areas of the locality and even of the country.

A new stadium can generate a whole new business and provide yet more funds to attract the world's best players. At the time of writing, it is understood that Saints chairman, Eamonn McManus, is near to realising his dream of announcing a new stadium complex closer to St Helens town centre. That must become a reality if other clubs, already settled in their new homes and welcoming new income streams, are not to overtake the Saints on the pitch.

Super League is a bigger, brighter, bolder and more media-orientated version of the game's previous Championship and league format, but the ingredients needed to win trophies in both it and the other competitions which run parallel, are the same as those of yesteryear. The success of the St Helens club in Super League lies in the fact that their management and coaches have never forgotten the recipe and continue to use it to the delight of the club's faithful fans and the many devotees of rugby league who simply want to watch a high-speed game played at fever pitch. Long may that continue.

But, hopefully, not at Knowsley Road.

● *A former captain of St Helens and Widnes, and a Great Britain player between 1961-71, ex-England rugby union convert Ray French has been the voice of rugby league on BBC TV's Grandstand for the past 25 years. A regular commentator and presenter on the game for BBC Radio Merseyside since 1975, he is an associate editor of the League Weekly newspaper and has written over eight books on the 13-a-side code, including "The Match of My Life", "100 Greats" and "My Kind of Rugby".*

15. Our Survey Says
...Family Fortunes

Angela Powers

No birth is easy. Never believe a woman who says she felt nothing. She is usually lying, deluded, in denial or has forgotten. But then, even these are just tactics to get you through one of the most traumatic ordeals a woman will ever face. It's true, you do eventually forget the pain, especially when you are rapt by the beauty and perfection of the child you have produced. But believe me, at the time and for a while afterwards, it hurts. A lot.

I first went through the trauma of childbirth 10 years ago. The scars may have faded, but one thing is for sure - despite the pain, the sleepless nights, the nostalgic sentimentalism for my life as it was before, the PTS, the stretch marks - I wouldn't change a thing.

Of course I wasn't the only one feeling labour pains in the spring and summer of 1995. There were thousands of us, and for some, the process was a lot more painful than for others. I am, of course talking about the birth of Super League. It was a long, arduous labour and I have reason to remember it very well. Heavily pregnant, with swollen ankles of elephantine proportions and a bladder under more pressure than a bouncy castle at a primary school open day, I was one of the happy band of reporters who spent hours hanging around an old club car park in Wigan. We spent a lot of time waiting for something to report, but very little time reporting.

Central Park was the labour ward for this much-anticipated, much-reviled birth. The chairmen of all the rugby league clubs met there, knowing they were to play a part in making one of the most momentous decisions the game would ever see. One by one they arrived, some looking worn and worried, others smug and assured, just like expectant fathers the world over.

As with any birth, Super League came along after much puffing and panting, hand-wringing and nail-biting and no doubt a great deal of shouting and swearing. The new arrival bore some resemblance to its parents; strong hints of St Helens and Wigan, Bradford and Leeds, but Warrington and Widnes, Castleford and Featherstone, Hull, Salford, Sheffield and Workington - well, of them there was nothing left but a trace of DNA that you'd have to use your imagination to spot. It was one of those babies that you could never coo over, not even to spare the feelings of its mum and dad. But then they do say that all new-borns appear looking like Winston Churchill. Luckily for us, this one soon changed shape, assuming features far more acceptable to a wider audience, and when Super League was ready to take its first tentative steps back in 1996, there was a real sense of hopeful anticipation. There was a feeling that we were witnessing the start of something new, something special.

Now, a decade later, when I look at my 10-year-old son, it's hard to see how he's changed over the years, though the fact that I don't have to carry a bottle and bag of nappies around for him anymore is clear evidence that he has matured somewhat. In a way, it's the same with Super League. It's still the same game, albeit with a few little changes in shape (40-20 rule, dominant tackle etc), but if you start looking more closely, you can see that it has come on in leaps and bounds over the last 10 seasons.

Back in 1996, Wilderspool Stadium was buzzing. It was a wonderful time to be a Warrington fan. We'd made the final cut and had a place in Super League. We had Iestyn Harris. We had Paul Sculthorpe. We loved the place...loved the fact that visiting supporters called it 'The Zoo', loved being part of the flow of the crowd as it crossed Bridge Foot, loved turning into Fletcher Street to hear the clattering of feet against the corrugated iron of the Fletcher end. It was old. It was tatty. It was ours. Best atmosphere in rugby league. Sadly, that was the best thing about it. In every other way it was lacking. It didn't bother us though that seating was restricted... we liked our particular little spot in the Fletcher end. I wasn't particularly peeved about the lack of loos. There was one ladies' toilet (not one block but one toilet) to service that end of the ground, but there was never a queue. That was because you got used to holding it in anyway until you got home, or into the Touchdown Club. I never bought the burgers or pies, or whatever they sold at the refreshment kiosks because we ate before we left home. And we never, ever took baby Michael. We never even considered it. If we wanted to go to see this new-born baby that was Super League, we had to call in baby-sitting favours. Or, quite simply, we didn't go.

Now don't get me wrong, we were not fickle fans. We used to pay our pound to watch the 'A' team even when the wind and rain were so bad they threatened to blow the roof off the main stand. We even got a BSB 'squariel' so we didn't miss a match. But once little Mickey came along the prospect of taking him to Wilderspool was one we never contemplated, never even debated. It was out of the question. A rugby league ground was no place for a baby, however much we loved our rugby.

Now I can't speak for other parents, but I would imagine many of them would have felt the same as us. Because you did not have to pay to take babies and young children into grounds, there are no figures to say how many used to go along to games, but I would hazard a guess that very few bothered to go through the hassle. Let me explain why with a little comparison:

Getting ready to go to home match - typical routine
Scenario 1 - Without baby

7.00am-2.00pm	Wake up at any time between these hours in gleeful anticipation of game ahead.
2.05-2.10pm	Get ready.
2.15-2.20pm	Leave house.
2.30-2.35pm	Park car at usual spot, start walking.
2.40-2.50pm	Arrive at ground.
2.55pm	Meet friends in usual spot on terraces, start singing/whinging.
3.00pm	Cheer at kick-off.
4.30pm	Match ends. Continue singing/whinging for a few minutes then go home.

181

Scenario 2 - With baby

6.30-7.00am	Baby's crying wakes you up. Put head under covers and try to pretend it's not happening.
7.05am	Dawning reality that it's matchday. Spring out of bed. You know you have already wasted too much time.
7.10am	Change baby's nappy. (NB this step will be repeated many, many times)
7.25-8.50am	Put on protective overall and goggles. Feed baby breakfast.
8.50-9.50am	Bath baby, make first attempt to get baby out of bath.
9.50-10.20am	Continue attempts to entice child from bath. Eventually pull out bath plug.
10.30-11am	Dress baby.
11.05am	Make first rallying call to rest of family to get out of bed.
11.10am	Turn on shower.
11.12am	Prise child's grip from your leg. Put him on bed with sleeping husband/wife/partner.
11.13-11.33am	Repeat above until husband/wife/partner actually starts to help.
11.34am	Get in shower.
11.36am	Get out of shower.
11.37-1.00pm	Make various attempts to get dressed while pandering to needs of everyone else.
1.05pm	Tell everyone to get their coats on and get in the car. Start packing nappies, dummies, spare clothes for child etc.
2.50pm	Start journey to ground.
3.00pm	Start looking for somewhere to park.
3.10-3.30pm	Find somewhere to park. Run to ground. Stop several times to catch breath/pick up dummy/wait for stragglers.
3.35pm	Get into ground. Find seats/place to stand.
3.40pm	Start to watch match.
4.20pm	Leave early to beat traffic. Miss match-winning try. Make mental note to bring umbrella next time.

As you can see, what was once a leisurely, fun experience becomes a process designed to raise your blood pressure. In short, it was better to invest in a good radio for your matchday enjoyment. And it is here that we hit upon the cause of the malaise that was eating into the great game of rugby league before Super League. The good old 'traditional' ground, with its lack of proper hand-washing facilities, corroded and cracking terraces, exposure to the elements, was not a nice place to take young babies, so parents simply wouldn't bother. As a result, the club lost revenue from the tickets they would have bought, the refreshments they would have consumed and the merchandise they might have been tempted to purchase. In turn, the club could not reinvest money in top-class players.

That's the short-term effect. Long term, this failure to be family friendly was potentially fatal. Every baby is a fledgling customer. Catch them young and by the time they are 18, you have created a full-price-paying devoted fan. Even earlier than that, when he joins the ranks of concessions, he's paying to get in, waving the foam finger he bought from the club shop and telling his mates how he meets his heroes after the match. In short, he is the future, a financial resource. Each club had a duty to try to attract these future spenders.

It was a fact not lost on the powers-that-be. Super League, they vowed, would make rugby league bigger, better and faster than it had ever been. But more than that, it would be the sport the whole family could enjoy.

Hmmm. Had we not heard this before? I remember feeling genuinely excited a couple of years prior to Super League when I opened a big brown envelope to find inside a document called "*Framing the Future*". It set out the minimum standards that would be required as the game sought to take itself into a modern era. One of these criteria was the provision of a crèche at each ground. Imagine that? A place you could leave your kids while you enjoyed 80 joyous minutes of unadulterated pleasure. This was a major step forward in creating a sport that really was for the whole family. Someone, somewhere had 'got it'. Sadly, those crèches stayed within the pages of "*Framing the Future*". And to be fair, a staffed playroom was hardly a priority when the men's toilet block had no roof and no running water, except for that created by the visitors themselves.

No, the greatest journeys start with the smallest of steps. And in 1996 the journey began. Step number one was the switch to summer. This one momentous decision more than any other paved the way to success, the misery of frozen toes and wet clothes consigned to the past. Hello ice-cream and cold beer on sun-baked terraces.

The next couple of steps were simple and cheap. Looking back now it's hard to imagine gameday, as it is now known, without cheerleaders or a furry mascot running up and down the touchline. Back then you might as well have given them horns and a whip and called them the devil incarnate, such was the response from some die-hard fans. Even worse, this 'ridiculous' idea of giving the teams tag names. Wolves? What's wrong with Wire? Bulls? My team always has been and always will be Northern. Squad numbering? Players' names on shirts? Aargh! The world will stop turning! Except it didn't. Instead, these 'gimmicks' became a huge marketing opportunity aimed squarely at kids. Wolves, Rhinos, Tigers, Broncos - these weren't just names, they turned each club into a brand with a logo, an attitude and a cuddly toy for sale in the club shop, appealing to all youngsters, from toddler to teenager.

And if there were stragglers still unconvinced that the Super League bandwagon was the right one to join, the Bradford Bulls soon persuaded them to get on board. The Bulls knew they had to invest in a good team on the pitch, but they also recognised they had to do the same off the field. With Brian Smith, ex-school teacher, on board as coach and the late Peter Deakin drafted in as marketing manager, they targeted kids and schools. "They put the players in the news pages as well as the sports pages of the papers," says Stuart Duffy, their current media manager. "Players got involved with all sorts of initiatives - anti-bullying, anti-drugs, healthy-eating. These were the images families were seeing of our players. The kids would go home and talk about these rugby stars they'd seen and pester their parents to take them to games."

Rugby league quickly went from a dads-and-lads Sunday afternoon activity to an event for the whole family. And to get these kids in, the Bulls made a brave decision. They gave away tickets. In schools, at clubs, in supermarkets…they handed them out with discount vouchers for adults. The kids got in free. Their parents got cheaper admission. It was a loss leader. But once inside they persuaded them to part with their cash. In the 10 years of Super League, profits on sales of refreshments inside the ground have quadrupled. They sell about 12,000 replica shirts per year. Half of these are children's. You do the sums. To me it adds up to good business. The brilliance of the Bulls' branding hit home for me when I took my son, then aged five, to watch Bradford play Warrington at Odsal. He insisted on having his face painted. In black, gold and red.

Where the Bulls led, other clubs followed. Now, you can go to a game of rugby league at most levels (not just Super League) and expect to enjoy more than just 80 minutes of sport. A decade on, rugby league is no longer a game that appeals to working class men alone. It appeals to pre-teen girls who want to be cheerleaders. It appeals to business leaders who want to schmooze new clients in the corporate boxes. It still appeals to the men in flat caps who watched with their dads 50 years ago. And now it appeals to families.

When my first son was born, Super League was just a twinkle in Maurice Lindsay's eye and the terraces of most grounds were inhospitable places for a babe in arms. In 2004, my second son arrived. Now I had the chance to see for myself whether the game really had become family friendly, or whether that was all marketing talk with no substance.

So, as Super League X kicked off, Sky Sports decided to put it to the test. Instead of watching the game from the comfort of the press box, I would take the whole clan - husband Chas, first born Michael and new addition Lucas. Oh, and a camera crew. We would road test every ground in Super League as away spectators, taking our chances with parking like everyone else. Wherever possible, we would buy our tickets on the day, rather than pre-order them. We would buy the refreshments (and sometimes even eat them), sit through the pre-match entertainment, use the facilities, check out the stewards and canvas the opinions of the other away fans. We wanted to get a snapshot of the gameday experience at each ground, not simply assess how nice (or otherwise) the surroundings were. At the end of each report, we would give each club marks out of 100. The results were very interesting.

We found that a new stadium was not necessarily a good indicator of quality of service. In a couple of instances we were downright disappointed. We travelled to the KC Stadium in Hull with great expectations. It was our first ever visit to a stadium that had opened only in 2003. All was going well until half-time when I went to look for baby-changing facilities. The stewards said they had none, instead letting me use the first aid room. I was later told there were facilities, but the stewards didn't know about them. We encountered the same problem at Widnes' home, the Halton Stadium. At the Halliwell Jones Stadium - Warrington's new ground - there were no baby-changing facilities. "An oversight" was the explanation. To give the club credit, they were installed immediately after our visit. Out of 12 clubs, only four had fitted facilities available to us when we visited.

Salford had them in the Willows Club, at the opposite end of the ground to the family stand, so not ideal. Leeds, Huddersfield and Bradford had changing facilities, so top marks for them.

Another of our marking criteria was value for money: how much would it cost us to sit down as a family and watch a game of Super League? The prices varied greatly. At Huddersfield, under 11s got in free and adult tickets cost £15 each. Compare that with Leeds where it cost £58 for a family like us to sit down, almost double the price. Leeds said their prices compared well with other sporting and entertainment events in and around the city. Still, it added up to an expensive day out compared with some other Super League grounds.

When it came to children's entertainment, some grounds knew how to put on a show. Top of the league here - still the best - were Bradford. From the minute you pass through the turnstiles, there's a feast for the senses. Bouncy castles, face painting, rodeo-riding - who needs a game of rugby league when you've got all this? They had a band on that sang classic pop songs we could all sing along to. There was a parade of bright and colourful floats, cars and motorcycles, led by their charismatic mascots. All around the ground there were refreshment outlets...not just burgers and hot-dogs, but doughnuts, ice-creams, steaks, pies and pasties, jacket potatoes, sweets and toffees. We spent more money there than at any other ground simply because they had such a great variety to choose from and the quality was fantastic. It seemed that as soon as we had entered the ground, there was a fan-fare and the kick-off. We didn't even notice we had the kids with us. Fabulous.

At Hull, they had cheerleaders. We had arrived early to beat the traffic and sat in the snow for an hour waiting for kick-off. The kids were bored and so were we. Earlier in the season, down in London, it was just as cold, but the Broncos got the fans involved in a kicking-for-touch game that made us laugh and kept the chill away. It cost nothing to stage and helped pass the time.

Finding somewhere to park may not seem important when you are an adult travelling alone or with other grown-ups. When you are travelling with children it's a major consideration. They don't do walking, at least not distances further than a couple of hundred metres. And you try carrying a squirming toddler for more than five minutes. A good car park close to the turnstiles is worth an extra few quid on the gameday budget, just to avoid the tantrums, whining and marital tension. Ditto an easy exit. This is where the modern stadia score highly. Hull, Wigan and Huddersfield have plenty of space (though getting away takes patience and Jaffa Cakes - always good for keeping toddlers quiet).

This is how the final table looked:

Bradford Bulls	77/100	London Broncos	71
Wigan Warriors	74	Salford City Reds	68
Huddersfield Giants	72	Widnes Vikings	68
Leeds Rhinos	72	Wakefield T Wildcats	66
Warrington Wolves	72	Leigh	64
Hull FC	71	St Helens	64

The age of a stadium didn't matter: we were solely interested in how welcome they made us feel as a family, how easy they made it for us to visit and how entertaining the whole experience was. But it was clear that age does have an impact. At places like Knowsley Road, St Helens and the Atlantic Solutions Stadium, Wakefield, toilet facilities with no running water were a big turn-off. Since then, both clubs have updated those facilities, but the general condition of a ground can have a big bearing on whether a family will make the decision to go to the game. Who wants to queue outside damp loos or run the risk of the kids getting wet because there's not enough cover? It doesn't take a genius to see that Warrington's recent success in raising attendances isn't purely down to attracting big-name players. Their new stadium has taken them onto a bigger and better stage, one that appeals to the die-hard fan on the terraces as well as the mother-of-two who wants quality time with her brood.

Baby-changing facilities may seem irrelevant to the vast majority of people watching a game. But to fans with babies they make the difference between deciding to go to the game or stay at home. And, no, the concrete floor of the disabled toilet doesn't count as a nappy-changing room.

Equally, pre-match entertainment may seem to some like an unwelcome extra cost, especially when money is short, but as Bradford have shown, it can become an integral part of the whole experience. I know my son doesn't complain when we go to visit Odsal. He does when we go to some grounds closer to home.

So, with all this in mind, is this game the fun-for-all-the-family spectacle it promised it would become 10 long years ago? Well, some clubs may have grasped the concept better than others, but every single one of them has made huge strides in the right direction. You only have to look at the faces in the crowd to see that it's a game that is attracting women and children in greater numbers than ever. Good clean facilities have made a big difference. But the sport's image has changed too. No longer does it rely on beer and fags for sponsorship. Now we get brands like engage, with its emphasis on family values, and sporting goods retailers like all:sports and JJB. St Helens even have the name of a firm of solicitors on their playing shirts. From 2006, smoking will be banned from the terraces at Warrington, and many other clubs are following suit. That is a long-overdue step that will make the whole experience infinitely more enjoyable and emphasise the healthy-lifestyle message that clubs are keen to spread.

The RFL's annual review of 2005 says that research shows rugby league to be *the* family sport: accessible, affordable, safe and exciting, with a communal sense of pride in the product. It's hard to disagree. It has produced many great players over the decade, the majority of whom are excellent role models to the next generation of spectators. They visit schools and promote the game at every opportunity. The atmosphere on the terraces is competitive but friendly and there's no need for fan segregation. None of the above can be said for football. I know which game I'd rather my children grew up supporting.

Is there room for improvement? Of course, but that makes it all the more exciting. If it is this good now, imagine what we can look forward to. We might even see crèches at every club by the time my grandchildren come along. The next generation will take warm, clean facilities for granted, while we amaze them with tales of the good old days, when the toilets had no roofs and the only thing we had to entertain us on matchdays was a game of rugby league.

● *Angela Powers is a member of Sky Sports' rugby league reporting team and produces features for the weekly magazine show "Boots 'n' All" and the broadcaster's live rugby league outside broadcasts. She joined Sky in 1998, after eight years with the BBC in Manchester, where she was a broadcast journalist and sports producer.*

16. Around the World in 80 Minutes

Tony Hannan

A global television audience of billions preferred to watch Bob Geldof and his Live 8 rockers giving their middle-aged beer bellies a work-out in London's Hyde Park but, on Saturday 2nd July 2005, we were where it really mattered. The Willows, Salford. All 2,682 of us.

For as the clock struck five-past six, around two-thirds of the way through Super League X, the mighty mid-table City Reds hosted Huddersfield Giants and their 25-strong travelling army of loyal fans, in a round-19 tea-time knee trembler. Action. Thrills. Glamour. Skills. A level of gladiatorial combat unseen since Russell Crowe and Eric Watson shared restaurant space. None of those qualities were in evidence as 34 players went through the motions, sorry, fought to the death for the ultimate prize: two precious Super League points.

Over the past decade, we have grown used to Sky Sports duo Eddie Hemmings and Mike "Stevo" Stephenson hailing every season as "the best yet". The critics may sneer, but it's not such a daft claim. Generally, playing standards and attendances have indeed risen year on year, although the 2002 season remains the high watermark, for mine. The downside to such hyperbole is that it can alienate as many viewers as it attracts; especially when what you have promised is an exciting Spanish paella and what you actually serve up is Lancashire hotchpotch.

Every sport has its off-days and, thankfully, rugby league has fewer than most. Truly terrible matches are rare, but few among that paltry attendance and the reported 38,000 (yes, that's 38,000) who admitted to having endured it on telly would have objected had Eddie and Stevo described this particular fizzer as "the worst yet". Was it traitorous to wonder what we were doing there? What manner of depraved naughtiness could justify such punishment? An earful of Mariah Carey's emetic yodelling would have been far, far preferable. Not that Salford were complaining. They edged an error-ridden, horror show of a match, 24-16.

This wasn't what was promised 10 years ago, was it? Those of us who, like legendary Aussie newspaper scribe Steve Mascord, collect air miles at the rate normal folk collect dust, were assured that rugby league's future lay in constant, exotic travel. While editing *Rugby League World*, I even dug out a handy technical term for it: dromomania. Eager television audiences right across the globe, from Outer Mongolia to Oldham, Townsville to Timbuktoo, were waiting with bated breath. What's the Icelandic for "gerremonside" again? Instead, a decade on and it's 38,000 for Salford v Huddersfield. Strewth. Satellite TV channel *Look4Love* gets bigger viewing figures (and don't ask how I know that).

The Willows, for those who have never had the pleasure, might euphemistically be described as "homely". In other words, it's an archetypal, perhaps even stereotypical English rugby league ground in that it lies just up the road from Weaste tram shed and nestles alongside row upon chimney-potted row of Coronation Street-style terrace houses. There's a good old-fashioned northern Variety Club at one end and a sparsely populated two-tier grandstand at the other, although the word grandstand is probably too lavish. If and when the club finally moves into what it calls its "iconic" super stadium at nearby Barton in 2007/08, the original Red Devils will luxuriate in state-of-the-art splendour. For now, their fans huddle in distinctly unglamorous wooden sheds, the dilapidated remnants of better days. As, indeed, are the tunnels and toilets beneath them, the majority of which, as the match goes on, develop a pungency not seen since the German army pioneered the use of mustard gas in 1915. Cut off your nose to spite your face here, and it would chase you back outside.

Meanwhile, in the surrounding environs, urban myths are rife of fans returning to parked cars only to find them devoid of radios, seat covers and even wheels, steering or otherwise. Whether they are true or not hardly matters. It feels as though they might be and that sense of insecurity extends to the rather dishevelled club car park, occasionally littered with broken glass. Driving into it ahead of a match against Bruges (or was it Bradford?), I was not a little alarmed to find myself the target of a sharp wooden javelin, springing up from nowhere and on a collision course with my windscreen. The culprit, it turned out, was the driven-over and now crushed head of a cunningly-hidden old wooden broom. God knows how that got there, although it's safe to assume it hadn't been used for sweeping up. No sirree, Roberto. The San Siro Stadium, this most definitely ain't.

Which, harking back to those 1995 promises, is precisely where we and several hundreds of thousands more enraptured spectators ought to have been as round 19 of the 10th season of the European Super League unfolded, perhaps enjoying a 2005 World Club Challenge clash between the Milano Miracoli and the Johannesburg Jaguars, or maybe just a bog-standard European derby between the Versace Super League's Italian giants and Manchester, that shiver-down-the-spine-inducing amalgamation of, er, Salford and Oldham.

Hindsight may indeed be a wonderful thing, but however much you bought or did not buy into the original Super League dream, a crystal ball wasn't really necessary to figure that unbridled global expansion was never going to be likely for a sport that had spent the past 100 years struggling to establish itself much beyond Doncaster, and certainly not on the timescale suggested. Despite all the talk down under of plundering markets right across Asia, the tit-for-tat answer to the ARL's World Sevens that was the Super League World Nines, and imaginative northern hemisphere proposals for setting up shop in Paris, Toulouse, Barcelona and Rome - the latter allegedly inspired by the ability of John Kirwan's wife to speak Italian - before you could say "loyalty bonus", reality set in and those wildest of expectations were downgraded to a point where the idea of a club in the west midlands seemed impossibly fanciful. With the arrival of Super League in March 1996, only Paris and London had made it from drawing board to starting gate.

Super League's early inability to deliver on its global promises were perfectly symbolised by those World Nines. Held over three days in Fiji, in February 1996, the inaugural tournament ("inaugural" in that it was the first of two - Townsville, north Queensland, hosted the next and so far last the following January) was intended to be a glorious celebration of a brave new world. In fact, it was an almighty damp squib, thanks to events in an Australian courtroom and political squabbling over the availability of ARL-affiliated players. Nor did water-logged pitches help, with day two completely washed out thanks to Fiji's worst levels of rainfall in years. It wasn't the first time extreme weather had rained upon a big rugby league parade, nor, in the coming Super League era, would it be the last.

On the political front, Wigan duo Gary Connolly and Martin Hall were pressured into withdrawal by the ARL on the eve of the competition, giving England and Wales late selection headaches. Nevertheless, the pair did continue to serve their countries in the somewhat ironic capacity of water carriers. Those two nations were joined by 14 more countries in four (metaphorical) pools; Scotland, Ireland, Tonga, Papua New Guinea, Western Samoa, New Zealand, France, Italy, Morocco, Cook Islands, USA, Japan, Australia and Fiji. Wins over Tonga (18-4), Morocco (34-0) and a fright against Italy (4-0) saw England end the first day on top of their group, meaning second-round clashes with Australia (who not surprisingly had done likewise), Western Samoa and Tonga. New Zealand and PNG were the other divisional leaders. Unfortunately, the downpour from those storm clouds completely submerged the pitch, with day two scrapped entirely as organisers made a wholesale restructure. The second round was ditched entirely and the truncated tournament moved straight to semi-finals. Even then, the whole thing came close to being cancelled, with hordes of workers and mechanical pumps called into action as the heavens continued to do their worst.

Given parallel developments back in Sydney, abandonment was unthinkable for the Super League bosses, so the teams struggled on until the rains broke, the sun risked offending the locals by once again getting its hat on, and New Zealand emerged eventual winners by beating Australia 10-8 in the semis before accounting for Papua New Guinea 26-10 in the final. Thankfully, the main event was

ABOVE: Willie Peters in action during Gateshead's one and so-far only Super League season in 1999

ABOVE: Skipper Chris Joynt lifts the Super League trophy after St Helens beat Bradford Bulls 8-6 to win the club's first Old Trafford Grand Final
BELOW & RIGHT: Leroy Rivett scored a record four tries as Leeds Rhinos celebrated the last-ever Challenge Cup final at the old Wembley Stadium by running out convincing 52-16 winners over Richard Branson's London Broncos

ABOVE: St Helens celebrate their third Super League title in the summer era after beating Wigan in the millennium Grand Final at Old Trafford. LEFT: Apollo Perelini upholds the code's family values

RIGHT: Paul Wellens shows off his Grand Final winners ring - a rugby league tradition imported from Australia's NRL competition

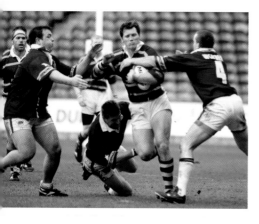

ABOVE: Barnsley-born Dale Laughton on the charge for the ill-fated merged club Huddersfield-Sheffield Giants

RIGHT: Tulsen Tollett, now a presenter with Sky Sports and BBC Radio Five Live, in action for London Broncos

BELOW: Leon Pryce goes tartan after Bradford Bulls beat Leeds 24-18, for the club's first Challenge Cup victory in 51 years at Murrayfield in Edinburgh

RIGHT: If crowds were generally low for the 2000 World Cup, there were many memorable moments

ABOVE: Iestyn Harris is tackled as Wales give the Kangaroos a scare in the semis. BELOW: Olympic rowing gold medalist, Sir Steve Redgrave, presents Australia with the Cup, as their dominance continues

BELOW: Nigel Vagana rounds Paul Wellens as England are whipped 49-6 by New Zealand in the semi-final. ABOVE: Cork's Brian Carney came to the fore for Ireland

ABOVE: PNG's Adrian Lam. BELOW: America v Morocco in the Emerging Nations competition

ABOVE & LEFT: World Club joy for a British club at last, as St Helens beat the mighty Brisbane Broncos 20-18 at Bolton's Reebok Stadium in January 2001

ABOVE: Aussie legend Alfie Langer shone for Warrington & then returned to Australia to star in the State of Origin series

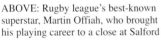

ABOVE: Rugby league's best-known superstar, Martin Offiah, who brought his playing career to a close at Salford

BELOW & RIGHT: Bradford Bulls enjoy a wet homecoming after their 2001 Grand Final annihilation of Wigan

ABOVE: A hypothetical end-of-season Dream Team, chosen by a panel of rugby league media personalities, has become an annual feature of every Super League season. Here, the 2002 team lines up for the cameras

LEFT: Warrington drop-out at Wilderspool - a ground soon to be consigned to the history books. ABOVE: Huddersfield Giants celebrate immediate promotion back to Super League

BELOW: Sean Long's late drop-goal for St Helens won the 2002 Grand Final against Bradford Bulls, extending Saints' run as the most successful club in the Super League era. BELOW RIGHT: Australian coach Ian Millward became one of the most controversial figures in the competition and one of its brightest personalities

LEFT: Captains of the 12 Super League teams gather together to launch the 2003 competition

RIGHT: Yorkshire skipper Ryan Hudson celebrates after leading his side to a 56-6 win over Lancashire in the Origin Game at Odsal, in July 2003. Intended to imitate Australia's State of Origin, but seen by fans and media alike as little more than a half-hearted international trial match, the three-year old concept was quietly shelved

St Helens comedian Johnny Vegas and a couple of Sydney Roosters fans watch Adrian Morley and the NRL premiers win the 2003 World Club Challenge

BELOW: A World Club Challenge win over Penrith Panthers in 2004 completed a haul of "All Four Modern Cups" for Bradford Bulls after their Challenge Cup, Super League Grand Final and Minor Premiership successes in 2003

ABOVE: Legendary rugby league figure Alex Murphy OBE celebrates, along with Leigh players and their coach Darren Abram, as the Centurions win promotion to Super League in 2004 by beating Whitehaven in the LHF National League One Grand Final. The following season Leigh finished bottom, Abram departed, and the long-running controversy surrounding promotion and relegation rumbled on. BELOW LEFT: Dejected Castleford head in the opposite direction

RIGHT: Leeds winger Marcus Bai speeds away from Bradford's Karl Pratt, as Tony Smith's Rhinos end a 32-year wait to win the Championship on a thrilling night at Old Trafford in October 2004

RIGHT: Fearsome Bradford Bulls winger Lesley Vainikolo scored a record six tries in one Super League match against Powergen Challenge Cup winners Hull in September 2005

BELOW: New Zealand international superstar Sonny-Bill Williams in action for NRL premiers Canterbury Bulldogs against Leeds in the 2005 Carnegie World Club Challenge at Elland Road. The Rhinos won 39-32

BELOW RIGHT: Andrew Johns - "the greatest player in the world" - made a massive impact in his three-match stay with Warrington Wolves

ABOVE: Hull players leap for joy as the black and whites end Super League's "Big Four" cartel with a Powergen Challenge Cup win over Leeds. RIGHT: Bradford captain Jamie Peacock lifts the trophy after the Bulls come from third in the table to beat Leeds in the 2005 Grand Final

watched by a large crowd, and PNG earned their place in it by narrowly edging England 15-14 in the semis, with Australia getting one over on the Poms, 14-10, in the third-place play-off. Not that anyone's mind was really on the football.

Despite the scaling down of his original plans for a pan-European competition, and with the expansionist bit as firmly between his teeth as ever, unabashed World Super League Board chairman Maurice Lindsay had continued to champion an equally ambitious if slightly more realistic way of sexing the game up, namely a trans-global competition for the new organisation's existing clubs in Australasia and Europe: the World Club Championship. There was to be one major snag, however. Much to the dismay of astonished officials gathered in the Fijian capital, Suva, as the south sea rains lashed down, the ARL successfully prevented the start of any Super League competition in Australia by gaining the swingeing support of Federal Court judge Justice James Burchett.

Among Burchett's original rulings were conditions that there would be no Super League involving Australian teams anywhere in the world until the year 2000; Super League-aligned coaches and players would be banned from participating in any competition other than the ARL, forfeiting payment if they refused to do so; and all Super League-branded clothing, mascots, advertising material, kits and promotional videos were to be handed over to the ARL. The Draconian legal beagle stopped short of ordering Super League bosses to bend over and take six of the best without blubbing but, for the rebels, that was about as good as it got. Even when, two days later, the Full Bench of the Federal Court granted stays on five of those orders ahead of an appeal, any Super League season down under in 1996 was a non-starter.

Nevertheless, the pugnacious Lindsay gave an early hint of what was to come through his plans for a breakaway "Global League", announced in conjunction with those 311 Super League-aligned players who were now apparently able to trade freely. Exactly how it would have worked was never made crystal clear but, in any case, the intention was almost immediately thwarted when those same Federal Court judges backtracked to Justice Burchett's original orders on player payment - i.e. that Super League-aligned players must take part in the ARL competition in order to be paid by News Ltd - after the withdrawal of labour forced the Super League clubs in that year's ARL into forfeiting their first-round matches.

When most of those player rebels returned to action as ordered the following week - Gorden Tallis and Ian Roberts being the two exceptions, the pair preferring to go without payment rather than back down on their principles - Lindsay's idea was stillborn. In one form or another, though, it refused to go away. And when on October 5th 1996, five days after St George won that year's Grand Final despite having been threatened with extinction at its start, three Sydney Appeal Court judges sensationally overturned just about every one of Justice Burchett's original orders, not only were two parallel Australian competitions for 1997 guaranteed, it was also full steam ahead for Lindsay's revolutionary international ambitions.

Revolutionary for rugby league, anyway. The now openly-professional rugby union had already reacted to the "threat" of Super League by launching its own Super 12s tournament, featuring shamelessly-manufactured state and provincial clubs from Australia, New Zealand and South Africa. Not that any of that worried Maurice Lindsay. "They (rugby union) should be congratulated on their Super 12s," he told reporters, "but ours will be bigger and better."

In a nutshell, the original and relatively sane Super League idea of staging a World Club Championship between the top four clubs in each hemisphere at season's end, perhaps taking in Paris and Auckland to give it that true planetary feel, was ditched. In its place came a far more elaborate and gung-ho scheme in which all 22 Super League clubs would participate in two phases of pool games during mid-domestic season breaks in June, July and August. Half of the European clubs would head down under on a three-week mini-tour, while 50 per cent of their Australasian counterparts would do likewise in the opposite direction, and vice versa in the second phase. Knock-out play-offs and a final would decide the ultimate winners. The sport's profile would be lifted right across Europe. ARL-loyal players would be tempted to jump ship and Britain's coaches and players, who apart from those at Wigan and Leeds had only recently turned full-time, would have the chance to learn from their far more capable and ruthless Antipodean cousins.

If anything should have sounded the PR alarm bells it was surely that last bit although, to be fair, it was a danger that Lindsay himself was aware of. "People ask 'what about Oldham playing the Brisbane Broncos'?" he admitted. "I accept that there could be some awful thrashings in the first year or two. That's the price you pay to get ahead. It is an opportunity for all our European clubs to play against the great Australian sides. It will accelerate the growth of our game."

While that visionary philosophy might have made complete sense in a sport prepared to come up with a development plan and stick with it - i.e. just about every other professional sport on planet earth - this was rugby league we were talking about. If a thing is broken, dump it. If a thing isn't broken, dump it anyway.

In the event, it was even worse than anticipated. After a creditable opening match down under, in which London gave Brisbane an early fright before succumbing 42-22, a tournament whose arrival had prompted Lindsay to declare: "No longer can we be accused of being a sport whose ambition is limited to the M62 corridor" went downhill faster than a runaway biscuit in Batley. In England, champions St Helens were first to face the awful truth that all this was about to turn quite nasty.

From the moment the side propping everybody else up in the Aussie comp, Auckland Warriors, trotted out onto the Knowsley Road turf, to the moment 80 minutes later when they left it with an emphatic 42-14 win in their Kiwi back pockets, there was only one side in it, and they didn't have a red chevron on their shirt. Nor did a 42-20 defeat for Leeds to the North Queensland Cowboys the following morning do much to relieve the nausea. That opening weekend concluded with five more defeats for the European sides and whilst Castleford and Paris Saint-Germain didn't do too badly against Perth and Hunter Mariners, losing 24-16 and 28-12 respectively, Warrington were walloped 40-12 by Cronulla, Adelaide stuffed Salford 50-8 and poor Halifax, already enduring comedy status thanks to their absurd "Blue Sox" nickname, were given the mother of all pastings, 70-6, by Canberra Raiders.

On the Monday, a brave effort by Wigan produced a brief glimmer of hope and a 22-18 away win over Canterbury Bulldogs, but normal service was soon resumed when runaway Euro Super

League leaders Bradford contrived to throw away a 16-6 lead before going down 20-16 in a last-minute loss to Penrith Panthers. Those 10 opening games had ended in nine Australasian victories, prompting the concept's architect-in-chief to reflect: "I always said we might not win a match."

World Club Challenges were nothing new, of course. The first half-hearted attempt at such a fixture featured Eastern Suburbs and St Helens in 1976, when the future Roosters came out on top 25-2 in what was by all accounts a less-than-thrilling spectacle at the Sydney Cricket Ground. But 11 years later, when Wigan met Manly and beat them 8-2 at Central Park, many would class it as the highlight of their rugby league watching lives.

From that point until the advent of Super League, there was an on-off stuttering procession of other games held under the WCC banner, including Widnes' 30-18 victory over Canberra at Old Trafford in the 1989-90 season, Wigan's 21-4 defeat of Penrith at Liverpool's Anfield the following year and, most notably, the Cherry and Whites' audacious 20-14 shocking of the all-powerful Brisbane Broncos at Queensland's ANZ Stadium in 1993-94. However, the concept had never really been guaranteed a place in the calendar. In fact, Wigan's scheduled clash with Canberra for June 1995 was another now-forgotten casualty of the revolution down under. This latest proposal, though, was rather different. As ideas go, it was big, it was bold, it was definitely before its time and, as the following weeks were to confirm, it was barmy.

After such a poor opening weekend, already disappointing crowds figures dipped even more. For this writer, few World Club Championship matches were more depressing than when Brisbane flew halfway around the world to be greeted by 3,255 people at Halifax's now-defunct Thrum Hall. Despite that ground's venerable past, it wasn't in its best shape by 1997 and scheduled to be written off when the "Sox" departed for the New Shay at season's end. On that less than August warm Monday evening, despite the presence of true world class talents like Alfie Langer, Steve Renouf and Wendell Sailor, its virtually empty terraces and stands cut a bleak sight indeed, as the vast majority of the Halifax public opted to stay at home and watch "Neighbours" rather than witness a predictable 54-10 beating.

At least it wasn't as bad as the 76-0 thrashing the club received in the reverse fixture down under. That game, it was joked, had ended with Brisbane's equine mascot "Bronco", who traditionally did a lap of honour whenever his team scored a try, having to be put down with exhaustion.

Not that there weren't any highlights; there were. London, for example, went a long way to proving that while attracting people to watch professional rugby league in the capital might be an uphill struggle when the likes of Castleford, Leigh and Wakefield are in town, give them a big game against glamourous opposition and it can be a different story. Nearly 8,000 turned up to watch Shaun Edwards inspire his team to a 38-18 win over Canberra while, the following week, almost 10,000 packed in to watch the battle of the Broncos, when Brisbane came out on top 34-16. Maybe the presence of so many ex-pat Aussies in the London line-up paid off, they were by far the most consistent European outfit throughout. And although the Broncos did lose their third clash on home soil, 44-22 to Canterbury Bulldogs, it was before another healthy attendance of around 7,000.

Elsewhere, in round two, Sheffield Eagles fought their way back from 22-8 half-time deficit to beat Perth Reds 26-22 with a Nick Pinkney try four minutes from time at the Don Valley, and there was a mighty punch-up between Gorden Tallis and Terry O'Connor during Wigan's 34-0 loss at Brisbane. The Warriors may have come up with a duck egg on the scoreboard, but O'Connor did at least have the pleasure of leaving Tallis with a broken nose after the Broncos forward launched a vicious assault that resulted in a letter from the Australian Super League threatening to cite him if it happened again.

In round three, an Andy Goodway-coached Paris had an unlikely 24-0 win over Perth at the Charlety Stadium. In round four, a length-of-the-field Paul Sterling try lit up a 22-14 win for Leeds over Adelaide Rams, while perhaps the most unlikely result of them all came when relegation-bound Oldham stunned North Queensland, 20-16. Wigan also accounted for the Bulldogs 31-24 and, in the last round of pool games, Salford edged Adelaide, 14-12.

Those surprise turnarounds notwithstanding, the over-riding impression of the World Club Championship was that of a farcical flop, further undermined by the tournament's arcane rule structure.

The former Iraqi Information Minister, Comical Ali, would have baulked at spinning how the October quarter-finals could boast four European Super League clubs. Most ridiculously, that meant Aussie club Penrith lost out on a last-eight place despite winning every single one of their pool matches, whilst Bradford and St Helens, who did qualify, had failed to notch a single victory between them. Saints did, however, win a quarter-final "play-off" with Paris, 42-4, in front of 3,641 at Knowsley Road. So that was all right then.

As it happened, such shenanigans only delayed the inevitable. Although Wigan ran the Hunter Mariners close before going down 22-18 at Central Park, London lost 40-16 to Cronulla at the Stoop, and a couple of 62-14 and 66-12 thrashings to England's two travelling sides saw the Bulls and Saints fly back from Auckland and Brisbane respectively with their tails between their legs and halos in a handcart. Fortunately the semis were far tighter, with Brisbane only just pipping Auckland 22-16 and the Sharks going down 22-18 to the Mariners in a clash originally intended for the UK but hastily switched to Cronulla. In the final, at Auckland's Ericcson Stadium, a crowd of 12,000 watched favourites Brisbane beat the ill-fated Hunter side to take out the title, as the Aussies like to put it, 36-12.

An unmitigated disaster, then? Well, not quite. Eight seasons on and the old spectacles don't have to be so rose-tinted to see that Lindsay's initial claims that such a tournament would help progress northern hemisphere playing standards weren't actually so wide of the mark. Even if the World Club Championship itself, to nobody's great shock, was deemed a financial disaster and quietly consigned to the back of that rugby league filing cabinet marked "Too Much Trouble", players and coaches alike declared the experience beneficial.

Three years later, in 2000, something like it reappeared in an abridged one-off World Club Challenge format, when NRL winners Melbourne flew in for a set-to with English champions St Helens at Wigan's shiny new JJB Stadium. Considering the subsequent 44-6 whitewash in favour of the Victorians, it's a miracle that the idea wasn't buried again just as quickly. Yet, remarkably, the sport's money men seemed more alive to giving the thing more time when it didn't prove so financially onerous.

The following year Saints again hosted the NRL champions - this time Brisbane - at Bolton's Reebok Stadium. Where a St Helens side coached by Ellery Hanley had given the impression of treating the game as a pre-season warm-up, leading to the usual hand-wringing over widening standards that always seems to accompany big defeats to Australian teams, with new coach Ian Millward in charge they had a different attitude entirely. So much so that, helped along by a second-half hail storm, they came up with a surprising 20-18 win.

When, in 2002, Bradford Bulls then took Newcastle Knights - Andrew Johns and all - to the cleaners 41-26, at Huddersfield's McAlpine Stadium, it was difficult to know whether the British game really was making ground on the NRL or whether the Aussies just weren't taking the event seriously enough. The latter view was reinforced when a fired-up Sydney Roosters had St Helens on toast 38-0 in Bolton in 2003, although subsequent years have seen Bradford demolish Penrith 22-4 at Huddersfield while, in 2005, Leeds Rhinos beat Canterbury Bulldogs 39-32 at Elland Road.

Ignoring a distressingly one-sided final, 2004's otherwise tightly-fought Gillette Tri-Nations tournament also seemed to indicate that the respective competitions might not be quite so far apart as the English game's critics suppose. Then again, at the time of writing, since Wigan's 1994 heroics no World Club Challenge match has been staged down under. Perhaps it would be to everybody's benefit if our Australian chums either put up or shut up on this one.

Meanwhile, a decade after the global vision was first unveiled, apart from Challenge Cup finals in Wales and Scotland, and the odd half-baked exotic road trip to the likes of Leicester and Northampton, since Paris were put out of their financial misery at the end of 1997, Tyneside is about as far as the European Super League's supposed wanderlust has taken it.

Married to a German-born lass raised in South Shields, like a lot of rugby league folk linked to or living in the north east, I invested a good deal of evangelical effort into promoting what was to be Gateshead Thunder's single ill-fated Super League season in 1999. I was hardly being selfless in that. All those weekends visiting the in-laws when I could "just pop out for a couple of hours"; it seemed too good to be true. Under the stewardship of giant Aussie Shane Richardson off the pitch and his equally svelte countryman Shaun

McRae on it, with additional support from Kath Hetherington and several hundred Geordie and Mackem stalwarts already at the heart of the region's steadily developing amateur scene, that supposedly inaugural season appeared to shape up very nicely. When they weren't impersonating Steve Cram and Jonathan Edwards, or shoving round balls up their shirts and pretending to be Paul "Gazza" Gascoigne, the sports-mad public of Tyneside had a history of showing willing where one-off rugby league representative fixtures and Charity Shield matches were concerned. With an opening night crowd of 5,960 against Leeds and an average attendance of 3,895 throughout a memorable first season in which the club finished sixth - a play-off position nowadays - the area seemed set to take to the game on a more regular basis. Gateshead's purple super hero mascot "Captain Thunder" quickly became a local celebrity and Super League's north east roots grew stronger by the week.

Behind the scenes, however, the project was not making any money. In fact, it was leaking it. Much of that cash had been invested by Richardson himself who, in true rugby league style, had only been allowed to bring the club into Super League in the first place on agreement that it would pay its own way. Little, if any, of the Sky TV money made it up the A1 and that, coupled with the fact that just about every player was flown in from Australia and set up in accommodation, meant the whole exercise was a costly one. Crowds, though generally encouraging in what was virtually a virgin area, were not as large as initially hoped, with a season high of 6,631 against Bradford Bulls offset by three woeful attendances of around 1,500 for the visits of Salford, Hull and Sheffield. Inevitably, when the bean counters of Super League (M62) dreamt up the financial escape route of a "twinning" with Hull that was more acquisition than merger, "Richo", "Bomber", Kath and Co were away down the east coast faster than any sprinter who ever graced the Gateshead International Stadium.

Shane Richardson, in particular, took plenty of stick for cutting his losses but, in all honesty, who amongst us would have acted any differently? If we need to apportion blame, it would be better to target the usual narrow self interest from the game's existing clubs. Either way, the abandonment of Gateshead Thunder represented a massive opportunity lost, and one that would surely have gone on to produce long-term benefits. Anyone doubting that needs only to look up the road to rugby union's Newcastle Falcons where - with a commercial department headed by former Thunder marketing guru Mick Hogan - Jonny Wilkinson and pals these days play to regular audiences of 5-6,000 people or more (when he's fit, of course). In the summer of 1999, it was the Falcons who played second fiddle to their 13-a-side neighbours. Upon rugby league's demise a new generation of fans simply flicked up their red "Thunderdome" seats and headed for Kingston Park instead. Others, outraged at what they rightly perceived as a major betrayal of the area and its people, drifted away from rugby all together, never to return.

I say "never to return"; some did, of course. In fact, as the supporters group "Thunder Storm" they went a stage further and rebuilt the club from scratch, enabling a reborn Gateshead Thunder to compete as a member of 2001's Northern Ford Premiership. Since then, it has been hardship all the way in the English game's most north-easterly outpost, with attendances refusing to climb much above 500 and weekly defeat almost guaranteed. Thankfully, under the canny stewardship of coach Dean Thomas and the latest board of directors, fortunes improved in 2005, with a place in the National League Two play-offs replacing the usual scrap to avoid the wooden spoon. In fact, a second Gateshead club, Gateshead Storm, born from that original supporters group, spent the 10th season of Super League competing in National League Three, thereby giving further cause for long-term optimism that the Thunder's Super League adventure may not have been such a complete waste of time after all.

Nevertheless, I still vividly remember the telephone call I took from another of this book's contributors, *Guardian* writer Andy Wilson, in which he passed on news of the original Thunder's "merger" with Hull, a club who have at least built upon that fortunate foundation by winning the 2005 Powergen Challenge Cup and rekindling interest in the sport along that more southerly stretch of England's east coast.

I was a resident of Carcassonne's Hotel Terminus at the time, using that historic old rugby league venue as a base camp from which to cover the first ever Mediterranean Cup, a qualifying competition for the 2000 World Cup that featured France, Italy, Morocco and eventual-winners Lebanon. The Terminus, a former Nazi HQ, earned its place in league history by being at the centre of the game's post-war revival in France after the Vichy government's ban back in the 1940s. At the risk of sounding like *un chemisier de la grande fille*, I spent the next couple of days drifting in and out of its elegantly-mirrored and marbled reception in a daze, not all of it brought on by Kronenbourg 1664. How could rugby league expansion be viewed with anything other than cynicism? After all, if the game couldn't extend its reach 80-odd miles north of York, what serious chance did it have of putting down roots in Beirut, Naples or Casablanca?

Fortunately, a combination of the enthusiasm shown by organiser Tas Baitieri, an inspirational battle with cancer by roguish Lebanon coach John Elias and the South of France's worst floods in 60 years - during which over 20 people lost their lives and the Italian squad's hotel had its ground floor destroyed by a terrifying wall of water - saw a bit of perspective reintroduced. Disaster is a word bandied about far too frequently in sporting circles.

As it happened, World Nines-style wet weather was to be a feature of the main event too, with the following November's World Cup proper also hit hard by the elements, together with a ticketing fiasco and the over-ambition of organisers who saw fit to include 16 teams in games staged at 28 different venues right across the United Kingdom, Ireland and France.

If the World Club Championship was an example of rugby league running before it could walk, then the Lincoln World Cup suffered from similar delusions of grandeur, writ even larger. Forged in the confidence created by a highly-successful 1995 tournament, in which 10 nations had taken part for the first time since the event (the first such World Cup in either code of rugby) began in 1954, the World Club lessons of 1997 were spectacularly ignored. With the exception of a relatively successful pool in France, the overall result was chronically low crowds, a media and public relations disaster and a financial meltdown that left the Rugby Football League mired deep in a £700,000 debt that took four years to clear. The sport's media critics could not believe their luck and stuck the boot in with glee. It was as though someone had sent them a big fat birthday cake with the

202

words "Rugby League Is Dead" spelled out in lovely pink icing, alongside 13 damp and smouldering candles.

In hindsight, however, even that ill-fated farrago was rather less gloomy in the bigger picture than might then have been imagined. For sure, one of the sticks with which the 2000 World Cup was beaten - an accusation of too many manufactured nations consisting almost entirely of second or even third generation Aussies - turned out to be ultimately beneficial in a couple of cases at least. Despite much initial derision at the inclusion of Lebanon, for example, vanquishers of a USA team that had itself beaten Canada and Japan to make a qualifying final at Disneyland, Orlando (cue Mickey Mouse jokes), a domestic league was subsequently launched in that middle eastern country based around its universities that continues to this day. Enthusiasts in Ireland were sparked into life too, giving new impetus to the development of rugby league in the Emerald Isle.

Since then, while the effects of the Super League war can still be felt in any number of ways, its more malign repercussions diminish by the year. At a small-scale amateur level, the game has never enjoyed such a wide presence in so many countries, from Georgia to Singapore, from Holland to Jamaica. Since those dark, wintry and waterlogged days of the 2000 World Cup, I myself have had the pleasure of watching rugby league played in, amongst other places, Moscow, Tatarstan and Beirut, by teams as diverse as Lebanon, Russia, the United States, France, Morocco and Serbia, usually in front of decent-sized audiences. Okay, many of those would struggle to beat your average northern English pub side, but what the hell. The game is played there and that's enough for me.

Where the sport's two major centres in Australia and England are concerned, despite continued struggles at the game's amateur and semi-pro levels, both top-flight professional domestic leagues have strengthened to the extent that the term golden era does not seem so far-fetched. In 2007, the Gold Coast will reappear on the Aussie rugby league map as a cautiously optimistic NRL again feels confident enough to flex its expansionist muscles. With the arrival of Les Catalans on a three-year guarantee against relegation from 2006, the European Super League will once again live up to its name, a moniker it will merit even more if the proposed entry of Toulouse and perhaps even the Bridgend-based Celtic Crusaders actually do come to pass in 2009.

As few will need reminding, the key word in the above paragraph is "if". For, as rugby league also contemplates its symbolically-perfect 13th World Cup, scheduled to celebrate the sport's Australian centenary (of 2007!) in 2008, featuring the first Australian-staged World Cup final since 1977, it's worth remembering that it should, in fact, be its 14th.

Can anyone recall these words? "This is a marker that rugby league has faith in its international future and we are excited by the prospect of yet another World Cup in this country."

Hmmm, "yet another" World Cup in this country. Spoken like a true Rugby Football League spokesperson immediately after a two-day meeting of International Federation delegates in Sydney, 2002. The "marker" in question was an announcement that Great Britain had been "awarded" its third consecutive World Cup to be held in, wait for it, 2005. Yes, that's 2005.

It's probably best not to splash out on sun tan lotion just yet.

● *Tony Hannan is the former editor of Rugby League World magazine and the now-defunct weekly newspaper Total Rugby League. A one-time sports journalist with the Press Association, he writes for a wide range of publications in the UK and abroad including The Times and Australian magazine Big League, for whom he is British correspondent. Since retiring as a Club 18-30 holiday rep, he has written, edited & contributed to several books, co-commentates on BBC GMR and dislikes sprouts.*

17. To In-Quin-ity ...and Beyond!

Dave Woods

Nothing dates as quickly as a prediction. You only have to watch the re-runs of *Tomorrow's World* to realise that. It's not just Judith Hann's curly perm that makes that programme seem so comically out of date; it's the confident claims that by 2006 we'd all be travelling to work in motorised moon-boots.

When the programme was first aired we watched with slack-jawed wonder, marvelling at how our lives were about to be revolutionised. We now look back and scoff at our own innocent gullibility. So, it's with a certain degree of caution that this chapter is written, lest you should wander into some musty second-hand book shop in a couple of decades time, pick up this volume and read predictions for the game that never came close to passing.

"Look at this, Martha," you would splutter, half-choking on the dry dust clouds billowing out from its long-forgotten pages. "This chump reckoned we'd be playing Grand Finals on the moon by 2025. Guffaw." Nice idea, by the way, were it not for the lack of atmosphere. There is, though, one prediction you can confidently make about rugby league - there will be change. It's a game of change, a game that has constantly evolved from the day it was born back in 1895.

The rugby league I watch today is not the game my dad first

introduced me to in the early Seventies. And in the early Seventies it was no longer the game he first began watching a couple of decades earlier. Rules have altered, styles been revised. Clubs have emerged, others have disappeared. Stadiums have been razed and raised. Some shiny cups are no longer played for, big ideas have come and gone.

Yet, rugby league is also the game it always was. It has always had that same honest, brutal beauty - a bone-crunching artistry that no other sport can match. It survives and often flourishes when those outside the game expect, and sometimes hope, it will flounder. But we keep on tinkering at the fringes and every so often someone comes along with the next big idea to keep the game evolving and revolving. Why? Because at its heart the game has a deep insecurity, a collective chip on the shoulder over the way we are dismissed as irrelevant by those who set the national sporting agenda. So we are always looking for ways to catch the eye of the wider world, hoping that at some undetermined future date we, the devotees of rugby league, will bask in the sunshine of universal consent that it really is the greatest game of all. Sadly, that day may never come. But it shouldn't stop us dreaming.

Part of the problem is our roots; the working-class northern-ness that was our *raison d'etre*. We think of our heartlands as we would a dotty old grandmother. Were it not for her we wouldn't be here, we love her to bits and we're immensely proud of her. But sometimes, in more cosmopolitan company, we're a little bit embarrassed by her presence. So, almost from the day the game was born, bellowing indignantly as it pushed and clawed its way into existence, rugby league has aspired to going global and expanding beyond the cotton mills and coal-mining towns in which it found itself.

We want to be the working-class lad who made good; able to mix in the same social circles as the rest of this nation's sporting elite, have the same social manners they have, to be recognised as an equal wherever we go, yet retain our flat vowels as a proud sign-post to where we came from. The problem is, rugby league's attempts at expansion in this country have, without exception, failed.

We've tried it in Cardiff, Carlisle, Chorley, Gateshead, Mansfield, Kent, Nottingham, Scarborough, Southend, Trafford, etc, etc, even Paris. They were all towns and cities into which professional clubs were planted, and where rugby league was meant to be the next big thing. But several years on, the local public remain largely ignorant of the sporting seeds that were scattered in their back gardens; that briefly sprouted, before withering back into the dark earth. Now we appear to have another bright horizon in terms of spreading the gospel. Two, to be precise, in London and in Perpignan. But before we can go there, there is a fundamental question to be addressed.

As rugby league looks to its future, it has to get its head around whether it really does want to carry on trying to expand, in the knowledge that pushing at the boundaries could lead to the demise of some of our most traditional clubs.

There is an argument which states: let's leave things as they are and concentrate for the most part on looking after our own. We've had a go at expanding and it's not worked. Maybe there is something curious about the game that makes it a delicacy to northern tastebuds but unpalatable to anyone else's - like tripe and dark mild. And, after all, if them southerners can't be bothered with us, why should we be bothered with them?

It's a viewpoint that has many supporters. Concentrating on the communities where rugby league has always been nurtured and remains strongest seems common sense. And few could argue with the fact that, these days, the game is as healthy and vibrant as it has ever been, thanks in the main to clubs like Hull, Leeds, Bradford, Wigan, St Helens and Warrington, strung out along the M62 corridor. But there is an uneasy feeling under-pinning the current prosperity. A fear that what we are currently looking at is a snap-shot and that if you run the movie on, a gloomier future is in store for the game if it doesn't push itself further.

The communities on which the sport has been built have changed dramatically; we can no longer rely on them to provide unswerving support for their local team. Their leisure time is in much greater demand from other sports and other activities than ever before. For all that Old Trafford and the Millennium Stadium are always packed for the big events and Super League crowds are growing, we still struggle for deserved recognition from the national media. And even though we have put into practice youth development programmes that are envied by other sports, our pool of talent is still too shallow for any real self-congratulation. In short, we have to broaden our outlook.

With expansion comes greater interest from the public, more coverage by the national media, larger sponsorship deals, a much bigger pool of potential playing talent - and a healthier rugby league that can look towards the future with confidence. But not just any old expansion, it has to be successful expansion, something we have never achieved before. We need clubs emerging and growing in the parts we have not yet reached, attracting new followers, new fanatics, new players and new interest.

And so to those two bright horizons. As we approach Super League's second decade, there is much interest in the emergence of its two newest teams - Les Catalans, the French club based in Perpignan, and Harlequins RL, the team created when London Broncos wriggled out of their old skin before being stitched onto the existing union club of that name. How they got to where they have is described in earlier chapters. This chapter, however, is all about what lies ahead and, in both clubs, we may have the future of rugby league. So, fingers crossed that they aren't strangled in infancy.

Les Catalans and Harlequins each represent a different formula for expansion that has never been properly adhered to before. In the case of the French team, it's about planting a club in an area where there is already a latent support for rugby league. The South of France has been, and remains, a potential hot-bed for the 13-man code. Largely, Paris failed because it was an artificial club in an artificial environment. By contrast, Les Catalans were organically created, carrying the club's supporters through the process of merging two strong teams into one regional giant.

Its success as a club is vital, not just to help continue the vibrancy of Super League by placing in its midst a new exotic opponent, but for the sake of the global game. The club is committed to developing local talent, so that, very quickly, its squad will be made up of a large majority of home-grown players. If it works as they intend it to, that can only mean the re-emergence of France as a force on the international stage.

Les Catalans have been given a three-year protection from relegation so that they can find their feet in their new surroundings.

But here's a prediction - they won't need it. They will be strong contenders for a top-six spot before those three years are up and the game will have its first successful expansion club. Another prediction - within five years, a second French club will also be looking to join Super League, having been encouraged by the success of Les Catalans. But there does need to be a little caution. A second French club should only be admitted once the player pool in that country is large enough to cope. A Super League side in Toulouse or Marseilles packed with Aussies, Kiwis and Brits is bound to fail. The locals will want indigenous talent carrying their hopes, not mercenaries from another land.

The Harlequins experiment is based on an altogether different blueprint. At the risk of being whipped and dragged bare-chested through the streets of every rugby league town, before being placed in stocks in front of the George Hotel, to be pelted by rotten tomatoes and cabbages (or the modern day equivalent - being slagged off on an internet messageboard), may I suggest that partnership with our oldest and dearest rivals, rugby union, is the only way to expand properly in this country.

Oh, I know they are the devil at the door and that the evil snobbery of Twickenham, with its fingers in every Establishment pie, has always forced us to feed off scraps rather than feast at the table with other elite sports. But times have changed. Like it or not, our friends in union offer our best hope of advancement. Remind yourself of that list of failed expansion attempts: Cardiff, Carlisle, Chorley, Gateshead, Mansfield, Kent, Nottingham, Scarborough, Southend, etc. All were go-it-alone league enterprises and all failed.

Now add London to that list. From Fulham to Brentford, the London experiment has so far been a failure too. There have been one or two highs along the way, like getting to Wembley and the day Canberra came to town, but there have been an awful lot of lows. In 2005, but for the support of the RFL and the other Super League clubs, the Broncos would have gone out of business and disappeared totally from the sporting map.

Alright, the club has succeeded in setting up schools programmes and supports a growing amateur scene in the capital. And its supporters will tell you that average crowds and achievements on the field compare reasonably with some other clubs in the north. But the whole point of an expansion club is that it must bring new prosperity to the game - whether measured in support, sponsorship, media coverage or playing talent. They have a different responsibility to rugby league than any of the heartland outfits.

There is no hard evidence of Fulham, London Crusaders, London Broncos - whichever incarnation you choose to give as an example - having achieved any of those, at a sustained level, for the greater good of the game. Failure has not necessarily been down to a lack of expertise or hard-work from those involved at the club. Rugby league in London, as in every other previous expansion attempt elsewhere, has failed to take hold because the game has acted like a shabby door-to-door salesman. It has turned up, uninvited, opened its battered suitcase and tried to hard-sell its wares to folk who are quite happy with the sporting pastimes they already buy into. The result - one or two persuaded, but lots more doors slammed shut in our face and the vast majority remaining totally indifferent.

Now, with the Harlequins tie-up, there is every chance that rugby league can make an impact on the psyche of both London and the nation. It's a model for expansion in the rest of the country. This time, we aren't trying to sneak our foot in the door; we have been invited in by potential customers who are glad to see us. It's the future - and that's just as well as that's what this chapter is supposed to be about. Instead of looking for millionaires who fancy bank-rolling new franchises, or two-bit businessmen with a good line in patter and half an idea, the game should be trying to nurture its relationship with rugby union to encourage more such partnerships.

Of course, the more successful the new Harlequins venture, the better the chances of a Leicester, or a Newcastle or a Wasps wanting a taste of the rugby league action as well. And if rugby league die-hards find it grating to have a team called Quins playing in Super League, just imagine how it sticks in the craw of your toffee-nosed rah-rah to have his beloved favourites playing the other code.

But let's put all that absurd, out-dated inter-code rivalry to one side. Union has much to gain from league and has admitted as much by taking many of our coaches, some of our players and a few of our rules. But they are not the dangerous enemy we sometimes perceive them to be. League also has much to gain from union, as the Quins partnership will hopefully prove. For a start, the Harlequins have an established fan base that can now be tempted, without prejudice, to join up with the small but dedicated clan of supporters who have propped up Fulham, the Crusaders and Broncos for years.

The tie-up guarantees to generate media interest at a level that no London-based rugby league club could ever hope to achieve on its own. Youngsters, only ever able to play and watch union, will now be exposed to rugby league at close quarters, giving them the chance to try the game for themselves. The more youngsters try it, the better the chance we have of expanding the talent pool. Just imagine how many Alex Murphys, Ellery Hanleys and Paul Sculthorpes have been lost to our game because they didn't get a chance to try it as a kid.

Rugby league is moving into an environment where running with the ball is already familiar and aesthetically appreciated. You are not trying to get a football crowd to turn its entire sporting upbringing on its head. The codes can form a partnership of sorts right across the country. If for Harlequins, you read Cardiff, Leicester, Newcastle and Gloucester, you have the makings of something very special. Still not convinced? Perhaps concerned that union is more of a bogey man than a genuine partner? You have too little faith in rugby league.

Surely, as regular devotees of the game, we can only be confident that given a proper platform rugby league can become the equal of union, maybe even the code of choice for many around the country who have, hitherto, only been able to watch and play union because it was the only code they had access to. And if there isn't to be a partnership with the other code, how else can expansion be successfully achieved, given all that we have learnt from history?

Of course, persuading rugby union clubs that their future lays in partnership with us is one thing, altering Super League's mechanics so that any new club can enter is quite another. There will be a tricky philosophical debate over the next few years as the whole subject of top-flight promotion and relegation comes sharply into focus.

In the middle of 2005, the RFL came up with its radical plan for the future. Younger fans were doubtless excited by the prospect of more dramatic change to the game they love; those of us of an older generation simply carved another notch into the bedpost of life in response to one more "big idea" being unveiled. The "*Whole Sport Plan*" will operate until 2009. In a nutshell, and without wishing to regurgitate the jargon of the modern-day executive, it's all about the game hitching up its trousers and straightening its tie.

Everyone involved in the professional game, from the RFL down through the clubs, will be encouraged to improve the sport's off-field standards. Marketing, media, business development, customer needs, facilities, sponsorship, education, training, nurturing talent and developing excellence - in fact every area of life that can be described by a word or phrase whose meaning you're not exactly sure of, will be put under examination.

Then, in 2009, comes the dawning of a bright new day on which the future of rugby league will become clear to us all. Except that, at the moment, the weather forecasters are predicting fog for that particular day - long, lingering fog with a few pile-ups expected, especially on the M62. You see, the plan seems to be that Super League will be turned into a quasi-closed shop. Once you're in, it will be damned difficult to get out. If you're out, it will take some impossibly hard work to get in. Every club in Super League XIV will be given a charmed life of three years, during which finishing bottom won't matter. There will be no relegation. Winning the National League One Grand Final will have less consequence too, because promotion won't be happening either. Once at the star-studded, A-list party that is Super League, the only way a club can be picked up by the lapels and thrown out onto the cold pavement along with the other has-beens and never-weres, is if they are letting themselves down on several fronts.

Failing to win matches will no longer be the only criteria for getting the big heave-ho. If in those three years a club has finished bottom consistently, but at the same time has grown its business, attracted more fans, and kept its ground looking ship-shape, the chances are it will survive. If, however, another side has done comparatively well on the playing field, but its finances are in a mess, crowds are poor and the stadium's falling down, then it is in danger of getting the boot once the three years are up.

But the reality is this. Most existing Super League clubs have either got or are in the process of getting some very nice new stadiums. Others have plans for renovation that a club outside Super League could not afford. Sharing the Super League's income pot over the next few years means that its existing clubs will be much better off financially than those in the National Leagues. And the Super League clubs are fully-professional, so are much more likely to have in place marketing and business development staff, that those outside can never hope to employ, until, that is, they get the chance to join the elite, which, for all the reasons above, is unlikely to happen.

In effect, it's the end of the dream of promotion for every club outside the top-flight. The truth is that the only clubs who will be invited to join Super League from 2009 and beyond are new franchises or merged concerns.

There is merit in the plan. It aims to create a league of genuine shared quality, in which clubs don't bankrupt themselves simply to survive. They can invest and grow, both in terms of talent on the field and business off it. And one season, in which plots were lost or injuries sustained at a freakish level, doesn't mean the descent into a financial meltdown that relegation has so often brought in the past.

One by-product of that, though, is the loss to the game of the terrifically tense relegation battles that have lit up recent seasons. Can the game find a way of keeping alive the vibrancy of the competition if two or three clubs find themselves out of the Challenge Cup early and adrift of the running for a play-off place? Is the sport strong enough to make every 'gameday' a must-see event, no matter what league table context it's played in?

And for the National League clubs to be appeased, the RFL needs to find a way to make their competition just as vital and meaningful to a cynical public in the absence of the goal of promotion. Good luck to them; they'll need it. I can't think of another sport that has succeeded in doing that. In producing the answer, the RFL has also created an awful lot of questions.

Of course, 2009 is - in rugby league terms - light years away. You get the feeling that the British public's love of relegation and promotion and the natural justice of that system will be strong enough to convince the architects of this latest design to incorporate it into their plans. Maybe promotion shouldn't be an unqualified right for the side that wins National League One, but they should be given the incentive of knowing that winning the league and satisfying certain criteria will be enough to lift them into the big-time.

We should never forget that rugby league is a family and most of the clubs have grown up together. It would be unwise to cut adrift those who seem unfashionable and frail at any given moment. After all, it isn't so long ago that you could have made a case for the likes of Bradford, Wigan and Hull to be put down in order to save them from any further misery.

It might even be the case that when you come to read this in that musty second-hand bookshop in 2025, you might be scratching your head about the whole idea of a *"Whole Sport Plan"*, because it changed beyond recognition or was simply forgotten about before 2009 ever came around.

Generally, however, there is a confidence in the game at the moment that hasn't been experienced for a long time; a belief that the future is bright. Then again, rugby league was bursting with energy in the Fifties and Sixties, before hitting a real slump in the Seventies. Maybe complacency played a part in that and the game certainly has to avoid complacency now.

Take yourself to a match on a weekend, at any level, and you can't help but marvel at the entertainment. The lung-bursting, limb-crushing, sharp-passing, quick-thinking, hair-raising, side-stepping, dummying, darting, dancing, daring of it all is simply wonderful. How many times have you turned to the person next to you and asked: "Why isn't everyone in love with this sport? And why aren't the broadcasters and newspapers simply falling over themselves to show us even more of the spectacle?"

Well, maybe in the future everyone will learn to love 'The Greatest Game'. In the meantime, we can only dream of rugby league's world domination. And motorised moon boots.

● *Dave Woods' school report read: "...a spotty child who can smell." His myopic careers' master read that as "...a sporty child who can spell" and directed him into a career in sports journalism. Woods spent five years with Barnes News, a freelance Press Agency in Wigan, reporting on that club's glory years of the late '80s. In 1990, he joined the BBC, working for Radio Leeds and then Radio 5 Live as a rugby league and football commentator. To his mother's enormous pride, he also occasionally pops up on the telly. A more recent career switch could have occurred courtesy of a late-night telephone call asking if he fancied coaching Castleford Tigers. He declined.*

18. A Decade of Action, Trev's Top Ten...

Trevor Hunt

① March 29th 1996 - Paris in the Springtime
Paris Saint-Germain 30...............................Sheffield Eagles 24

The dream finally became a reality amid a fanfare of publicity, the crackle of rocket fire and French revolution. At a rocking and rolling Charlety Stadium, Sheffield Eagles were served up as edible fare for hungry expansionists desperate to see a Paris Saint-Germain victory.

The most optimistic of Super League advocates viewed this first televised game for the controversial new set-up with trepidation. Would Paris be competitive? Would the fans turn up? Could Rupert Murdoch's Sky deliver the presentation, passion and style the game deserved? It must have been a time of considerable soul-searching in the hours leading up to kick-off, as the TV crews moved into the empty stadium, the giant TV screen was erected and the press started to arrive with varying degrees of pessimism and foreboding.

Sheffield arrived on the back of their best ever season in 1995's truncated Centenary campaign. Still two years away from their most glorious moment - a 1998 Challenge Cup final win over Wigan - the Eagles didn't have many big stars. Keith Senior, Paul Broadbent, Andy Hay, Dale Laughton and Ryan Sheridan were players whose best moments lay ahead of them, although captain and scrum-half

Mark Aston was in his pomp. Paris had a decent scrum-half of their own in Patrick Entat. Laurent Lucchese, Didier Cabestany, Pierre Chamorin and Frederic Banquet were other French internationals in a hastily-drawn together squad. Aussie signings Jason Sands and Todd Brown, plus Kiwi Darren Adams, added overseas experience. Then, as kick-off approached the stadium filled to the tune of 17,873 people and a memorable opening night was guaranteed.

In keeping with the stereotype, Paris showed lots of Gallic flair, and they opened the scoring when Banquet grabbed the historic first-ever Super League try in the 10th minute, as Freddie Mercury blasted out: "We Will Rock You!" The referee was future RFL Director of Referees, Stuart Cummings, and he was assisted by an innovation that would become a fixture and fitting of televised matches in the decade to come. The giant video screen was responsible for disallowing three tries, with Banquet also becoming the first man to have a try denied by this method just before the one that counted. It all added to the tension.

Dean Lawford scored the Eagles' first try in a lively combination with Ryan Sheridan and paved the way for another from Andy Hay. Moldovan winger Mikhail Piskunov's one and only try of the season levelled the scores at 10-10 for the break. Nine minutes after the restart, Darren Adams crashed over for Paris, but Matt Crowther and then Paul Carr crossed in quick succession. With Lawford adding a second conversion, all looked set for an Eagles victory.

Paris, though, blazed back and when Vea Bloomfield boosted their flagging pack, the magnificent Chamorin charged over for a Patrick Torreilles-goaled try and a 58th-minute 22-20 lead they were never to surrender. Nine minutes from time, Arnaud Cervello added a second try to an earlier length-of-the-field effort and although Senior crossed for Sheffield, it could not deny a marvellous opening victory for Paris, their coach, Michel Mazaré and Super League.

PARIS 30: Laurent Lucchese; Mikhail Piskunov, Frederic Banquet, Pierre Chamorin, Arnaud Cervello; Todd Brown, Patrick Entat; Gregory Kacala, Patrick Torreilles, Jason Sands, Darren Adams, Didier Cabestany, Jacques Pech. Subs: Ian Turner, Vea Bloomfield, Regis Pastre-Courtine, Fabien Devecchi.
Paris tries: Banquet, Piskunov, Adams, Chamorin, Cervello 2; G- Torreilles 3.
SHEFFIELD 24: Waisale Sovatabua; Joe Dakuitoga, Lynton Stott, Jean-Marc Garcia, Matt Crowther; Ryan Sheridan, Dean Lawford; Paul Broadbent, Johnny Lawless, Danny McAllister, Andy Hay, Paul Carr, Mick Cook. Subs: Keith Senior, Mark Aston, Anthony Farrell, Dale Laughton.
Sheffield tries: Carr, Crowther, Hay, Lawford, Senior; G- Crowther 4, Mycoe 1; DG- Stott.
Referee: Stuart Cummings; Half-time: 10-10; Attendance: 17,873.

2 October 19th 2002 - Long Drops, Joynt's Tackle

Bradford Bulls 18 ....St Helens 19

Sean Long snatched the headlines and a sensational last-gasp victory for St Helens with the most important drop-goal in Super League history - a 20-metre match winner that broke Bradford hearts with just 51 seconds left on the clock. "I thought I had blown it when I missed an earlier one," Long explained. "But Tony Stewart made a great break, Joynty (Chris Joynt) took it right to the sticks and Keiron (Cunningham) laid it on a plate for me."

There was still time for more controversy. With six seconds remaining, Joynt took the ball from dummy-half and dropped to the feet of Lee Gilmour and Paul Deacon. Whether he was anticipating the tackle or going down voluntarily has been debated ever since, but the Bulls players laid off him and screamed for a penalty. From 45 metres out, they would have backed a Deacon kick to win the game but Joynt leapt to his feet and the game was over.

The 2002 Grand Final started in devastating fashion as Saints full-back Paul Wellens fractured a cheekbone in Bradford's very first attack, after colliding with Brandon Costin. Michael Withers then put Scott Naylor in for a third-minute try and Deacon goaled. Man of the match Deacon later missed a penalty, kicked a penalty and had a try disallowed by the video referee - for a Jamie Peacock knock-on as he grappled with Paul Newlove - a decision that newly-appointed controller of referees, Stuart Cummings, later admitted was wrong.

Mike Bennett grabbed Saints' first before Cunningham sent Long in for a second converted try and a 12-8 interval lead. On the restart, Robbie Paul raced 30 metres for a Deacon-goaled score before Withers hared in off Naylor's inside pass. Saints again fought back through a Gleeson try and Long penalty to level the scores at 18-18 before Long's calm boot ensured an unforgettable finale.

BRADFORD 18: Michael Withers; Tevita Vaikona, Scott Naylor, Brandon Costin, Lesley Vainikolo; Robbie Paul, Paul Deacon; Joe Vagana, James Lowes, Stuart Fielden, Daniel Gartner, Jamie Peacock, Mike Forshaw. Subs: Brian McDermott, Leon Pryce, Paul Anderson, Lee Gilmour.
Bradford tries: Naylor, Paul, Withers; G- Deacon 3.
ST HELENS 19: Paul Wellens; Anthony Stewart, Martin Gleeson, Paul Newlove, Darren Albert; Paul Sculthorpe, Sean Long; Darren Britt, Keiron Cunningham, Barry Ward, Tim Jonkers, Mike Bennett, Chris Joynt. Subs: John Stankevitch, Mick Higham, Peter Shiels, Sean Hoppe.
St Helens tries: Bennett, Long, Gleeson; G- Long 3; DG- Long.
Referee: Russell Smith; Half-time: 8-12; Attendance: 61,138.

③ September 22nd 2000 - "That" Try!

St Helens 16 ....Bradford Bulls 11

"Joynt scores! Joynt scores! Joynt scores! Joynt scoreeeeeeessssss!" Sky Sports commentator Eddie Hemmings wasn't the only one to nearly lose his wig. That was the breathless way BBC GMR listeners heard me describe Chris Joynt's unbelievable match-winner, unarguably the try of the decade if not the best in RL history.

Bradford led 11-10 with a mere three seconds to go as Paul Sculthorpe played the ball on the Saints left-hand side, some 25 metres from his own line. Who could predict what came next? In the very last play of the game, Keiron Cunningham passed to Sean Long, who kicked cross-field. Kevin Iro plucked the ball out of the air and found Steve Hall on the right. Hall inside to Hoppe, to Hall again, to Jim Jonkers, to Long again. The scrum-half sped along the Saints 20-metre line before arcing to the left-centre position and finding Joynt. Joynt shipped it to Dwayne West, who lifted his legs high out of a despairing tackle and tore down the left wing. With Michael Withers covering, West threw an inside pass that the supporting Joynt took to his chest before pinning back his ears for a 40 metre sprint.

The Saints skipper didn't need the help of supporting speedster Anthony Sullivan as he left the devastated Bradford chasers in his wake and, with an arm raised high in triumph, charged over the whitewash before being mobbed by ecstatic team-mates and delirious fans. By contrast, shell-shocked Bulls coach Matthew Elliott slipped from his seat in sheer disbelief.

Long added the extras with the St Bernard mascot's head on, but nobody cared. Knowsley Road was alight with excitement and St Helens were on their way to back-to-back Grand Final victories. The comeback kings had delivered the fightback to end all fightbacks. After this great escape, no game seemed beyond their redemption.

ST HELENS 16: Paul Wellens; Sean Hoppe, Kevin Iro, Paul Newlove, Anthony Sullivan; Tommy Martyn, Sean Long; Apollo Perelini, Keiron Cunningham, Julian O'Neill, Chris Joynt, Tim Jonkers, Paul Sculthorpe. Subs: Steve Hall, Dwayne West, Fereti Tuilagi, John Stankevitch.
St Helens tries: Hoppe, Martyn, Joynt; G- Long 2.
BRADFORD 11: Stuart Spruce; Leon Pryce, Michael Withers, Scott Naylor, Tevita Vaikona; Henry Paul, Paul Deacon; Brian McDermott, James Lowes, Paul Anderson, Jamie Peacock, Mike Forshaw, Brad Mackay. Subs: Nathan McAvoy, Stuart Fielden, Hudson Smith, Robbie Paul.
Bradford tries: Peacock, Pryce. G- H Paul. DG- H Paul.
Referee: Russell Smith; Half-time: 0-4; Attendance: 8,864.

❹ August 1st 1999 - Thunder Over Edinburgh

Gateshead Thunder 20 .... Wigan Warriors 16

Gateshead Thunder's finest hour. A magnificent victory over the reigning champions of Wigan and an early eye-catching performance from a certain young Irish wingman named Brian Carney, in only his third Super League game ever.

The only pity was that this most entertaining of Sunday afternoon matches wasn't staged in Gateshead, where the home fans would have savoured it even more than those who made the trip up to Edinburgh. Nevertheless, it provided a tasty appetiser for future rugby league events in the Scottish capital.

The home of Scottish soccer club Heart of Midlothian erupted into life from the kick-off, as Thunder struck like lightning thanks to a second-minute try from Carney, despite the attentions of five would-be tacklers. Four minutes later Craig Wilson and Ben Sammut combined to put Craig Simon away, and when he kicked to the corner, Matt Daylight touched down for try number two, before adding his second and Thunder's third on the nod of the video ref. A Craig Wilson try and Sammut goal made it 18-0.

The introduction of Greg Florimo sparked a Wigan revival and a Denis Betts try and Andy Farrell goal earned an 18-6 interval scoreline. It could have been closer but the video referee disallowed a second Wigan 'score' for the smallest of Farrell knock-ons in first-half injury-time.

Despite being under immense pressure at the start of the second half, a well-taken Wilson drop-goal increased Gateshead's lead before tries to Betts and Farrell helped close the gap to three points. But Thunder hung on and Willie Peters slotted over another drop-goal three minutes from time. "Something special is evolving," beamed Gateshead coach Shaun McRae.

GATESHEAD 20: Ben Sammut; Brian Carney, Brett Grogan, Craig Simon, Matt Daylight; Will Robinson, Willie Peters; Danny Lee, Mick Jenkins, Luke Felsch, Craig Wilson, Tony Grimaldi, Deon Bird. Subs: Kerrod Walters, David Maiden, Adam Maher, Garreth Carvell.
Gateshead tries: Daylight 2, Carney, Wilson; G- Sammut; DG- Wilson, Peters.
WIGAN 16: Kris Radlinski; Jason Robinson, Gary Connolly, Danny Moore, Paul Johnson; Tony Smith, Gavin Clinch; Terry O'Connor, Mark Smith, Neil Cowie, Denis Betts, Mick Cassidy, Andy Farrell. Subs: Lee Gilmour, Brett Goldspink, Greg Florimo, Chris Chester.
Wigan tries: Betts 2, Farrell; G- Farrell 2.
Referee: Stuart Cummings; Half-time: 18-6; Attendance 4,978.

⑤ February 21st 2004 - Merry Halliwell

Warrington Wolves 34 ....Wakefield Trinity Wildcats 20

Nathan Wood earned a place in Warrington folklore by scoring the first ever try at the Halliwell Jones Stadium, just five minutes into this Super League clash with Wakefield Trinity Wildcats. It was typical Wood. He backed up Mike Forshaw's burst off a Chris Leikvoll pass and slid over for a touchdown that Lee Briers goaled to ensure the happiest of housewarmings for the delirious Wolves.

Almost three long years of hard work, negotiation and planning had come to fruition. Before a packed house, in a turbo-charged atmosphere, any fears that the fans might have preferred to remain at Wilderspool were swept away. Ironically, the Wildcats were the opposition in the final Super League game at the old ground exactly five months earlier, when a hat-trick of tries and 10 goals from Graham Appo brought the primrose and blue curtain down in style.

After Dean Gaskell notched Warrington's second try, goaled by Briers, Rooney added to an earlier penalty by kicking through for the scoring Ben Jeffries. A Briers penalty on the stroke of half-time gave the Wolves a narrow 14-8 interval lead. Five minutes after the restart, a magnificent solo Briers try from the base of the scrum set the crowd alight again. Mark Gleeson then put Paul Wood in before Westwood and Gaskell combined on the end of a Briers break to make Wood's second try. The new ground was rocking!

The Wildcats, though, came oh so close to spoiling the party when Gareth Ellis sparked a brilliant comeback by putting Justin Ryder in on the hour. Rooney carried on that good work by pouncing on an angled Jeffries kick and Colum Halpenny squeezed in at the corner. Warrington, though, steadied the ship and Briers' seventh goal with seconds remaining meant the celebrations could begin. Despite unbearable tension,the HJ Stadium had made a winning start.

WARRINGTON 34: Graham Appo; John Wilshere, Brent Grose, Ben Westwood, Dean Gaskell; Lee Briers, Nathan Wood; Chris Leikvoll, Jon Clarke, Mark Hilton, Darren Burns, Mike Wainwright, Mike Forshaw. Subs: Mark Gleeson, Paul Wood, Danny Lima, Paul Noone.
Warrington tries: N Wood 2, Gaskell, Briers, P Wood; G- Briers 7.
WAKEFIELD 20: Jason Demetriou; Justin Ryder, Gareth Ellis, Sid Domic, Semi Tadulala; Jamie Rooney, Ben Jeffries; Darrell Griffin, David March, Michael Korkidas, David Solomona, Dallas Hood, Jamie Field. Subs: Colum Halpenny, David Wrench, Steve Snitch, Albert Talipeau.
Wakefield tries: Jeffries, Ryder, Rooney, Halpenny; G- Rooney 2.
Referee: Ian Smith; Half time: 14-8; Attendance 14,206.

⑥ September 5th 1999 - Goodbye, Central Park

Wigan Warriors 28 ....St Helens 20

Grounds have come and gone but few matches have sparked as much emotion as the last game at Wigan's Central Park. The end finally arrived for this most famous of rugby league venues some 96 years and 364 days after it hosted its first game against Batley.

A pre-match parade of legends like Mick Sullivan, Eric Ashton, Andy Gregory and Billy Boston set the mood, with a brass band providing a melancholy backdrop. Overall, though, the day was one of celebration, with the club almost doubling its average gate for the season. Selling up to supermarket giants Tesco wasn't to everyone's taste, even if that did mean a farewell to the old 'river caves' urinals!

If anyone could rain on Wigan's parade, it was arch-enemies Saints, especially with ex-Wigan legend Ellery Hanley in charge. A Tommy Martyn penalty gave them the lead but Jason Robinson soon struck. He took a clearing kick on his own 10-metre line, weaved upfield and sent Denis Betts racing in for an opening try which Andy Farrell goaled. Paul Sculthorpe crossed for Saints but Wigan hit back when Gary Connolly claimed Wigan's second, before a Robinson 70-metre special. Even so, an Anthony Sullivan try and Martyn goal meant Wigan led just 16-12 at the break.

Home hearts fluttered when Saints levelled through Kevin Iro on the hour. But just when it looked like the hallowed turf might sign off with a defeat, 'Billy Whizz' Robinson raced over from 50 metres and Farrell added the extras. Paul Johnson claimed the fifth and final Wigan try, as Farrell landed his fourth goal. Ironically, it was a Saint - Tommy Martyn - who had the honour of scoring the ground's last-ever four-pointer. Grown men and women embraced, wiped away a tear and headed home. The following day the office staff moved out and the bulldozers moved in. Central Park was just a happy memory.

WIGAN 28: Kris Radlinski; Jason Robinson, Gary Connolly, Paul Johnson, Danny Moore; Chris Chester, Gavin Clinch; Neil Cowie, Mark Smith, Terry O'Connor, Mick Cassidy, Denis Betts, Andy Farrell. Subs: Tony Mestrov, Brett Goldspink, Simon Haughton, Lee Gilmour.
Wigan tries: Robinson 2, Connolly, Betts, Johnson; G- Farrell 4.
ST HELENS 20: Anthony Stewart; Chris Smith, Kevin Iro, Paul Newlove, Anthony Sullivan; Paul Sculthorpe, Tommy Martyn; Julian O'Neill, Keiron Cunningham, Apollo Perelini, Des Clark, Sonny Nickle, Chris Joynt. Subs: Freddie Tuilagi, Vila Matautia, Steve Hall, Gareth Price.
St Helens tries: Sculthorpe, Sullivan, Iro, Martyn; G- Martyn 2.
Referee: Stuart Cummings; Half time: 16-12; Attendance: 18,179.

⑦ October 24th 1998 - A Grand (& Wet) Day Out
Leeds Rhinos 4 ....Wigan Warriors 10

Rugby league is a game for fearless people; and not just where the players are concerned. Jason Robinson's wonderful solo try through the heart of a momentary spellbound Leeds defence might be the abiding image of the first ever Super League Grand Final, but the game was more about the future of Super League than any since that opening day clash in Paris.

It is always good to be first at anything and Wigan Warriors added to a list that includes a 1929 Wembley win over Dewsbury and their 1986 World Club Championship defeat of Manly. Yet the build-up saw the critics out in force with many predicting a sparsely-filled Theatre of Dreams and a Super League nightmare.

Their dire predictions looked like becoming reality when the pre-match heavens opened and down fell a Biblical deluge not seen since Noah built his ark. Nevertheless, almost 44,000 fans fought their way to a soggy Manchester to be rewarded not only with a sporting extravaganza, but also by a cabaret spectacular with dancing troupes, musical performers and fireworks that was nothing less than a sporting and presentational triumph. It also further enhanced the legend of John Monie. The former Parramatta boss guided Wigan to four league and cup doubles on his first spell at the club from 1989-1993, and returned to replace Eric Hughes for Super League lll.

On the field, Iestyn Harris and Ryan Sheridan combined to put Richie Blackmore in for the opener, before Robinson's wonder try from a Kris Radlinski inside pass and Andy Farrell's conversion secured a 6-4 interval lead. The only second-half scores were two Farrell goals. There were plenty of errors on the rain-sodden surface but the intensity of the defence took the domestic game to new levels. This had been winner-take-all and didn't it show?

LEEDS 4: Iestyn Harris; Leroy Rivett, Richie Blackmore, Brad Godden, Francis Cummins; Daryl Powell, Ryan Sheridan; Martin Masella, Terry Newton, Darren Fleary, Adrian Morley, Anthony Farrell, Marc Glanville. Subs: Jamie Mathiou, Marcus St Hilaire, Graham Holroyd, Andy Hay.
Leeds try: Blackmore.
WIGAN 10: Kris Radlinski; Jason Robinson, Danny Moore, Gary Connolly, Mark Bell; Henry Paul, Tony Smith; Terry O'Connor, Robbie McCormack, Tony Mestrov, Lee Gilmour, Stephen Holgate, Andy Farrell. Subs: Neil Cowie, Mick Cassidy, Paul Johnson, Simon Haughton.
Wigan try: Robinson. G- Farrell 3.
Referee: Russell Smith; Half time: 4-6; Attendance: 43,553.

8 August 8th 2003 - Revenge Not So Sweet

Leeds Rhinos 18..Bradford Bulls 20

Bruising, sometimes brutal, but with more than enough finesse and flair to keep the packed Headingley stadium on its toes to the final tackle. It was a repeat of the May Challenge Cup final, in which the Bulls had held on for a similar two-point advantage at a sold out Millennium stadium in Cardiff. Although the teams had met at Odsal since then, with Leeds winning 48-22, this was the Rhinos' chance for revenge on own turf.

At the time, it was the second-biggest crowd of the Super League era - the clash between Yorkshire's big two drawing 24,020 at Odsal in 1999 - but this time the heat and humidity were stifling. And what a ferocious start! Matt Adamson and Mike Forshaw were both yellow-carded for letting off steam before the Bulls broke the deadlock on 18 minutes. Lesley Vainikolo took Andrew Dunemann's cross-field kick on his own line and raced the length of the pitch for a breathtaking score which Paul Deacon goaled. The Rhinos upped an already high tempo by hitting pay dirt with two tries in three minutes through Gary Connolly and Keith Senior, with two Kevin Sinfield goals. Danny McGuire then broke clear and looked set for a third home score until Stuart Reardon made an incredible tackle and Leeds had to settle for a 10-6 half-time lead.

After Matt Diskin had a try ruled out by the video referee, Rob Parker got the Bulls' second-half rolling with a try that Deacon goaled for the lead. Minutes later, Forshaw was in for another Deacon goaled six-pointer before Rob Burrow and Sinfield's boot cut the margin back to two points. Incredibly, despite there being over 20 minutes to go, in a frenzied finish there were no further scores. "It was as good a defensive display in this country as I have ever seen," heralded Bulls coach, Brian Noble. Few disagreed.

LEEDS 18: Gary Connolly; Mark Calderwood, Chris McKenna, Keith Senior, Francis Cummins; Kevin Sinfield, Andrew Dunemann; Danny Ward, Matt Diskin, Barrie McDermott, David Furner, Matt Adamson, Willie Poching. Subs: Chris Feather, Wayne McDonald, Danny McGuire, Rob Burrow.
Leeds tries: Connolly, Senior, Burrow; G- Sinfield 2.
BRADFORD 20: Stuart Reardon; Tevita Vaikona, Scott Naylor, Shontayne Hape, Lesley Vainikolo; Leon Pryce, Paul Deacon; Joe Vagana, James Lowes, Paul Anderson, Lee Radford, Jamie Peacock, Mike Forshaw. Subs: Rob Parker, Stuart Fielden, Jamie Langley, Lee Gilmour.
Bradford tries: Vainikolo, Parker, Forshaw; G- Deacon 3.
Referee: Karl Kirkpatrick; Half time 10-6; Attendance 23,035.

⑨ September 10th 2005 – King "Joey" Rules, UK

Warrington Wolves 33 . . . . Leeds Rhinos 16

We came, we saw, he conquered! Andrew Johns lived up to his billing as the best player in the world with a five-star performance that fired Warrington's dreams of a Grand Final date at Old Trafford. His stay may have been short and ultimately unsuccessful, but Johns was the biggest Super League signing ever - the current Australian captain at the height of his powers. The fans lapped up every minute.

All the pre-match media hype was matched in unforgettable style on the field. When Henry Fa'afili tore in at the corner with less than 60 seconds on the clock, the man reported to be on £10,000 a game coolly slotted over the touchline conversion for a dream start.

After a Richard Mathers try and Kevin Sinfield goal levelled matters, it was a Johns penalty that edged the Wolves back in front. Yet aside from a personal haul of 13 points, it was his sublime orchestration of the players around him that was most impressive. "He extracted gears and levels from other players that I didn't think existed," enthused his temporary coach, Paul Cullen.

More tries from Martin Gleeson and Brent Grose, against a late Matt Diskin effort, made it 18-12 to Warrington at the break. But Leeds came out firing and Marcus Bai's early unconverted try left the Wolves fans sweating. Cometh the hour, cometh the man! 'Joey' reached inside his pouch of tricks, pulled out a sidestep and a couple of body swerves and sent Logan Swann charging in by the posts.

Leeds still didn't lie down and after an unlucky Danny McGuire was brought back for offside when clean away, Johns added a penalty and 72nd-minute drop-goal, before Nathan Wood took advantage of Leeds' preoccupation with the Aussie skipper and hared in for try of his own. Johns claimed afterwards: "This game was right up there with any of the big games I have ever played."

WARRINGTON 33: Brent Grose; Henry Fa'afili, Martin Gleeson, Toa Kohe-Love, Chris Bridge; Lee Briers, Andrew Johns; Chris Leikvoll, Nathan Wood, Paul Wood, Logan Swann, Paul Noone, Jon Clarke. Subs: Chris Riley, Andrew Bracek, Mark Gleeson, Danny Lima.
Warrington tries: Fa'afili, Mathers, Martin Gleeson, Grose, Swann, N Wood; G- Johns 7; DG- Johns 1.
LEEDS 16: Richard Mathers; Mark Calderwood, Chev Walker, Lee Smith, Marcus Bai; Kevin Sinfield, Rob Burrow; Jamie Jones-Buchanan, Andrew Dunemann, Danny Ward, Ali Lauitiiti; Willie Poching, Gareth Ellis. Subs: Danny McGuire, Matt Diskin, Nick Scruton, Barrie McDermott.
Leeds tries: Mathers, Diskin, Bai; G- Sinfield 2.
Referee: Ashley Klein; Half-time: 18-12; Attendance: 13,024.

10 September 18th 2004 - Relegation at the Double

Hull FC 20 .... Widnes Vikings 18
Castleford Tigers 28 .... Wakefield Trinity Wildcats 32

One 80 minutes - two great games! The relegation battle in Super League IX boiled down to one super-charged night in East and West Yorkshire. It didn't matter which game you were at. For 80 pulsating minutes, the Super League lifeblood of Castleford and Widnes ebbed and flowed until the final hooter signalled salvation for one and despair for the other.

The mathematical permutations were these: Widnes had two more league points and a +23 better points average. But Hull had hammered Widnes 70-4 earlier in the season. Anything similar, allied to a Cas win, would send Frank Endacott's boys down and reprieve the Tigers.

Semi Tadulala swept in for the first try after two minutes, to put Wakefield ahead. Castleford's Damien Gibson responded to tie the scores. In the 11th minute: Hull's Richard Whiting charged down a clearance kick, hacked on and re-gathered to score for the lead against Widnes. Tom Saxton swept in for a second Castleford try only for a Colum Halpenny touchdown and David March conversion to edge Wakefield in front again.

Back to the KC Stadium and Daniel Frame sliced through for a Jules O'Neill-goaled try. But soon the Widnes fans were groaning again as Castleford's jubilation flashed on the big screen when Paul Mellor and Michael Smith bagged Tiger touchdowns before Francis Maloney added a goal for an 18-10 lead on 23 minutes. Widnes faces were glum, especially when Hull's Whiting crashed in for his second unconverted try two minutes later. Matt Whittaker grabbed an O'Neill-goaled try three minutes from half-time to make it 12-8 to Widnes just as the Wildcats hit back at Castleford with a March penalty and conversion to a David Solomona try in the 39th minute to tie the Jungle scores at 18-18.

Solomona didn't know it, but he was proving to be the Vikings saviour, as he bamboozled his way in for his second Wakefield try on 43 minutes. Moments later, O'Neill increased the Widnes lead with a penalty-goal. Paul Handforth crossed for the Wildcats and his goal pushed Castleford 10 points adrift. Widnes fans started to celebrate, but their joy was dampened when Richie Barnett Jr and Peter Lupton claimed un-goaled Hull tries in quick succession.

Even so, Castleford could see their Super League life dripping away before a second Mellor try gave them hope in the last quarter. Cruelly, though, Solomona made room for Halpenny's second and for Castleford the writing was well and truly on the wall. Widnes celebrated with a Sala Fa'alogo try but then fell behind to a Colin Best effort with 10 minutes remaining, as Wayne Godwin kept a flicker of hope alive at the Jungle with a sixth Tigers touchdown.

But the hooter at the Jungle sounded four minutes earlier than at Hull and as realisation of safety dawned, 'Happy' Frank Endacott had a smile as wide as the Humber. Widnes stayed up and Castleford were down for the first time since joining the Rugby Football League in 1926.

HULL 20: Shaun Briscoe; Colin Best, Kirk Yeaman, Gareth Raynor, Richie Barnett Jr; Richard Whiting, Peter Lupton; Nick Scruton, Richard Swain, Ewan Dowes, Andy Bailey, Paul McNicholas, Graeme Horne. Subs: Richard Fletcher, Garreth Carvell, Liam Higgins, Andy Last.
Hull tries: Whiting 2, Barnett, Lupton, Best.
WIDNES 18: Tim Holmes; Paul Devlin, Deon Bird, Adam Hughes, Justin Murphy; Jules O'Neill, Stephen Myler; David Mills, Shane Millard, Steve McCurrie, Daniel Frame, Andy Hay, Simon Finnigan. Subs: Matt Whittaker, Andy Hobson, Tom Gallagher, Sala Fa'alogo.
Widnes tries: Frame, Whittaker, Fa'alogo. G- O'Neill 3.
Referee: Richard Silverwood; Half-time: 8-12; Attendance 9,544.

CASTLEFORD 28: Damien Gibson; Waine Pryce, Paul Mellor, Tom Saxton, Darren Rogers; Brad Davis, Francis Maloney; Craig Greenhill, Wayne Godwin, Andy Lynch, Lee Harland, Michael Smith, Ryan Hudson. Subs: Nathan Sykes, Mark Tookey, Jon Hepworth, Paul Jackson.
Castleford tries: Gibson, Saxton, Mellor 2, Smith, Godwin; G- Maloney 2.
WAKEFIELD 32: Mark Field; Colum Halpenny, Jason Demetriou, Sid Domic, Semi Tadulala; Gareth Ellis, Ben Jeffries; Chris Feather, David March, Michael Korkidas, David Solomona, Duncan MacGillivray, Rob Spicer. Subs: Darrell Griffin, Paul Handforth, Oliver Elima, Justin Ryder.
Wakefield tries: Tadulala, Halpenny 2, Solomona 2, Handforth; G- March 3, Handforth.
Referee: Ian Smith; Half-time: 18-18; Attendance: 11,055.

● *Trevor Hunt has been a rugby league commentator with BBC GMR for 20 years and a freelance writer on the sport for over three decades. A former University International, amateur player with Leigh Miners and BARLA Tour manager, he has reported on games from all over France along with equally exotic locations such as the Cook Islands, Fiji, New Zealand, Samoa, Tonga, South Africa, Millom and Beverley.*

Statistical Records

SUPER LEAGUE I   1996

Champions: St Helens. Runners–up: Wigan Warriors.

STONES SUPER LEAGUE FINAL TABLE

	P	W	D	L	F	A	D	PTS
St Helens	22	20	0	2	950	455	495	40
Wigan	22	19	1	2	902	326	576	39
Bradford	22	17	0	5	767	409	358	34
London	22	12	1	9	611	462	149	25
Warrington	22	12	0	10	569	565	4	24
Halifax	22	10	1	11	667	576	91	21
Sheffield	22	10	0	12	599	730	-131	20
Oldham	22	9	1	12	473	681	-208	19
Castleford	22	9	0	13	548	599	-51	18
Leeds	22	6	0	16	555	745	-190	12
Paris	22	3	1	18	398	795	-397	7
Workington	22	2	1	19	325	1021	-696	5

● All individual records on the following pages include play-offs & Grand Finals. They do not include WCC, Premiership or Challenge Cup games

TOP TRY SCORERS
1 Paul Newlove
   St Helens 28
2 Jason Robinson
   Wigan...............................24
3 John Bentley
   Halifax.............................21
4 Henry Paul
   Wigan...............................20
5 Danny Arnold
   St Helens 19

TOP GOAL KICKERS
1 Bobbie Goulding
   St Helens.......................117
2 Andy Farrell
   Wigan.............................103
3 John Schuster
   Halifax..........................101
4 Mark Aston
   Sheffield.........................86
5 Frano Botica
   Castleford 84

TOP POINTS SCORERS
1 Bobbie Goulding
   St Helens 257
2 John Schuster
   Halifax..........................236
3 Andy Farrell
   Wigan.............................226
4 Graham Holroyd
   Leeds 198
5 Frano Botica
   Castleford 190

● *The 1996 Super League Championship was decided by a first-past-the-post system*

PREMIERSHIP SEMI-FINALS
Wigan 42 ....Bradford 36
St Helens 25 ....London 14

PREMIERSHIP FINAL
Wigan 44 ....St Helens 14

HARRY SUNDERLAND AWARD WINNER
Andy Farrell (*Wigan*)

1995 PRE-SUPER LEAGUE AVERAGE ATTENDANCES
Wigan...............................11,947
Leeds...............................11,594
St Helens..........................7,143
Castleford.........................5,012
Warrington 4,922
Halifax..............................4,657
Bradford............................4,593
Oldham 3,187
Sheffield...........................3,106
Workington 3,061
London..............................2,386
Paris ....N/A

MAN OF STEEL
Andy Farrell (*Wigan*)

COACH OF THE YEAR
Shaun McRae (*St Helens*)

YOUNG PLAYER OF THE YEAR
Keiron Cunningham (*St Helens*)

PLAYER OF THE YEAR
Robbie Paul (*Bradford*)

RUGBY LEAGUE WRITERS PLAYER OF THE YEAR
Apollo Perelini (*St Helens*)

CHALLENGE CUP FINAL
Bradford 32 ....St Helens 40

LANCE TODD WINNER
Robbie Paul (*Bradford*)

AVERAGE ATTENDANCES
Bradford...........................10,346
St Helens..........................10,221
Wigan...............................10,152
Leeds.................................8,581
Paris 8,092
London...............................5,418
Warrington 5,157
Halifax 5,080
Castleford...........................4,072
Sheffield.............................4,534
Oldham 3,629
Workington 2,322

SUPER LEAGUE II 1997

Champions: Bradford Bulls. Runners–up: London Broncos.

STONES SUPER LEAGUE FINAL TABLE

	P	W	D	L	F	A	D	PTS
Bradford	22	20	0	2	769	397	372	40
London	22	15	3	4	616	418	198	33
St Helens	22	14	1	7	592	506	86	29
Wigan	22	14	0	8	683	398	285	28
Leeds	22	13	1	8	544	463	81	27
Salford	22	11	0	11	428	495	-67	22
Halifax	22	8	2	12	524	549	-25	18
Sheffield	22	9	0	13	415	574	-159	18
Warrington	22	8	0	14	437	647	-210	16
Castleford	22	5	2	15	334	515	-181	12
Paris	22	6	0	16	362	572	-210	12
Oldham	22	4	1	17	461	631	-170	9

TOP TRY SCORERS
1 Nigel Vagana
  Warrington......................17
2 Paul Sterling
  Leeds 15
= Alan Hunte
  St Helens 15
= Anthony Sullivan
  St Helens 15
= Jason Robinson
  Wigan..............................15
= Tony Smith
  Wigan..............................15

TOP GOAL KICKERS
1 Andy Farrell
  Wigan............................106
2 Steve McNamara
  Bradford 98
3 Mark Aston
  Sheffield..........................74
4 Steve Blakeley
  Salford 73
5 Iestyn Harris
  Leeds 63

TOP POINTS SCORERS
1 Andy Farrell
  Wigan............................243
2 Steve McNamara
  Bradford 225
3 Steve Blakeley
  Salford 171
4 Mark Aston
  Sheffield........................161
5 Iestyn Harris
  Leeds 155

● *The 1997 Super League Championship was decided by a first-past-the-post system*

● The 1997 Premiership competition was contested by all 12 teams, with the bottom eight in a preliminary round

PREMIERSHIP PRELIMINARY ROUND
Halifax 18 ....Castleford 23
Salford 48 ....Paris 6
Sheffield 26 ....Warrington 16
Leeds 42...................Oldham 14

PREMIERSHIP QUARTER-FINALS
Bradford 12 ....Castleford 25
London 16 ....Sheffield 58
St Helens 26..............Salford 12
Wigan 38 ....Leeds 22

PREMIERSHIP SEMI-FINALS
St Helens 32.........Castleford 18
Wigan 22 ....Sheffield 10

PREMIERSHIP FINAL
St Helens 20 ....Wigan 33

HARRY SUNDERLAND AWARD WINNER
Andy Farrell (*Wigan*)

MAN OF STEEL
James Lowes (*Bradford*)

COACH OF THE YEAR
Matthew Elliott (*Bradford*)

YOUNG PLAYER OF THE YEAR
Lee Briers (*Warrington*)

PLAYER OF THE YEAR
James Lowes (*Bradford*)

RUGBY LEAGUE WRITERS PLAYER OF THE YEAR
Andy Farrell (*Wigan*)

CHALLENGE CUP FINAL
St Helens 32 ....Bradford 22

LANCE TODD WINNER
Tommy Martyn (*St Helens*)

AVERAGE ATTENDANCES
Bradford..........................15,159
Leeds..............................11,005
Wigan..............................8,866
St Helens..........................8,824
Paris 5,489
Halifax 5,408
Warrington 5,404
Salford 5,202
London.............................5,076
Castleford.........................5,004
Sheffield..........................4,310
Oldham 3,453

SUPER LEAGUE III   1998

Champions: Wigan Warriors. Runners–up: Leeds Rhinos.

JJB SPORTS SUPER LEAGUE FINAL TABLE

	P	W	D	L	F	A	D	PTS
Wigan	23	21	0	2	762	222	540	42
Leeds	23	19	0	4	662	369	293	38
Halifax	23	18	0	5	658	390	268	36
St Helens	23	14	1	8	673	459	214	29
Bradford	23	12	0	11	498	450	48	24
Castleford	23	10	1	12	446	522	-76	21
London	23	10	0	13	415	476	-61	20
Sheffield	23	8	2	13	495	541	-46	18
Hull	23	8	0	15	421	574	-153	16
Warrington	23	7	1	15	411	645	-234	15
Salford	23	6	1	16	319	575	-256	13
Huddersfield	23	2	0	21	288	825	-537	4

ELIMINATION PLAY-OFF
St Helens 46 .... Bradford 24

QUALIFYING PLAY-OFF
Leeds 13 .... Halifax 6

ELIMINATION SEMI-FINAL
Halifax 30 .... St Helens 37

QUALIFYING SEMI-FINAL
Wigan 17 .... Leeds 4

ELIMINATION PLAY-OFF
St Helens 46 .... Bradford 24

FINAL ELIMINATOR
Leeds 44 .... St Helens 16

GRAND FINAL
Wigan 10 .... Leeds 4

LEEDS: Iestyn Harris (C); Leroy Rivett; Richie Blackmore; Brad Godden; Francis Cummins; Daryl Powell; Ryan Sheridan; Martin Masella; Terry Newton; Darren Fleary; Adrian Morley; Anthony Farrell; Marc Glanville. *Subs*: Jamie Mathiou; Marcus St Hilaire; Graham Holroyd; Andy Hay. *Try*: Blackmore (20). WIGAN: Kris Radlinski; Jason Robinson; Danny Moore; Gary Connolly; Mark Bell; Henry Paul; Tony Smith; Terry O'Connor; Robbie McCormack; Tony Mestrov; Lee Gilmour; Stephen Holgate; Andy Farrell (C). *Subs*: Neil Cowie; Mick Cassidy; Paul Johnson; Simon Haughton. *Try*: Robinson (37). *Goals*: Farrell 3. *Referee*: Russell Smith (Castleford). *Half-time*: 4-6. *Attendance*: 43,553.

HARRY SUNDERLAND AWARD WINNER
Jason Robinson (*Wigan*)

TOP TRY SCORERS
1   Anthony Sullivan
     St Helens 24
2   Francis Cummins
     Leeds 21
3   Paul Newlove
     St Helens 17
4   Gary Connolly
     Wigan 15
=   Tony Smith
     Wigan 15

TOP GOAL KICKERS
1   Andy Farrell
     Wigan 120
2   Iestyn Harris
     Leeds 110
3   Sean Long
     St Helens 86
4   Steve McNamara
     Bradford 77
5   Martin Pearson
     Halifax 69

TOP POINTS SCORERS
1   Iestyn Harris
     Leeds 275
2   Andy Farrell
     Wigan 265
3   Sean Long
     St Helens 227
4   Steve McNamara
     Bradford 161
5   Martin Pearson
     Halifax 154

MAN OF STEEL
Iestyn Harris (*Leeds*)

COACH OF THE YEAR
John Pendlebury (*Halifax*)

YOUNG PLAYER OF THE YEAR
Lee Gilmour (*Wigan*)

PLAYERS' PLAYER
Iestyn Harris (*Leeds*)

RUGBY LEAGUE WRITERS PLAYER OF THE YEAR
Iestyn Harris (*Leeds*)

CHALLENGE CUP FINAL
Sheffield 17 .... Wigan 8

LANCE TODD WINNER
Mark Aston (*Sheffield*)

AVERAGE ATTENDANCES
Bradford 13,026
Leeds 12,111
Wigan 10,803
St Helens 7,238
Castleford 6,395
Hull 5,741
Halifax 5,651
Huddersfield 5,142
Warrington 4,897
Salford 4,675
Sheffield 4,595
London 3,625

SUPER LEAGUE IV   1999

Champions: St Helens. Runners–up: Bradford Bulls.

JJB SPORTS SUPER LEAGUE FINAL TABLE

	P	W	D	L	F	A	D	PTS
Bradford	30	25	1	4	897	445	452	51
St Helens	30	23	0	7	1034	561	473	46
Leeds	30	22	1	7	910	558	352	45
Wigan	30	21	1	8	877	390	487	43
Castleford	30	19	3	8	712	451	261	41
Gateshead	30	19	1	10	775	576	199	39
Warrington	30	15	1	14	700	717	-17	31
London	30	13	2	15	644	708	-64	28
Halifax	30	11	0	19	573	792	-219	22
Sheffield	30	10	1	19	518	818	-300	21
Wakefield	30	10	0	20	608	795	-187	20
Salford	30	6	1	23	526	916	-390	13
Hull	30	5	0	25	422	921	-499	10
Huddersfield	30	5	0	25	463	1011	-548	10

QUALIFYING PLAY-OFF
St Helens 38 .... Leeds 14

ELIMINATION PLAY-OFF
Wigan 10 .... Castleford 14

ELIMINATION SEMI-FINAL
Leeds 16 .... Castleford 23

QUALIFYING SEMI-FINAL
Bradford 40 .... St Helens 4

ELIMINATION PLAY-OFF
St Helens 46 .... Bradford 24

FINAL ELIMINATOR
St Helens 36 .... Castleford 6

GRAND FINAL
Bradford 6 .... St Helens 8

BRADFORD: Stuart Spruce; Tevita Vaikona; Scott Naylor; Michael Withers; Leon Pryce; Henry Paul; Robbie Paul (C); Paul Anderson; James Lowes; Stuart Fielden; David Boyle; Bernard Dwyer; Steve McNamara.
Subs: Paul Deacon; Nathan McAvoy; Mike Forshaw; Brian McDermott.
Try: H Paul (18). *Goal*: H Paul.
ST HELENS: Paul Atcheson; Chris Smith; Kevin Iro; Paul Newlove; Anthony Sullivan; Paul Sculthorpe; Tommy Martyn; Apollo Perelini; Keiron Cunningham; Julian O'Neill; Fereti Tuilagi; Sonny Nickle; Chris Joynt (C).
Subs: Paul Wellens; Sean Hoppe; Vila Matautia; Sean Long.
Tries: Iro (65). *Goals*: Long 2.
Referee: Stuart Cummings (Widnes).
Half-time: 6-2. *Attendance*: 50,717.

HARRY SUNDERLAND AWARD WINNER
Henry Paul (*Bradford*)

TOP TRY SCORERS
1 Anthony Sullivan
  St Helens 27
2 Matt Daylight
  Gateshead 25
= Francis Cummins
  Leeds 25
= Toa Kohe-Love
  Warrington 25

TOP GOAL KICKERS
1 Iestyn Harris
  Leeds 135
2 Sean Long
  St Helens 108
3 Ian Herron
  Gateshead 105
4 Andy Farrell
  Wigan 96
5 Steve McNamara
  Bradford 95

TOP POINTS SCORERS
1 Iestyn Harris
  Leeds 343
2 Sean Long
  St Helens 306
3 Ian Herron
  Gateshead 226
4 Andy Farrell
  Wigan 213

CHALLENGE CUP FINAL
Leeds 52 .... London 16

LANCE TODD WINNER
Leroy Rivett (*Leeds*)

MAN OF STEEL
Adrian Vowles (*Castleford*)

COACH OF THE YEAR
Matthew Elliott (*Bradford*)

YOUNG PLAYER OF THE YEAR
Leon Pryce (*Bradford*)

PLAYERS' PLAYER
Sean Long (*St Helens*)

RUGBY LEAGUE WRITERS PLAYER OF THE YEAR
Iestyn Harris (*Leeds*)

RUGBY LEAGUE WORLD GOLDEN BOOT
Andrew Johns (*Australia*)

AVERAGE ATTENDANCES
Leeds 13,703
Bradford 13,398
Wigan 9,466
St Helens 8,460
Castleford 6,877
Warrington 5,110
Salford 4,505
Halifax 4,483
Hull 4,346
Wakefield 4,235
Gateshead 3,895
Huddersfield 3,727
Sheffield 3,590
London 2,935

231

SUPER LEAGUE V   2000

Champions: St Helens. Runners–up: Wigan Warriors.

TETLEY'S SUPER LEAGUE FINAL TABLE

	P	W	D	L	F	A	D	PTS
Wigan	28	24	1	3	960	405	555	49
St Helens	28	23	0	5	988	627	361	46
Bradford	28	20	3	5	1004	408	596	43
Leeds	28	17	0	11	692	626	66	34
Castleford	28	17	0	11	585	571	14	34
Warrington	28	13	0	15	735	817	-82	26
Hull	28	12	1	15	630	681	-51	25
Halifax	28	11	1	16	664	703	-39	23
Salford	28	10	0	18	542	910	-368	20
Wakefield	28	8	0	20	557	771	-214	16
London	28	6	0	22	456	770	-314	12
Hudds-Sheff	28	4	0	24	502	1026	-524	8

QUALIFYING PLAY-OFF
St Helens 16 ....Bradford 11

QUALIFYING PLAY-OFF
Leeds 22 ....Castleford 14

QUALIFYING SEMI-FINAL
Wigan 16 ....St Helens 54

ELIMINATION SEMI-FINAL
Bradford 46 ....Leeds 12

FINAL ELIMINATOR
Wigan 40 ....Bradford 12

GRAND FINAL
St Helens 29 ....Wigan 16

ST HELENS: Paul Wellens; Steve Hall; Kevin Iro; Sean Hoppe; Anthony Sullivan; Tommy Martyn; Sean Long; Apollo Perelini; Keiron Cunningham; Julian O'Neill; Chris Joynt (C); Tim Jonkers; Paul Sculthorpe.
Subs: Fereti Tuilagi; Sonny Nickle; John Stankevitch; Scott Barrow.
Tries: Hoppe (7), Joynt (28, 50), Tuilagi (69), Jonkers (80). *Goals*: Long 4.
Drop-goal: Sculthorpe.
WIGAN: Jason Robinson; Brett Dallas; Kris Radlinski; Steve Renouf; David Hodgson; Tony Smith; Willie Peters; Terry O'Connor; Terry Newton; Neil Cowie; Mick Cassidy; Denis Betts; Andy Farrell (C).
Subs: Brady Malam; Tony Mestrov; Chris Chester; Lee Gilmour.
Tries: Farrell (13), Hodgson (58), Smith (61). *Goals*: Farrell 2.
Referee: Russell Smith (Castleford).
Half-time: 11-4. *Attendance*: 58,132.

HARRY SUNDERLAND AWARD WINNER
Chris Joynt (*St Helens*)

TOP TRY SCORERS
1 Sean Long
  St Helens 22
  Tommy Martyn
  St Helens 22
3 Darren Rogers
  Castleford........................20
= Steve Renouf
  Wigan 20
= Jason Robinson
  Wigan 20

TOP GOAL KICKERS
1 Andy Farrell
  Wigan 160
2 Sean Long
  St Helens 151
3 Henry Paul
  Bradford 150
4 Iestyn Harris
  Leeds 106
5 Steve Blakeley
  Salford & Warrington 72

TOP POINTS SCORERS
1 Sean Long
  St Helens 390
2 Andy Farrell
  Wigan 357
3 Henry Paul
  Bradford 342
4 Iestyn Harris
  Leeds 256
5 Lee Briers
  Warrington 179

RUGBY LEAGUE WORLD GOLDEN BOOT
Brad Fittler (*Australia*)

MAN OF STEEL
Sean Long (*St Helens*)

COACH OF THE YEAR
Frank Endacott (*Wigan*)

YOUNG PLAYER OF THE YEAR
Stuart Fielden (*Bradford*)

PLAYERS' PLAYER
Tommy Martyn (*St Helens*)

RUGBY LEAGUE WRITERS PLAYER OF THE YEAR
Tommy Martyn (*St Helens*)

CHALLENGE CUP FINAL
Bradford 24 ....Leeds 18

LANCE TODD WINNER
Henry Paul (*Bradford*)

AVERAGE ATTENDANCES
Bradford....................15,350
Leeds...............................12,740
Wigan.............................11,329
St Helens..........................8,830
Castleford.........................7,975
Warrington 6,872
Hull..................................5,943
Halifax 5,714
Wakefield..........................4,615
Salford 4,448
Huddersfield-Sheffield 3,422
London...............................3,419

SUPER LEAGUE VI   2001

Champions: Bradford Bulls. Runners-up: Wigan Warriors.

TETLEY'S SUPER LEAGUE FINAL TABLE

	P	W	D	L	F	A	D	PTS
Bradford	28	22	1	5	1120	474	646	45
Wigan	28	22	1	5	989	494	495	45
Hull	28	20	2	6	772	630	142	42
St Helens	28	17	2	9	924	732	192	36
Leeds	28	16	1	11	774	721	53	33
London	28	13	1	14	644	603	41	27
Warrington	28	11	2	15	646	860	-214	24
Castleford	28	10	1	17	581	777	-196	21
Halifax	28	9	0	19	630	819	-189	18
Salford	28	8	0	20	587	956	-369	16
Wakefield*	28	8	0	20	529	817	-288	14
Huddersfield	28	6	1	21	613	926	-313	13

* Wakefield deducted two points for breach of salary cap

QUALIFYING PLAY-OFF
Wigan 27 ....Hull 24

ELIMINATION PLAY-OFF
St Helens 38................Leeds 30

ELIMINATION SEMI-FINAL
Hull 20 ....St Helens 24

QUALIFYING SEMI-FINAL
Bradford 24 ....Wigan 18

FINAL ELIMINATOR
Wigan 44 ....St Helens 10

GRAND FINAL
Bradford 37 ....Wigan 6

BRADFORD: Michael Withers; Tevita Vaikona; Scott Naylor; Graham Mackay; Leon Pryce; Henry Paul; Robbie Paul (C); Joe Vagana; James Lowes; Brian McDermott; Daniel Gartner; Jamie Peacock; Mike Forshaw.
Subs: Stuart Fielden; Paul Anderson; Shane Rigon; Paul Deacon.
Tries: Lowes (9), Withers (11, 27, 31), Fielden (65), Mackay (72).
Goals: H Paul 5, Mackay. *Drop-goal*: H Paul.
WIGAN: Kris Radlinski; Brett Dallas; Gary Connolly; Steve Renouf; Brian Carney; Matthew Johns; Adrian Lam; Terry O'Connor; Terry Newton; Harvey Howard; Mick Cassidy; David Furner; 13 Andy Farrell (C).
Subs: Paul Johnson; Neil Cowie; Denis Betts; Chris Chester.
Try: Lam (63). *Goal*: Furner.
Referee: Stuart Cummings (Widnes).
Half-time: 26-0. *Attendance*: 60,164

HARRY SUNDERLAND AWARD WINNER
Michael Withers (*Bradford*)

TOP TRY SCORERS
1 Kris Radlinski
  Wigan 30
2 Michael Withers
  Bradford 25
3 Paul Sculthorpe
  St Helens 24
4 Tevita Vaikona
  Bradford 22
= Tonie Carroll
  Leeds 22

TOP GOAL KICKERS
1 Henry Paul
  Bradford 178
2 Andy Farrell
  Wigan 176
3 Paul Sculthorpe
  St Helens 82
4 Lee Briers
  Warrington 79
5 Iestyn Harris
  Leeds 76

TOP POINTS SCORERS
1 Andy Farrell
  Wigan 425
2 Henry Paul
  Bradford 392
3 Paul Sculthorpe
  St Helens 260
4 Lee Briers
  Warrington 186
5 Iestyn Harris
  Leeds 185

RUGBY LEAGUE WORLD GOLDEN BOOT
Andrew Johns (*Australia*)

MAN OF STEEL
Paul Sculthorpe (*St Helens*)

COACH OF THE YEAR
Ian Millward (*St Helens*)

YOUNG PLAYER OF THE YEAR
Rob Burrow (*Leeds*)

PLAYERS' PLAYER
Paul Sculthorpe (*St Helens*)

RUGBY LEAGUE WRITERS PLAYER OF THE YEAR
Paul Sculthorpe (*St Helens*)

CHALLENGE CUP FINAL
Bradford 6 ....St Helens 13

LANCE TODD WINNER
Sean Long (*St Helens*)

AVERAGE ATTENDANCES
Leeds................12,881
Bradford........................12,379
Wigan................11,795
St Helens........................8,779
Castleford....................7,102
Hull 6,710
Warrington........................6,422
Halifax 4,832
Salford 4,170
Huddersfield 3,681
Wakefield........................3,651
London................3,177

233

SUPER LEAGUE VII 2002

Champions: St Helens. Runners–up: Bradford Bulls.

TETLEY'S SUPER LEAGUE FINAL TABLE

	P	W	D	L	F	A	D	PTS
St Helens	28	23	0	5	927	522	405	46
Bradford	28	23	0	5	910	519	391	46
Wigan	28	19	1	8	817	475	342	39
Leeds	28	17	0	11	865	700	165	34
Hull	28	16	0	12	742	674	68	32
Castleford	28	14	2	12	736	615	121	30
Widnes	28	14	1	13	590	716	-126	29
London	28	13	1	14	661	635	26	27
Halifax	28	8	0	20	558	856	-298	16
Warrington	28	7	0	21	483	878	-395	14
Wakefield	28	5	2	21	566	899	-333	12
Salford	28	5	1	22	490	856	-366	11

ELIMINATION PLAY-OFF
Leeds 36 .... Hull 22

ELIMINATION PLAY-OFF
Wigan 26 .... Castleford 14

ELIMINATION SEMI-FINAL
Wigan 41 .... Leeds 18

QUALIFYING SEMI-FINAL
St Helens 26 .... Bradford 28

FINAL ELIMINATOR
St Helens 24 .... Wigan 8

GRAND FINAL
Bradford 18 .... St Helens 19

BRADFORD: Michael Withers; Tevita Vaikona; Scott Naylor; Brandon Costin; Lesley Vainikolo; Robbie Paul (C); Paul Deacon; Joe Vagana; James Lowes; Stuart Fielden; Daniel Gartner; Jamie Peacock; Mike Forshaw. *Subs*: Lee Gilmour; Paul Anderson; Brian McDermott; Leon Pryce.
Tries: Naylor (3), Paul (44), Withers (47).
Goals: Deacon 3.
ST HELENS: Paul Wellens; Darren Albert; Martin Gleeson; Paul Newlove; Anthony Stewart; Paul Sculthorpe; Sean Long; Darren Britt; Keiron Cunningham; Barry Ward; Mike Bennett; Tim Jonkers; Chris Joynt (C). *Subs*: Sean Hoppe; Peter Shiels; John Stankevitch; Mick Higham.
Tries: Bennett (24), Long (32), Gleeson (56).
Goals: Long 3. *Drop-goal*: Long.
Referee: Russell Smith (Castleford).
Half-time: 12-8. *Attendance*: 61,138.

HARRY SUNDERLAND AWARD WINNER
Paul Deacon (*Bradford*)

TOP TRY SCORERS
1 Dennis Moran
  London 22
2 Mark Calderwood
  Leeds 21
= Keith Senior
  Leeds 21
4 Tevita Vaikona
  Bradford 19
= Darren Albert
  St Helens 19

TOP GOAL KICKERS
1 Paul Deacon
  Bradford 147
2 Paul Sculthorpe
  St Helens 113
3 Wayne Bartrim
  Castleford 104
4 Ben Walker
  Leeds 100
5 Matt Crowther
  Hull 91
Tony Martin
  London 91

TOP POINT SCORERS
1 Paul Deacon
  Bradford 319
2 Paul Sculthorpe
  St Helens 287
3 Wayne Bartrim
  Castleford 240
4 Ben Walker
  Leeds 232
5 Matt Crowther
  Hull 222

RUGBY LEAGUE WORLD GOLDEN BOOT
Stacey Jones (*New Zealand*)

MAN OF STEEL
Paul Sculthorpe (*St Helens*)

COACH OF THE YEAR
Neil Kelly (*Widnes*)

YOUNG PLAYER OF THE YEAR
Richard Horne (*Hull*)

PLAYERS' PLAYER
Adrian Lam (*Wigan*)

RUGBY LEAGUE WRITERS PLAYER OF THE YEAR
Adrian Lam (*Wigan*)

CHALLENGE CUP FINAL
St Helens 12 .... Wigan 21

LANCE TODD WINNER
Kris Radlinski (*Wigan*)

AVERAGE ATTENDANCES
Leeds 12,192
Bradford 11,524
St Helens 10,580
Wigan 10,480
Hull 6,928
Castleford 6,914
Widnes 6,584
Warrington 6,153
Salford 4,199
Halifax 4,080
Wakefield 3,890
London 3,760

SUPER LEAGUE VIII 2003

Champions: Bradford Bulls. Runners–up: Wigan Warriors.

TETLEY'S SUPER LEAGUE FINAL TABLE

	P	W	D	L	F	A	D	PTS
Bradford	28	22	0	6	878	529	349	44
Leeds	28	19	3	6	751	555	196	41
Wigan	28	19	2	7	776	512	264	40
St Helens*	28	16	1	11	845	535	310	31
London	28	14	2	12	643	696	-53	30
Warrington	28	14	1	13	748	619	129	29
Hull*	28	13	3	12	701	577	124	27
Castleford	28	12	1	15	612	633	-21	25
Widnes	28	12	1	15	640	727	-87	25
Huddersfield	28	11	1	16	628	715	-87	23
Wakefield	28	7	1	20	505	774	-269	15
Halifax*	28	1	0	27	372	1227	-855	0

* St Helens, Hull & Halifax deducted two points each for breach of salary cap

ELIMINATION PLAY-OFF
St Helens 24 ....London 6

ELIMINATION PLAY-OFF
Wigan 25 ....Warrington 12

ELIMINATION SEMI-FINAL
Wigan 40 ....St Helens 24

QUALIFYING SEMI-FINAL
Bradford 30 ....Leeds 14

FINAL ELIMINATOR
Leeds 22 ....Wigan 23

GRAND FINAL
Bradford 25 ....Wigan 12

BRADFORD: Stuart Reardon; Tevita Vaikona; Michael Withers; Shontayne Hape; Lesley Vainikolo; Karl Pratt; Paul Deacon; Joe Vagana; James Lowes; Stuart Fielden; Daniel Gartner; Jamie Peacock; Mike Forshaw.
Subs: Paul Anderson; Lee Radford; Leon Pryce; Robbie Paul (C).
Tries: Reardon (51), Hape (59), Lowes (75).
Goals: Deacon 6. Drop-goal: Deacon.
WIGAN: Kris Radlinski; Brian Carney; Martin Aspinwall; David Hodgson; Brett Dallas; Sean O'Loughlin; Luke Robinson; Quentin Pongia; Terry Newton; Craig Smith; Mick Cassidy; Danny Tickle; Andy Farrell (C).
Subs: Paul Johnson; Terry O'Connor; Gareth Hock; Mark Smith.
Tries: Tickle (17), Radlinski (72).
Goals: Farrell 2.
Referee: Karl Kirkpatrick (Warrington).
Half-time: 4-6. Attendance: 65,537.

HARRY SUNDERLAND AWARD WINNER
Stuart Reardon (*Bradford*)

TOP TRY SCORERS
1 Dennis Moran
   London 24
2 Graham Appo
   Warrington 23
3 Lesley Vainikolo
   Bradford 22
4 Mark Calderwood
   Leeds 20
5 Brandon Costin
   Huddersfield 19
= Colin Best
   Hull 19

TOP GOAL KICKERS
1 Paul Deacon
   Bradford 137
2 Kevin Sinfield
   Leeds 112
3 Sean Long
   St Helens 98
4 Jules O'Neill
   Wigan & Widnes 95
5 Andy Farrell
   Wigan 88

TOP POINTS SCORERS
1 Paul Deacon
   Bradford 313
2 Sean Long
   St Helens 249
3 Kevin Sinfield
   Leeds 242
4 Graham Appo
   Warrington 216
= Jules O'Neill
   Wigan & Widnes 216

RUGBY LEAGUE WORLD GOLDEN BOOT
Darren Lockyer (*Australia*)

MAN OF STEEL
Jamie Peacock (*Bradford*)

COACH OF THE YEAR
Brian Noble (*Bradford*)

YOUNG PLAYER OF THE YEAR
Gareth Hock (*Wigan*)

PLAYERS' PLAYER
Jamie Peacock (*Bradford*)

RUGBY LEAGUE WRITERS PLAYER OF THE YEAR
Jamie Peacock (*Bradford*)

CHALLENGE CUP FINAL
Bradford 22 ....Leeds 20

LANCE TODD WINNER
Gary Connolly (*Leeds*)

AVERAGE ATTENDANCES
Bradford.........................15,259
Leeds..............................13,143
Hull 11,598
Wigan..............................11,217
St Helens.........................9,643
Castleford.......................7,199
Warrington 7,031
Widnes 6,511
Huddersfield 4,722
Wakefield........................4,017
London............................3,546
Halifax 2,977

SUPER LEAGUE IX 2004

Champions: Leeds Rhinos. Runners–up: Bradford Bulls.

TETLEY'S SUPER LEAGUE FINAL TABLE

	P	W	D	L	F	A	D	PTS
Leeds	28	24	2	2	1037	443	594	50
Bradford	28	20	1	7	918	565	353	41
Hull	28	19	2	7	843	478	365	40
Wigan	28	17	4	7	736	558	178	38
St Helens	28	17	1	10	821	662	159	35
Wakefield	28	15	0	13	788	662	126	30
Huddersfield	28	12	0	16	518	757	-239	24
Warrington	28	10	1	17	700	715	-15	21
Salford	28	8	0	20	507	828	-321	16
London	28	7	1	20	561	968	-407	15
Widnes	28	7	0	21	466	850	-384	14
Castleford	28	6	0	22	515	924	-409	12

ELIMINATION PLAY-OFF
Hull 18..................Wakefield 28

ELIMINATION PLAY-OFF
Wigan 18...............St Helens 12

ELIMINATION SEMI-FINAL
Wigan 18..............Wakefield 14

QUALIFYING SEMI-FINAL
Leeds 12.................Bradford 26

FINAL ELIMINATOR
Leeds 40.....................Wigan 12

GRAND FINAL
Bradford 8....................Leeds 16

BRADFORD: Michael Withers; Stuart Reardon; Paul Johnson; Shontayne Hape; Lesley Vainikolo; Iestyn Harris; Paul Deacon; Joe Vagana; Robbie Paul (C); Stuart Fielden; Jamie Peacock; Logan Swann; Lee Radford. *Subs*: Paul Anderson; Karl Pratt; Rob Parker; Jamie Langley.
Tries: Vainikolo (7), Hape (43).
LEEDS: Richard Mathers; Mark Calderwood; Chev Walker; Keith Senior; Marcus Bai; Kevin Sinfield (C); Danny McGuire; Danny Ward; Matt Diskin; Ryan Bailey; Chris McKenna; Ali Lauitiiti; David Furner. *Subs*: Willie Poching; Barrie McDermott; Rob Burrow; Jamie Jones-Buchanan.
Tries: Diskin (15), McGuire (75).
Goals: Sinfield 4.
Referee: Steve Ganson (St Helens).
Half-time: 4-10. *Attendance*: 65,547.

HARRY SUNDERLAND
AWARD WINNER
Matt Diskin (*Leeds*)

TOP TRY SCORERS
1 Lesley Vainikolo
  Bradford 38
= Danny McGuire
  Leeds.................................38
3 Marcus Bai
  Leeds.................................26
4 Shontayne Hape
  Bradford 24
5 Shaun Briscoe
  Hull 22
= Sid Domic
  Wakefield 22

TOP GOAL KICKERS
1 Kevin Sinfield
  Leeds...............................140
2 Paul Deacon
  Bradford 123
3 Paul Cooke
  Hull 115
4 Andy Farrell
  Wigan..............................104
5 David March
  Wakefield 77

TOP POINT SCORERS
1 Kevin Sinfield
  Leeds...............................299
2 Paul Deacon
  Bradford 276
3 Paul Cooke
  Hull 250
4 Andy Farrell
  Wigan..............................243
5 Lee Briers
  Warrington.....................180

RUGBY LEAGUE WORLD
GOLDEN BOOT
Andy Farrell (*Great Britain*)

MAN OF STEEL
Andy Farrell (*Wigan*)

COACH OF THE YEAR
Shane McNally (*Wakefield*)

YOUNG PLAYER
OF THE YEAR
Shaun Briscoe (*Hull*)

PLAYERS' PLAYER
Andy Farrell (*Wigan*)

RUGBY LEAGUE WRITERS
PLAYER OF THE YEAR
Danny McGuire (*Leeds*)

CHALLENGE CUP FINAL
St Helens 32...............Wigan 16

LANCE TODD WINNER
Sean Long (*St Helens*)

AVERAGE ATTENDANCES
Leeds.............................16,608
Bradford.........................13,500
Wigan.............................13,333
Hull 11,397
Warrington 9,889
St Helens 9,507
Castleford........................7,035
Widnes 6,167
Wakefield.........................4,804
Huddersfield 4,362
Salford 3,994
London.............................3,458

236

SUPER LEAGUE X   2005

Champions: Bradford Bulls. Runners–up: Leeds Rhinos.

ENGAGE SUPER LEAGUE FINAL TABLE

	P	W	D	L	F	A	D	PTS
St Helens	28	23	1	4	1028	537	491	47
Leeds	28	22	0	6	1150	505	645	44
Bradford	28	18	1	9	1038	684	354	37
Warrington	28	18	0	10	792	702	90	36
Hull	28	15	2	11	756	670	86	32
London	28	13	2	13	800	718	82	28
Wigan	28	14	0	14	698	718	-20	28
Huddersfield	28	12	0	16	742	791	-49	24
Salford	28	11	0	17	549	732	-183	22
Wakefield	28	10	0	18	716	997	-281	20
Widnes	28	6	1	21	598	1048	-450	13
Leigh	28	2	1	25	445	1210	-765	5

ELIMINATION PLAY-OFF
Bradford 44 ....London 22

ELIMINATION PLAY-OFF
Warrington 6.................Hull 40

QUALIFYING SEMI-FINAL
St Helens 16...............Leeds 19

ELIMINATION SEMI-FINAL
Bradford 71 ....Hull 0

FINAL ELIMINATOR
St Helens 18 ....Bradford 23

GRAND FINAL
Leeds 6 ....Bradford 15

LEEDS: Richard Mathers; Mark Calderwood; Chev Walker; Chris McKenna; Marcus Bai; Danny McGuire; Rob Burrow; Ryan Bailey; Andrew Dunemann; Danny Ward; Gareth Ellis; Willie Poching; Kevin Sinfield (C).
Subs: Ali Lauitiiti; Matt Diskin; Jamie Jones-Buchanan; Barrie McDermott.
Try: McGuire (22).
Goal: Sinfield.
BRADFORD: Michael Withers; Leon Pryce; Ben Harris; Shontayne Hape; Lesley Vainikolo; Iestyn Harris; Paul Deacon; Stuart Fielden; Ian Henderson; Jamie Peacock (C); Paul Johnson; Brad Meyers; Lee Radford.
Subs: Robbie Paul; Adrian Morley; Joe Vagana; Jamie Langley.
Tries: Pryce (30), Vainikolo (53).
Goals: Deacon 3. *Drop-goal*: Harris
Referee: Ashley Klein (London).
Half-time: 6-8. *Attendance*: 65,536.

HARRY SUNDERLAND
AWARD WINNER
Leon Pryce (*Bradford*)

TOP TRY SCORERS
1 Lesley Vainikolo
   Bradford......................32
2 Mark Calderwood
   Leeds 27
3 Darren Albert
   St Helens 25
4 Keith Senior
   Leeds 24
5 Luke Dorn
   London 23
= Henry Fa'afili
   Warrington 23

TOP GOAL KICKERS
1 Paul Deacon
   Bradford....................153
2 Kevin Sinfield
   Leeds..........................129
3 Paul Sykes
   London 119
4 Danny Tickle
   Wigan 103
5 Chris Thorman
   Huddersfield................99

TOP POINT SCORERS
1 Paul Deacon
   Bradford....................359
2 Paul Sykes
   London 288
3 Kevin Sinfield
   Leeds 283
4 Chris Thorman
   Huddersfield...............274
5 Danny Tickle
   Wigan 259

MAN OF STEEL
Jamie Lyon (*St Helens*)

COACH OF THE YEAR
Tony Smith (*Leeds*)

YOUNG PLAYER
OF THE YEAR
Richard Whiting (*Hull*)

PLAYERS' PLAYER
Jamie Lyon (*St Helens*)

RUGBY LEAGUE WRITERS
PLAYER OF THE YEAR
Jamie Lyon (*St Helens*)

CHALLENGE CUP FINAL
Hull 25 ....Leeds 24

LANCE TODD WINNER
Kevin Sinfield (*Leeds*)

AVERAGE ATTENDANCES
Leeds............................17,006
Wigan...........................13,894
Bradford........................13,090
Warrington 11,085
St Helens......................10,817
Hull 10,639
Widnes...........................6,794
Huddersfield...................5,411
Wakefield.......................5,099
Leigh..............................4,750
Salford 4,093
London 4,038

THE DECADE AS A WHOLE

10th ANNIVERSARY COMPOSITE SUPER LEAGUE TABLE

		P	W	D	L	F	A	D	PTS	
DOES NOT include play-offs & Grand Finals	Bradford	265	199	7	59	8799	4880	3919	405	
	Wigan	265	190	11	64	8200	4498	3702	391	
	St Helens *	265	190	7	68	8782	5596	3186	385	
	Leeds	265	175	8	82	7940	5685	2255	358	
	London	265	116	13	136	6051	6454	-403	245	
	Warrington	265	115	6	144	6221	7165	-944	236	
	Hull *	221	108	10	103	5287	5205	82	224	
	Castleford	237	102	10	125	5069	5607	-538	214	
	Halifax *	209	76	4	129	4646	5912	-1266	154	
	Salford	215	65	3	147	3948	6268	-2320	133	*± Wakefield deducted two points for breach of 2001 salary cap*
+ includes 2000 season as Huddersfield-Sheffield	Wakefield ±	198	63	3	132	4269	5715	-1446	127	
	Huddersfield +	193	52	2	139	3754	6051	-2297	106	
	Widnes	112	39	3	70	2294	3341	-1047	81	
	Sheffield =	97	37	3	57	2027	2663	-636	77	
	Gateshead	30	19	1	10	775	576	199	39	** St Helens, Hull & Halifax deducted two points each for breach of 2003 salary cap*
= DOES NOT include 2000 season as Huddersfield-Sheffield	Oldham	44	13	2	29	934	1312	-378	28	
	Paris	44	9	1	34	760	1367	-607	19	
	Workington	22	2	1	19	325	1021	-696	5	
	Leigh	28	2	1	25	445	1210	-765	5	

SUPER LEAGUE TITLES
Bradford.....................4
St Helens...................4
Wigan........................1
Leeds........................1

CHALLENGE CUPS
St Helens...................4
Bradford....................2
Wigan........................1
Leeds........................1
Sheffield...................1
Hull.........................1

TABLE BASED ON LEAGUE VICTORY PERCENTAGE
Bradford....................75
Wigan (*11 draws*)..........72
St Helens (*7 draws*).......72
Leeds.......................66
Gateshead...................63
Hull........................49
London......................44
Castleford (*10 draws*).....43
Warrington (*6 draws*)......43
Sheffield...................38
Halifax.....................36
Widnes......................35
Wakefield...................32
Salford (*3 draws*).........30
Oldham (*2 draws*)..........30
Huddersfield................27
Paris.......................20
Workington..................09
Leigh.......................07

AGGREGATE ATTENDANCES
1996 6,545
1997 6,933
1998 7,087
1999 6,409
2000 7,555
2001 7,223
2002 7,377
2003 8,188
2004 8,833
2005 8,977

MOST TRIES IN A SUPER LEAGUE MATCH
Lesley Vainikolo.................6
Bradford v Hull, 2005
Mike Umaga.......................5
Halifax v Workington, 1996
Jason Robinson...................5
Wigan v Leeds, 1996
Tony Smith.......................5
Wigan v Sheffield, 1997
Anthony Sullivan.................5
St Helens v London, 1998
Kevin Iro........................5
St Helens v Huddersfield, 2000
Lesley Vainikolo.................5
Bradford v Wigan, 2004
Danny McGuire....................5
Leeds v Widnes, 2004
Ali Lauitiiti....................5
Leeds v Wakefield, 2005

MOST GOALS IN A SUPER LEAGUE MATCH
(*including drop-goals*)
Henry Paul......................14
Bradford v Salford, 2000
Iestyn Harris...................13
Leeds v Huddersfield, 1999

MOST POINTS IN A SUPER LEAGUE MATCH
Iestyn Harris 42 (4t, 13g)
Leeds v Huddersfield, 1999
Graham Appo............34 (4t, 9g)
Warrington v Halifax, 2003

HIGHEST SUPER LEAGUE SCORELINE
Bradford 96..............Salford 16
25th June, 2000

WIDEST SUPER LEAGUE WINNING MARGIN
Bradford 96.............Salford 16
25th June, 2000
Leed 86 v Huddersfield 6
16th July, 1999

LOWEST SUPER LEAGUE SCORELINE
Salford 4.................Castleford 0
16th March, 1997

MOST SL APPEARANCES
Keith Senior.........................258
(*Leeds 166, Sheffield 92*)

Official Dream Teams

1996

Full-back	Gary Connolly (Wigan)
Wing	Jason Robinson (Wigan)
Centre	Va'aiga Tuigamala (Wigan)
Centre	Paul Newlove (St Helens)
Wing	Anthony Sullivan (St Helens)
Stand-off	Henry Paul (Wigan)
Scrum-half	Bobbie Goulding (St Helens)
Prop	Apollo Perelini (St Helens)
Hooker	Keiron Cunningham (St Helens)
Prop	Terry O'Connor (Wigan)
Second row	Paul Sculthorpe (Warrington)
Second row	Peter Gill (London)
Loose forward	Andy Farrell (Wigan)

1997

Full-back	Stuart Spruce (Bradford)
Wing	Jason Robinson (Wigan)
Centre	Danny Peacock (Bradford)
Centre	Alan Hunte (St Helens)
Wing	Anthony Sullivan (St Helens)
Stand-off	Graeme Bradley (Bradford)
Scrum-half	Tony Smith (Wigan)
Prop	Paul Broadbent (Sheffield)
Hooker	James Lowes (Bradford)
Prop	Tony Mestrov (London)
Second row	Peter Gill (London)
Second row	Mike Forshaw (Bradford)
Loose forward	Andy Farrell (Wigan)

1998

Full-back	Kris Radlinski (Wigan)
Wing	Jason Robinson (Wigan)
Centre	Gary Connolly (Wigan)
Centre	Brad Godden (Leeds)
Wing	Anthony Sullivan (St Helens)
Stand-off	Iestyn Harris (Leeds)
Scrum-half	Gavin Clinch (Halifax)
Prop	Neil Cowie (Wigan)
Hooker	Robbie McCormack (Wigan)
Prop	Dale Laughton (Sheffield)
Second row	Steele Retchless (London)
Second row	Adrian Morley (Leeds)
Loose forward	Andy Farrell (Wigan)

1999

Full-back	Kris Radlinski (Wigan)
Wing	Jason Robinson (Wigan)
Centre	Gary Connolly (Wigan)
Centre	Paul Newlove (St Helens)
Wing	Matt Daylight (Gateshead)
Stand-off	Iestyn Harris (Leeds)
Scrum-half	Willie Peters (Gateshead)
Prop	Dean Sampson (Castleford)
Hooker	James Lowes (Bradford)
Prop	Barrie McDermott (Leeds)
Second row	Chris Joynt (St Helens)
Second row	Adrian Morley (Leeds)
Loose forward	Adrian Vowles (Castleford)

2000

Full-back	Kris Radlinski (Wigan)
Wing	Jason Robinson (Wigan)
Centre	Steve Renouf (Wigan)
Centre	Michael Eagar (Castleford)
Wing	Graham Mackay (Leeds)
Stand-off	Tommy Martyn (St Helens)
Scrum-half	Sean Long (St Helens)
Prop	Terry O'Connor (Wigan)
Hooker	Keiron Cunningham (St Helens)
Prop	Stuart Fielden (Bradford)
Second row	Jamie Peacock (Bradford)
Second row	Denis Betts (Wigan)
Loose forward	Andy Farrell (Wigan)

2001

Full-back	Kris Radlinski (Wigan)
Wing	Tevita Vaikona (Bradford)
Centre	Tonie Carroll (Leeds)
Centre	Steve Renouf (Wigan)
Wing	Brett Dallas (Wigan)
Stand-off	Paul Sculthorpe (St Helens)
Scrum-half	Adrian Lam (Wigan)
Prop	David Fairleigh (St Helens)
Hooker	Keiron Cunningham (St Helens)
Prop	Terry O'Connor (Wigan)
Second row	David Furner (Wigan)
Second row	Jamie Peacock (Bradford)
Loose forward	Andy Farrell (Wigan)

2002

Full-back	Kris Radlinski (Wigan)
Wing	Darren Albert (St Helens)
Centre	Keith Senior (Leeds)
Centre	Martin Gleeson (St Helens)
Wing	Tevita Vaikona (Bradford)
Stand-off	Danny Orr (Castleford)
Scrum-half	Adrian Lam (Wigan)
Prop	Terry O'Connor (Wigan)
Hooker	Keiron Cunningham (St Helens)
Prop	Stuart Fielden (Bradford)
Second row	Michael Smith (Castleford)
Second row	Jamie Peacock (Bradford)
Loose forward	Paul Sculthorpe (St Helens)

2003

Full-back	Gary Connolly (Leeds)
Wing	Lesley Vainikolo (Bradford)
Centre	Gareth Ellis (Wakefield)
Centre	Keith Senior (Leeds)
Wing	Brian Carney (Wigan)
Stand-off	Graham Appo (Warrington)
Scrum-half	Adrian Lam (Wigan)
Prop	Craig Smith (Wigan)
Hooker	Terry Newton (Wigan)
Prop	Andy Lynch (Castleford)
Second row	Jamie Peacock (Bradford)
Second row	Matt Adamson (Leeds)
Loose forward	Andy Farrell (Wigan)

2004

Full-back	Shaun Briscoe (Hull)
Wing	Lesley Vainikolo (Bradford)
Centre	Keith Senior (Leeds)
Centre	Sid Domic (Wakefield)
Wing	Marcus Bai (Leeds)
Stand-off	Danny McGuire (Leeds)
Scrum-half	Richard Horne (Hull)
Prop	Andy Farrell (Wigan)
Hooker	Matt Diskin (Leeds)
Prop	Paul King (Hull)
Second row	Ali Lauitiiti (Leeds)
Second row	David Solomona (Wakefield)
Loose forward	Paul Sculthorpe (St Helens)

2005

Full-back	Paul Wellens (St Helens)
Wing	Mark Calderwood (Leeds)
Centre	Jamie Lyon (St Helens)
Centre	Martin Gleeson (Warrington)
Wing	Darren Albert (St Helens)
Stand-off	Paul Cooke (Hull)
Scrum-half	Rob Burrow (Leeds)
Prop	Jamie Thackray (Hull)
Hooker	Keiron Cunningham (St Helens)
Prop	Paul Anderson (St Helens)
Second row	Jamie Peacock (Bradford)
Second row	Ali Lauitiiti (Leeds)
Loose forward	Kevin Sinfield (Leeds)

● *Each contributor was asked for a Dream Team of their favourite (not necessarily best) players. (Dave Hadfield's common thread is that all had made just one SL start on day of selection):*

Dave Hadfield

Full-back	Jason Laurence (Salford)
Wing	Blake Cannova (Widnes)
Centre	Dean Bell (Leeds)
Centre	Maea David (Hull)
Wing	Anderson Okiwe (Sheffield)
Stand-off	Kevin Walters (Warrington)
Scrum-half	Andrew Johns (Warrington)
Prop	Phil Adamson (St Helens)
Hooker	Martin Dermott (Warrington)
Prop	Jon Hamer (Bradford)
Second row	Craig Richards (Oldham)
Second row	Sione Faumuina (Hull)
Loose forward	Billy McGinty (Workington)

Mike Rylance

Full-back	Richie Barnett Sr
Wing	Jason Robinson
Centre	Jamie Lyon
Centre	Paul Newlove
Wing	Brian Carney
Stand-off	Iestyn Harris
Scrum-half	Adrian Lam
Prop	Terry O'Connor
Hooker	Keiron Cunningham
Prop	Craig Smith
Second row	David Solomona
Second row	Andy Farrell
Loose forward	Paul Sculthorpe

Christopher Irvine

Full-back	Robbie Paul
Wing	Jason Robinson
Centre	Jamie Lyon
Centre	Paul Newlove
Wing	Lesley Vainikolo
Stand-off	Iestyn Harris
Scrum-half	Sean Long
Prop	Apollo Perelini
Hooker	Keiron Cunningham
Prop	Barrie McDermott
Second row	Chris Joynt
Second row	Paul Sculthorpe
Loose forward	Andy Farrell

Paul Rowley

Full-back	Paul Wellens
Wing	Jason Robinson
Centre	John Schuster
Centre	Va'aiga Tuigamala
Wing	Fereti Tuilagi
Stand-off	Henry Paul
Scrum-half	Sean Long
Prop	Karl Harrison
Hooker	Keiron Cunningham
Prop	Barrie McDermott
Second row	Adrian Morley
Second row	Andy Farrell
Loose forward	Paul Sculthorpe

John Ledger

Full-back	Kris Radlinski
Wing	Jason Robinson
Centre	Paul Newlove
Centre	Keith Senior
Wing	Lesley Vainikolo
Stand-off	Danny McGuire
Scrum-half	Brad Davis
Prop	Dale Laughton ('98 Wembley try)
Hooker	James Lowes
Prop	Andy Farrell
Second row	Adrian Morley
Second row	Jamie Peacock
Loose forward	Kevin Sinfield

David Lawrenson

Full-back	Kris Radlinski
Wing	Jason Robinson
Centre	Jamie Lyon
Centre	Gary Connolly
Wing	Martin Offiah
Stand-off	Iestyn Harris
Scrum-half	Adrian Lam
Prop	David Fairleigh
Hooker	Keiron Cunningham
Prop	Stuart Fielden
Second row	Adrian Morley
Second row	Andy Farrell
Loose forward	Paul Sculthorpe

Malcolm Andrews

Full-back	Kris Radlinski
Wing	Lesley Vainikolo
Centre	Paul Newlove
Centre	Gary Connolly
Wing	Jason Robinson
Stand-off	Iestyn Harris
Scrum-half	Robbie Paul
Prop	Stuart Fielden
Hooker	Richard Swain
Prop	Adrian Morley
Second row	Andy Farrell
Second row	David Furner
Loose forward	Paul Sculthorpe

Harry Edgar

Full-back	Kris Radlinski
Wing	Jason Robinson
Centre	Martin Gleeson
Centre	Graeme Bradley
Wing	Lesley Vainikolo
Stand-off	Henry Paul
Scrum-half	Robbie Paul
Prop	Paul Anderson
Hooker	Keiron Cunningham
Prop	Terry O'Connor
Second row	David Solomona
Second row	Paul Sculthorpe
Loose forward	Andy Farrell

Ian Laybourn

Full-back	Kris Radlinski
Wing	Jason Robinson
Centre	Paul Newlove
Centre	Va'aiga Tuigamala
Wing	Martin Offiah
Stand-off	Shaun Edwards
Scrum-half	Allan Langer
Prop	Terry O'Connor
Hooker	Keiron Cunningham
Prop	Stuart Fielden
Second row	Jamie Peacock
Second row	Andy Farrell
Loose forward	Paul Sculthorpe

Mike Latham

Full-back	Steve Prescott
Wing	Jason Robinson
Centre	Jamie Lyon
Centre	Kirk Yeaman
Wing	Brett Dallas
Stand-off	Tommy Martyn
Scrum-half	Lee Briers
Prop	Stuart Fielden
Hooker	Paul Rowley
Prop	Dean Sampson
Second row	Warren Jowitt
Second row	Andy Farrell
Loose forward	Paul Sculthorpe

Andy Wilson

Full-back	Steve Prescott
Wing	Brian Carney
Centre	Martin Gleeson
Centre	Sid Domic
Wing	Darren Rogers
Stand-off	Tommy Martyn
Scrum-half	Danny McGuire
Prop	Brian McDermott
Hooker	James Lowes
Prop	Darren Fleary
Second row	Steele Retchless
Second row	Chris Joynt
Loose forward	Stanley Gene

Gareth Walker

Full-back	Kris Radlinski
Wing	Richie Barnett Sr
Centre	Jamie Lyon
Centre	Gary Connolly
Wing	Anthony Sullivan
Stand-off	Tommy Martyn
Scrum-half	Bobbie Goulding
Prop	Stuart Fielden
Hooker	Keiron Cunningham
Prop	Barrie McDermott
Second row	Adrian Morley
Second row	Andy Farrell
Loose forward	Paul Sculthorpe

superleague.co.uk visitors

Full-back	Kris Radlinski
Wing	Jason Robinson
Centre	Gary Connolly
Centre	Keith Senior
Wing	Lesley Vainikolo
Stand-off	Paul Sculthorpe
Scrum-half	Sean Long
Prop	Terry O'Connor
Hooker	Keiron Cunningham
Prop	Barrie McDermott
Second row	Jamie Peacock
Second row	Chris Joynt
Loose forward	Andy Farrell

Ray French

Full-back	Kris Radlinski
Wing	Darren Albert
Centre	Paul Newlove
Centre	Jamie Lyon
Wing	Lesley Vainikolo
Stand-off	Danny McGuire
Scrum-half	Robbie Paul
Prop	Stuart Fielden
Hooker	Keiron Cunningham
Prop	David Fairleigh
Second row	Ali Lauitiiti
Second row	Paul Sculthorpe
Loose forward	Andy Farrell

Angela Powers

"This dream team is not by position, it is made up of great players & nice guys who have made our job easier" -AP

	Richard Mathers
	Danny McGuire
	Kris Radlinski
	Stuart Fielden
	Brian Carney
	Brad Davis
	Luke Robinson
	Terry & Barrie!
	Robbie Paul
	Apollo Perelini
	Adrian Morley
	Tawera Nikau
	Mike Forshaw

Tony Hannan

Full-back	Richie Barnett Sr
Wing	Brian Carney
Centre	Graeme Bradley
Centre	Jamie Lyon
Wing	Lesley Vainikolo
Stand-off	Paul Sculthorpe
Scrum-half	Robbie Paul
Prop	Terry O'Connor
Hooker	James Lowes
Prop	Barrie McDermott
Second row	Steele Retchless
Second row	David Solomona
Loose forward	Andy Farrell

Dave Woods

Full-back	Kris Radlinski
Wing	Jason Robinson
Centre	Paul Newlove
Centre	Jamie Lyon
Wing	Lesley Vainikolo
Stand-off	Tommy Martyn
Scrum-half	Allan Langer
Prop	Stuart Fielden
Hooker	Keiron Cunningham
Prop	Barrie McDermott
Second row	Jamie Peacock
Second row	Andy Farrell
Loose forward	Steve McNamara

Trevor Hunt

Full-back	Kris Radlinski
Wing	Jason Robinson
Centre	Keith Senior
Centre	Paul Newlove
Wing	Lesley Vainikolo
Stand-off	Tommy Martyn
Scrum-half	Sean Long
Prop	Terry O'Connor
Hooker	Keiron Cunningham
Prop	Barrie McDermott
Second row	Jamie Peacock
Second row	Paul Sculthorpe
Loose forward	Andy Farrell

World Club Challenges

WORLD CLUB CHAMPIONSHIP - 1997
PHASE ONE

Round 1 - Pool A
Brisbane Broncos 42 ....London Broncos 22
Canberra Raiders 70 ....Halifax Blue Sox 6
St Helens 14..................................Auckland Warriors 42
Warrington Wolves 12 ....Cronulla Sharks 40
Canterbury Bulldogs 18 ....Wigan Warriors 22
Bradford Bulls 16 ....Penrith Panthers 20
Pool B
Adelaide Rams 50.....................................Salford Reds 8
Castleford Tigers 16 ....Perth Reds 24
N Queensland Cowboys 42....................Leeds Rhinos 28
Paris Saint-Germain 24....................Hunter Mariners 28

Round 2 - Pool A
Bradford Bulls 16 ....Auckland Warriors 20
Warrington Wolves 22.....................Penrith Panthers 52
Canberra Raiders 66.........................London Broncos 20
Canterbury Bulldogs 58....................Halifax Blue Sox 6
Brisbane Broncos 34..........................Wigan Warriors 0
St Helens 8 ....Cronulla Sharks 48
Pool B
Castleford Tigers 14 ....Hunter Mariners 42
Adelaide Rams 34...................................Leeds Rhinos 8
N Queensland Cowboys 54 ....Oldham Bears 16
Sheffield Eagles 26 ....Perth Reds 22

Round 3 - Pool A
Bradford Bulls 10.............................Cronulla Sharks 30
Brisbane Broncos 76 ....Halifax Blue Sox 0
Canberra Raiders 56..........................Wigan Warriors 22
St Helens 30.....................................Penrith Panthers 50
Warrington Wolves 28 ....Auckland Warriors 56
Canterbury Bulldogs 34 ....London Broncos 18
Pool B
Adelaide Rams 42 ....Oldham Bears 14
N Queensland Cowboys 44 ....Salford Reds 8
Paris Saint-Germain 24 ....Perth Reds 0
Sheffield Eagles 4 ....Hunter Mariners 40

PHASE TWO

Round 4 - Pool A
Auckland Warriors 64 ....Bradford Bulls 14
Cronulla Sharks 28 ....St Helens 6
Halifax Blue Sox 22..................Canterbury Bulldogs 40
London Broncos 38.........................Canberra Raiders 18
Penrith Panthers 48.....................Warrington Wolves 12
Wigan Warriors 4...........................Brisbane Broncos 30
Pool B
Hunter Mariners 26...........................Castleford Tigers 8
Leeds Rhinos 22...................................Adelaide Rams 14
Oldham Bears 20 ....N Queensland Cowboys 16
Perth Reds 48 ....Sheffield Eagles 12

Round 5- Pool A
Auckland Warriors 70...................................St Helens 6
Cronulla Sharks 44 ....Warrington Wolves 0
Halifax Blue Sox 12 ....Canberra Raiders 42
London Broncos 16 ....Brisbane Broncos 34
Penrith Panthers 54 ....Bradford Bulls 14
Wigan Warriors 31 ....Canterbury Bulldogs 24

PHASE TWO (*Continued*)

Pool B
Hunter Mariners 32......................Paris Saint-Germain 0
Oldham Bears 2 ....Adelaide Rams 18
Perth Reds 24 ....Castleford Tigers 14
Salford Reds 14 ....N Queensland Cowboys 24

Round 6 - Pool A
Auckland Warriors 16...................Warrington Wolves 4
Cronulla Sharks 40..............................Bradford Bulls 12
Halifax Blue Sox 10 ....Brisbane Broncos 54
London Broncos 22 ....Canterbury Bulldogs 44
Penrith Panthers 32.......................................St Helens 26
Wigan Warriors 10.........................Canberra Raiders 50
Pool B
Hunter Mariners 58 ....Sheffield Eagles 12
Leeds Rhinos 14...................N Queensland Cowboys 48
Perth Reds 30.............................Paris Saint-Germain 12
Salford Reds 14 ....Adelaide Rams 12

Play-off for quarter-final place
St Helens 42 ....Paris Saint-Germain 4

Quarter-finals
Auckland Warriors 62 ....Bradford Bulls 14
Brisbane Broncos 66....................................St Helens 12
London Broncos 16 ....Cronulla Sharks 40
Wigan Warriors 18 ....Hunter Mariners 22

Semi-finals
Brisbane Broncos 22....................Auckland Warriors 16
Cronulla Sharks 18 ....Hunter Mariners 22

Final
Brisbane Broncos 36 ....Hunter Mariners 12
at Ericcson Stadium, Auckland

WORLD CLUB CHALLENGE MATCHES
2000
St Helens 6....................................Melbourne Storm 44
at JJB Stadium, Wigan

2001
St Helens 20....................................Brisbane Broncos 18
at Reebok Stadium, Bolton

2002
Bradford Bulls 41 ....Newcastle Knights 26
at McAlpine Stadium, Huddersfield

2003
St Helens 0.....................................Sydney Roosters 38
at Reebok Stadium, Bolton

2004
Bradford Bulls 22 ....Penrith Panthers 4
at McAlpine Stadium, Huddersfield

2005
Leeds Rhinos 39.......................Canterbury Bulldogs 32
at Elland Road, Leeds

Timeline to Super League

30th August 1994

The Rugby Football League publishes its "*Framing The Future*" document, a specially-commissioned report which calls for a soccer-style Premier League and club mergers.

4th April 1995

After attempting to launch a breakaway "Star League" down under, Rupert Murdoch's News Ltd make first confirmed approach to RFL over a European Super League. Chief Executive Maurice Lindsay heads to London for talks with BSkyB.

5th April 1995

Rugby League Council meets at Headingley, Leeds, reportedly to debate a possible switch to summer rugby. During the meeting, Lindsay reveals News Ltd's approach.

Some newspapers report that Murdoch wants to pay £50m for a summer Super League. Talks are arranged between the RFL Board of Directors and News Ltd, the results of which are to be reported back to a special meeting of club chairmen in three days' time.

6th April 1995

Australian newspapers quote Murdoch's second-in-command, Ken Cowley, who describes Super League as a done deal.

7th April 1995

Super League details outlined for the first time at a meeting of First Division club chairmen, plus one from Second Division Hull KR, with Lindsay and RFL chairman Rodney Walker.

8th April 1995

The decision is made official at Wigan's Central Park. It is agreed unanimously that a 14-club Super League will begin in 1996, for which News Ltd will pay £77m, over five years.

However, controversy reigns when it is revealed that 15 clubs will have to merge. There will be two new clubs in France and a South Wales side will enter the new First Division.

Each Super League club will receive £1m per year, with First Division clubs pocketing a one-off payment of £100,000.

The 14 Super League teams will be: Bradford Northern, Calder (Castleford, Featherstone & Wakefield), Cheshire (Warrington & Widnes), Cumbria (Barrow, Carlisle, Whitehaven & Workington), Halifax, Humberside (Hull & Hull KR), Leeds, London, Manchester (Oldham & Salford), Paris, South Yorkshire (Sheffield & Doncaster), St Helens, Toulouse and Wigan.

The First Division will be comprised of: Batley, Bramley, Dewsbury, Highfield, Huddersfield, Hunslet, Keighley Cougars, Leigh, Rochdale Hornets, Ryedale York, Swinton and a Welsh XIII.

There is to be no relegation or promotion in the first two seasons and the top four Super League clubs will play in a World Club Championship with the leading Australian and New Zealand clubs.

9th April 1995

The first protests take place at Sunday afternoon matches featuring clubs who will be affected by mergers.

10th April 1995

ARL boss Ken Arthurson accuses Lindsay of betrayal and says that Super League will mean the end of British Lions and Kangaroo tours.

12th April 1995

Halifax board decides to seek merger with Bradford - leading to resignation of chairman Tony Gartland nine days later. Ryedale York consider move to Gateshead, but Salford and Oldham fail to agree on Manchester merger.

13th April 1995

A meeting of Super League chairmen rejects the inclusion of Keighley Cougars, who promise legal action.

14th April 1995

France opts to enter just one club - Paris - meaning merger of Widnes and Warrington is abandoned.

20th April 1995

Labour Party moves to refer Super League to the Office of Fair Trading and the Monopolies and Mergers Commission.

23rd April 1995

RFL announces intention to pay top players "loyalty bonuses", after British players such as Ellery Hanley are targetted by the Kerry Packer-backed Australian ARL. Castleford pull out of Calder merger.

25th April 1995

Some Super League clubs threaten a breakaway as eight lower-division clubs seek legal advice regarding an "unconstitutional lack of consultation".

26th April 1995

A Super League debate in the House of Commons lasts 90 minutes. Sports Minister Ian Sproat calls for a Commons committee investigation into the plans.

30th April 1995

A six-hour meeting of clubs at the Hilton Hotel, near Huddersfield, sees a withdrawal of the highly-unpopular merger proposals and a return to three divisions with a 12-team Super League.

Clubs will now be allocated places on the basis of their finish in the 1994-95 season, with the exceptions of London, Paris and National Conference club Chorley.

The Super League will now be: Bradford Northern, Castleford, Halifax, Leeds, London Broncos, Oldham, Paris, St Helens, Sheffield, Warrington, Wigan and Workington Town.

An 11-team First Division will feature: Batley, Dewsbury, Featherstone, Huddersfield, Hull, Keighley, Rochdale, Salford, Wakefield, Whitehaven and Widnes.

With the idea of a Welsh team now dropped and Doncaster in administration, a 10-team Second Division will include: Barrow, Bramley, Carlisle, Chorley, Highfield, Hull KR, Hunslet, Leigh, Ryedale York and Swinton.

Murdoch increases his financial input into the restructure from £77m to £87m. It also emerges that soccer's Newcastle United have enquired about Super League. They later "put back" entry until 1997.

2nd May 1995

Widnes join Keighley in sueing the RFL after losing their place when Super League was reduced to 12 clubs. On 26th May, they lose their case.

29th March 1996

After one last truncated winter season, the European Super League finally kicks off with a 30-24 win for Paris over Sheffield at the Charlety Stadium.

● *Timeline reference: Rothmans Rugby League Yearbook 1995-96, Raymond Fletcher and David Howes (Headline).*